SCIENCE AND PHILOSOPHY IN ANCIENT INDIA

SCIENCE AND PHILOSOPHY IN ANCIENT INDIA

Debiprasad Chattopadhyaya

Science and Philosophy in Ancient India
Debiprasad Chattopadhyaya

First Published 2013
Reprinted 2020
Reprinted 2024

ISBN 978-81-89833-44-2 (Hb)

Published by
AAKAR BOOKS
28 E Pocket IV, Mayur Vihar Phase I
Delhi 110 091, India
www.aakarbooks.com

Printed at
D.K. Fine Art Press, Delhi

Contents

Introduction

Debiprasad Chattopadhyaya (1918-1993) generally preferred to present his research in the form of book-length studies. Although best known for his highly influential work, *Lokayata: A Study in Ancient Indian Materialism* (1959), in the last years of his life he had concentrated on the study of History and Philosophy of Science in ancient India. It began with *Science and Society in Ancient India* (1977), a work devoted exclusively to the sociology and philosophy of medicine and surgery as found in the two great medical compilations, the *Caraka Saṃhitā* and the *Suśruta Saṃhitā* respectively. Later he led a whole team of collaborators to study the origin and development of science and technology in India from a radically novel point of view. Unlike his predecessors he chose to begin from the pre-Vedic Harappan civilisation. Thus archaeological findings were given precedence over purely literary sources. An avowed externalist in his approach, Chattopadhyaya followed the line formulated by Joseph Needham whose first two volumes of *Science and Civilisation in China* were his constant companions. Yet he knew that the development of science and technology in India had been quite dissimilar to that of China.

Chattopadhyaya, therefore, was forced to build a new model for his study and the first volume of his *magnum opus* was a path-breaking work. It went against all previous attempts at constructing the history of science and technology in India and gave birth to a new method, combining archaeology, philology and philosophy, reminiscent of D.D. Kosambi's *Combined Method in Indology*.

While Chattopadhyaya was engaged in writing this multi-volume history he was invited to deliver lectures and present papers at conferences and seminars all over the world. He also contributed a number of essays to Festschrifts. This book is a compilation of these lectures and articles that have so far remained scattered in journals and felicitation volumes published from different centres of learning. Some of his earlier lectures and papers had already been included in his lifetime in *Knowledge and Intervention* (Calcutta, 1985); some others have been posthumously collected in *Musing in Ideology*, (Bangalore, 2001) and *Some Thoughts on Marxism* (Bangalore, 2002).

The reader of the present volume will find fresh light thrown on three basic disciplines, namely, astronomy, mathematics and medicine in India. The first essay seeks to uphold the claim of Uddālakā Āruṇi, an Upaniṣadic seer, as the first scientist in the world. Chattopadhyaya controverts the euro-centric orthodoxy that Thales of Miletus was the first scientist. Step by step Chattopadhyaya shows quite convincingly that Uddālakā Āruṇi was the originator of the true scientific method by promoting experimentation as the means of arriving at knowledge of the external world.

The second seeks to establish the view that Vedāṇga Jyotiṣa was based on the data preserved by the pre-Aryans. He has resurrected the hypotheses of Lokamanya Bal Gangadhar Tilak and Hermann Jacobi. Chattopadhyaya here mentions an interesting anecdote. Jacobi told Tilak in 1909 that even if they were quite sure that Vedic culture was not older than 1200 or 1500 BCE they could not establish Tilak's findings concerning Kṛttikā. Tilak wished to enter upon a campaign against all opponents, but Jacobi dissuaded him by saying that "the discussion would have no definite result unless excavation in ancient sites in India should bring forth unmistakable evidence of the enormous antiquity of Indian civilisation." Chattopadhyaya adds that the discovery of the

Indus Valley Civilisation only twelve years after this statement "settled this question once for all" in favour of Tilak and Jacobi.

The third and fourth essays open up a new approach to the understanding of the scientific potential of the Śulbasūtras, works of proto-geometry and mensuration recorded in ancillary Vedic literature. The Śulbasūtras form a part of the Śrautasūtras, themselves belonging to Kalpa, rulebooks of Yajurvedic sacrifices (*Yajñas*). The Śulbasūtras exhibit the unity of head and hand in the birth of science, with brick technology providing the link.

The fifth and sixth essays review the *Caraka Saṃhitā and Suśruta Saṃhitā* as two great compilations in which science and its opposite are made to coexist. Chattopadhyaya here demonstrates how the physicians and surgeons of ancient India had to pay ransom to the powers that be. They were forced to accommodate superstition in their scientific works in order to preserve and further pursue their study of the human body. To prove that such a compromise is not unique, Chattopadhyaya refers to the lot of Brahmagupta as observed by al-Bīrūnī, the first "visiting scientist" in India known to us.

The seventh, eighth and ninth essays concern themselves with the very roots of idealist philosophy as found in the Upaniṣads. The former is a masterly analysis of the monarch (Kṣatriya)-seer (Brahmin) nexus vividly recorded in the tale of Janaka, king of Mithila, and Yājñavalkya, the first propounder of idealism in India. The eighth essay was written as early as in 1958 but has never been reprinted in full. Only a part of it was extracted as an Appendix to his *Lokāyata*. The ninth essay offers a sociological analysis of Upaniṣadic Idealism in a vivid way.

The tenth and the last essay proposes to place Rabindranath Tagore in the Indian philosophical traditions but it also raises a significant question: Was the poet after his visit to the then USSR in 1930 so impressed by her economic programme that he sought to reinterpret the words of the Upaniṣad, "Do not covet," in an altogether new sense by "putting a condition to his old conviction? Could it be that he was accepting the [*Iśa*] Upaniṣad on condition that it accepted the Bolshevist programme?" Chattopadhyaya concludes: "The question is important because without answering it we [can] hardly understand the last phase of the poet's life."

The editor wishes to thank Ms Aditi Chattopadhyaya for giving him free access to the private papers of her late father which led to the discovery of the off-prints and mimeographed copies of the lectures and articles. He would also like to thank the publisher for readily agreeing to bring out this collection. Grateful acknowledgement is made to Messrs. Amitava Bhattacharyya, Siddhartha Dutta, Bhabesh Mitra, Tirthankar Mitra and Pinaki Mukhopadhyaya for providing all sorts of assistance.

3 Mohanlal Street
Kolkata 700 004

Ramkrishna Bhattacharya

Debiprasad Chattopadhyaya: A Profile

Debiprasad Chattopadhyaya was born in Kolkata on November 19, 1918. He had his early schooling in the Mitra Institution, Bhowanipur, Kolkata and studied philosophy in the Presidency College, Kolkata and Calcutta University, standing first in the first class both in B.A. (Hons.) and M.A. in 1939 and 1942 respectively. It is ironical that he took Indian Philosophy (Vedanta Group) as his Special Paper in the M.A. since throughout his later life he waged a relentless battle against Vedanta and other forms of idealist philosophy.

An indefatigable worker and prolific writer, he has more than fifty volumes (some of which are quite bulky) and a number of edited works to his credit. He was recognised as a litterateur in Bengal, distinct for his extremely lucid style and way of exposition. In the 1940s and early 50s he was better known as an author of juvenile literature, writing stories, novels, popular science titles and biographies for school children. He also co-edited the Bengali journal *Rangmashal* with his elder brother, Kamakshiprasad. Earlier still, in his student days he was a budding poet, associated with an *avant-garde* group which wanted to sound a new note after Rabindranath Tagore. *Kayekti Nayak* (A Few Heroes), a slim book of verse (never reprinted in his lifetime since its first publication in 1942) remains the only testimony to his youthful ventures.

Samar Sen, the poet (later editor of the radical weekly *Frontier*) introduced him to the *Manifesto of the Communist Party* by Marx and Engels. Association with

Bankim Mukherjee, the labour leader, and Radharaman Mitra of Meerut Conspiracy Case fame, extended his acquaintance with the theory and practice of Marxism. After a brief stint with the Labour Party, he joined the Communist Party of India in the early 1940s. It was Bhowani Sen, the CPI leader, who urged him to apply Marxism to the study of ancient Indian philosophy. This seems to have changed the whole orientation of his life. Single-mindedly he devoted himself to the exploration of the rational and materialist contents in our heritage and continued this work to the end of his life.

The first product of this research was *Lokayat Darsana*, published first in Bengali (1956) and then rewritten in English (1959). It has been reprinted several times and translated into a number of Indian and foreign languages, including Chinese and Japanese. To date this remains the most popular of his works. As the reviews in leading journals and personal letters from savants such as Joseph Needham and J.B.S. Haldane demonstrate, the work supplied a long-felt need and opened a new vista in the study of materialism in India. It will be no exaggeration to say that *Lokāyata* has taught and will continue to teach generations of readers both at home and abroad how to view philosophy in a new light. He eschewed all existing models of enquiry and searched for the roots of materialism in anthropology, took a radical view of Tantra and studied the evidence of the Vedas in a way never attempted before.

A small 'Popular Introduction' to *Indian Philosophy* came next. Published in 1964, the work provides a bird's-eye view of the major schools. Planned as a direct antithesis to Sāyaṇa's compendium, the *Sarvadarśana-Saṃgraha*, which started from Lokāyata and stopped at Vedanta, Chattopadhyaya's book moves in a more orderly manner, following the developments of different Indian philosophical schools in terms of their historical origin.

In *Indian Atheism* (1969), Chattopadhyaya included even the *āstika* schools to bring out the atheistic contents inherent in them. The Ur-Samkhya and Ur-Nyaya, he demonstrated, were definitely atheistic as was Mīmāmsā itself. This is a more scholarly work than the preceding one, more closely argued and widely documented.

What is Living and What is Dead in Indian Philosophy (1976) explores new grounds, covering a broader area. Chattopadhyaya's level-headed analysis helped to resurrect a number of positive elements in both early Buddhism and Nyaya. A work of stupendous scholarship and meticulous research, the book is a follow-up of the *Lokāyata* and remains a classic of its kind.

Chattopadhyaya was already making forays into new territories as was evident in his *Science and Society in Ancient India* (1977). In a sense it is a continuation of his previous work where his endeavour was to excavate the scientific kernel out of the theological mumbo-jumbo that marred the two basic works of Indian medicine and surgery, the *Caraka-Samhitā* and the *Suśruta-Samhitā.* S.N. Dasgupta had said something about the 'philosophy' of our medical schools but Chattopadhyaya went much further. He showed that the forces of 'counter-ideology', i.e. the Hindu law-makers in league with the ruling powers had compelled the scientists to pay ransom to the state-approved orthodoxy, forcing them to include much that is extrinsic and detrimental to science. This is why, he argued, medicine and surgery in India could not develop into a more exact science after a brilliant beginning. Chattopadhyaya exhibited his true acumen as a historian of ideas in this work. He was the first to point out how tangled the basic texts of medicine and surgery are, containing both science and its opposite, and he accounted for this by pointing out the authoritarian intervention of hide-bound religion.

This work may very well be considered a watershed in Chattopadhyaya's career. His focus of interest now shifted to history and philosophy of science in ancient India. After retirement from the teaching post at City College, Kolkata, in 1978 (where for nearly thirty years he had taught the rudiments of logic and philosophy to the undergraduate students), he started afresh as a student, teaching himself different branches of ancient science. With the avid interest of an explorer, he now studied astronomy and geometry. His magnum opus, *History of Science and Technology in Ancient India* in three volumes (1986, 1991, and 1996, the last published posthumously) differs from all the other works of its kind. Instead of taking off from the more convenient area of the Vedas, he concentrated on the Indus Valley civilisation. This yielded excellent results, provide as it did the very important missing link vainly sought so far by Tilak and Jacobi. It also clinched the problem of dating the Vedāṇga Jyotiṣa. Relating the rise of science to the two periods of urbanisation in ancient India, he created a new model for the study of the history of science and technology in the East. He rescued the discipline from the conventional cataloguing of achievements without any reference to the socio-historical perspective. At the same time the way he linked the technique of brick-making and the geometry of the *Śulbasūtras* (the art of making altars) also established the continuity of the Indus Valley tradition beyond the Harappan sites in the Vedic age.

The last work on philosophy he wrote is *In Defence of Materialism in Ancient India: A Study in Carvaka/Lokayata* (1989), a "populariser" (in his own words) that seeks to present his mature views on the subject with which he had burst upon the world of Indian philosophy to the horror and dismay of the academic world forty years ago.

Ill health, lack of basic amenities, inordinate delay in publications—all this dogged his steps to the last day of his life. But over and above the works mentioned above, he brought out and edited a scholarly journal, *Indian Studies: Past and Present* (since 1959), translated with Dr. Mrinalkanti Gangopadhyaya the *Nyāyasūtra* with the commentary of Vātsyāyana as also of the annotations by M.M. Phanibhushana Tarkavagisa (in five volumes), edited the first ever English translation of Lama Taranatha's *History of Buddhism in India*, the Niharranjan Ray Festschrift, *History and Society* (1978), a three-volume anthology of studies in the

History of Indian Philosophy: Eastern and Western Views (1978-79), a two-volume *Studies in the History of Science in India* (1980), a collection of essays on *Marxism and Indology* (1981), *Carvaka/Lokayata: An Anthology of Source Materials and Some Recent Studies* (1990) and an eight-volume *Global Philosophy for Everyman* (1990-91). The range is breathtaking, so is the grip and control over such diverse material.

Official honours came late in his life, and those too first came from abroad. He was made a Member of the Academy of Sciences of the then German Democratic Republic in 1975, awarded D. Sc. *honoris causa* by the Academy of Sciences of the then USSR in 1981. The University Grants Commission, New Delhi, gave him the Science and Society Award in 1982, and the Government of West Bengal, the Vidyasagar Award in 1992. He was elected National Fellow of the Indian Council of Philosophical Research, New Delhi, with which he was associated from its very inception. He was also a Fellow and then a Council Member of the Indian Council of Historical Research, New Delhi, from 1987, and a member of the National Commission of the History of Science in India, Indian National Science Academy, New Delhi. He also worked as a Guest Scientist of the National Institute of Science, Technology and Development Studies (a Constituent Organisation of the Council for Scientific and Industrial Research, New Delhi). In spite of all these honours, he felt more gratified when he found young activists making use of his works in the ideological struggle against obscurantist forces. He edited a Reader called *Pratirodh* (Resistance) in 1991 on behalf of the Bengali monthly, *Utsa Manush*, which contained excerpts form the writings of the illustrious men of letters of Bengal, from Rammohun Roy to Satyendranath Bose, highlighting the constant battle of reason against conservatism and orthodoxy.

Besides Marx, Engels and Lenin, V. Gordon Childe, George Thomson and Joseph Needham wielded a lifelong influence on him. He used J.D. Bernal's *Science in History* as a handbook. He had the highest regard for Walter Ruben,

John Somerville and Barrows Dunham. With D.D. Kosambi, Trevor Ling and Dale Riepe he was on terms of the warmest friendship. He was associated with several Encyclopaedia projects, assisted workers in the rationalist and people's science movement, and went out of his way to help young scholars. A man of very strong likes and dislikes, he was, however, never reluctant to revise his opinions. The new trends of so-called Western Marxism and the New Left, however, left him cold, and he was totally out of sympathy with postmodernist pyrotechnics.

An unrepentant Marxist to the last day of his life, a firm believer in human progress, science and reason, Chattopadhyaya was overtaken by death on May 8, 1993. To say that the void created by his absence can never be filled is a statement of fact, not a mere cliché.

1

Uddālaka Āruni: The Pioneer of Science*

Most of the histories of science written so far would like us to believe that the first prodigious step to natural science was taken in ancient Greece by Thales of Miletus in the sixth century B.C. How far such an assertion is inspired by the widespread Eurocentrism of the historians is for others to judge. What I shall be emphasising instead is how far it is really based on ignorance. I shall try to show that, objectively speaking, the honour of first opening the gates to natural science should be given to one who belonged to the ancient Indian subcontinent and who, if not actually a century or more earlier than Thales, must have at least been his senior contemporary. In any case, his contributions to the making of natural science must have been immensely important, though we meet him where a natural scientist is least expected, namely in the Upaniṣads and even in a legend of what is called the Brāhmaṇa literature, to which the Upaniṣads were somehow appended.

It may, however, prove to be a procedural advantage if we begin with certain clarifications both about Thales and the Upaniṣads.

---

* This paper was delivered as the "Zakir Husain Memorial Lecture" in New Delhi on February 8, 1988. It forms part of the second volume of my book, *History of Science and Technology in Ancient India* (sponsored by the National Institute of Science, Technology and Development Studies, New Delhi), where the material background of the first making of conscious nature science is intended to be discussed.

Thales first. Really speaking, not much is actually known about Thales; modern writers depend mainly on certain floating legends and counter-legends for an account of him.[1] He is said to have predicted an eclipse, though understanding the phenomenon itself in a fantastic way and though, as it is admitted these days, depending on deductions of the ancient Babylonians who "were equally ignorant of the subject and yet predicted eclipses with tolerable accuracy by means of a cycle of 223 lunations".[2] Another legend imputes to him the technique of calculating the height of the pyramids from their shadows, though, again, depending on the knowledge of similar right-angled triangles—a knowledge for which he was indebted to the ancient Egyptians.[3] Thus, although we may accept the veracity of such legends, we may at best give him the credit of adding a certain amount of elegance or new applicability to pre-existing astronomy and geometry instead of really laying their foundations. But the great fame of Thales is based on the new line of cosmological speculation he is said to have started. As Burnet sums it up:

> According to Aristotle, Thales said that the earth floats on water and he doubtless thought of it as a flat disc.... It seems primitive enough, but in reality it marks a notable advance... This was no doubt connected with what Aristotle regards as the principal tenet of Thales, namely that everything is made out of water, or as he puts it in his own terminology, that water is the material cause of all things.[4]

Cornford[5] and others[6] express strong doubts, of course, about Aristotle's version of the view of Thales. Still, it somehow creeps into the standard histories of science and philosophy, though as a scientific view its value is at best rudimentary. As is observed, "His greatness, however, would lie in having asked the question rather than in the particular answer he gave it".[7]

But the problem remains: what was it that led Thales to ask the question at all—the question namely of some natural cause that ultimately accounts for the infinite multiplicity of things in the world? Farrington answers:

> The great renown of Thales, however, rests not on his geometry or his turn of affairs, but on a new commonsense way of looking at the world of things. The Egyptians and the Babylonians had old cosmogonies, part of their religious inheritance, which told how the world had come to be. Since in both countries, in cold fact, the land on which they lived had been won in a desperate struggle with nature by draining the swamps beside their rivers, naturally enough their cosmogonies embodied the idea that there was too much water about, and that the beginning of things, in any sense that mattered to men, was when some divine being did the equivalent of saying, *Let the dry land appear.* The name of the Babylonian creator was Marduk.... What Thales did was to leave Marduk out. He, too, said that everything else had been formed out of water by a natural process, like the silting up of the delta of the Nile..... It is an admirable beginning, the whole point of which is that it gathers together into a coherent picture a number of observed facts *without letting Marduk in* (emphasis added).[8]

Burnet and Mieli, whom Farrington quotes[9] with approval, though also with some reservation, substantially agree with such a view of the transition from pre-science to science. The stupendous step taken by Thales and his immediate successors is thus described: "They observe the phenomena which present themselves to their eyes, and putting aside all supernatural or mystical intervention, they endeavour to give strictly natural explanations of them."

With this preliminary note on Thales, let us now turn to the scientist we are going to discuss at length. His name comes down to us as Uddālaka Āruṇi, often also referred to by his clan name Gautama.

We first meet him in the Brāhmaṇas, which eminent Vedic scholars like Louis Renou[10] would not allow us to place outside the time-range of the tenth and seventh century B.C. A legend about Uddālaka is found codified in the *Śatapatha Brāhmaṇa*.[11] Admitting what is most plausible—that the legend itself must have been earlier than its codification—we have to place Uddālaka much earlier than Thales. Be that as it may, the legend itself has its own interest as it sheds some light on Uddālaka's bent of mind. We may therefore quote it in brief.

Though already famous for his learning as a Brāhmaṇa of Kuru-Pañcāla, the heartland of Āryāvarta culture, Uddālaka once visited the northern region, then considered culturally backward from the viewpoint of Brāhmanical learning. There he threw out a piece of gold, which was then the mode of challenging the local élite, something like a bet. Panic prevailed among the people there, till Svaidāyana, alias Śaunaka, moved forward to accept the challenge. He wanted Uddālaka to answer three questions, which, peculiarly enough, are of interest even for our times.

First: "Whereby it is that men here are born toothless, whereby the teeth grow with them, whereby these decay with their growth, whereby these grow again to remain long with them, whereby in the last stage of life these all decay again, whereby the lower ones grow first and then the upper ones, whereby the lower ones are smaller and the upper ones are broader, whereby the incisors are larger and whereby the molars are of equal size"?

Second: "Whereby men here are born with hair, whereby for the second time as it were the hair of the beard and the arm-pits and other parts of the body grow on them, whereby it is on the head that one first becomes grey, and then again in the last stage of life one becomes grey all over"?

Third: "Whereby the seed of the boy is not productive, whereby in the middle age it is productive and whereby again in his last stage of life it is not productive"?

According to our text, Uddālaka frankly confessed that the questions were beyond his depth. Hence he humbly approached Svaidāyana to become his pupil and learn the mystery of all these.

Not that we expect a text as ancient as the *Śatapatha Brāhmaṇa* to provide the real answers to the questions and it may even be embarrassing to ask ourselves if we are aware of the answers to these. One point, nevertheless, should be noted. Such questions are not prompted only by *a priori* curiosity, but are rather based on solid observations. Uddālaka's eagerness to know the answers to these questions which led him to become a student of somebody belonging to a comparatively backward area—and this in spite of coming from a centre of Āryāvarta culture—does throw some light on his bent of mind. Questions raised by direct observations were too important for him to be left unexplained. By contrast, he had little patience—or at least no anxiety at all—about the empty speculations then enjoying great prestige and patronage in the holy Āryāvarta. This we can easily guess from an Upaniṣadic text.[12] Some flatterers of the king of Pañcāla asked him if he knew anything about the path along which the departed soul moved towards the realm of the fathers (*pitṛyāna*) and the realm of the gods (*devayāna*). Uddālaka frankly confessed he had no knowledge of this. In fact, he seems to have no curiosity to dabble in such useless quests though such were the questions that the Āryāvarta élite then delighted discussing. Uddālaka was evidently going against the stream. Not that he was averse to the use of the word soul or *ātman*, about which speculations ran riot in Upaniṣadic India. As a matter of fact, as we shall presently see, he did use the word in his own discourse. What he actually understood by it, however, was something most peculiar.

In one of the principal Upaniṣads,[13] he was made to face the question concerning the concept of soul. A certain nobleman mentioned as "King" of the age, called Aśvapati Kaikeya, wanted him to explain his view of *ātman*. He came out with a remarkable answer:

> The king said to Uddālaka Āruṇi: 'Gautama,
> whom do you revere as the *ātman*'?
> 'The earth, indeed, sir, oh king', said he.

The answer is quaint indeed. Was this a way of showing his indifference to the concept itself, which was in fact a basic plank of the mystical idealism dominating the Upaniṣads?

Did it mean that for him the concept was an empty fiction? In any case, he appears to have been much too earth-minded to allow any room for the "pure spirit"—or, what is described by the great mystical idealist of the age called Yājñavalkya "as a mass of consciousness" (*vijñānaghana*)–within the general scheme of his own world-view, not to speak of raising it to the status of the ultimate reality. It remains for us to see the interesting theories he tried to work out—going even to the extent of experimental demonstration—of the origin of "speech" (*vāc*), "life" (*prāṇa*) and "mind" (*manas*), evidently understood by him as the differentia of man.

All this brings us to the Upaniṣads, our principal source of information about Uddālaka. The entire sixth chapter of the *Chāndogya Upaniṣad* is devoted exclusively to summing up his main view. Before dealing with it, however, we shall make a few comments about the Upaniṣads in general.

Winternitz[14] once observed, "it proved fatal for the development of Indian philosophy that the Upaniṣads should have been pronounced to be revelations". The importance of the observation can hardly be overrated, for the resulting disaster had been multi-dimensional. We note here only one of these. Knowledge alleged to be revealed can leave hardly any scope for internal inconsistency. Hence the strenuous effort of the Indian orthodoxy to read a single or monolithic view out of the entire corpus of the Upaniṣadic literature. Such a tendency was officially endorsed and even shared by most of the modern scholars, in spite of the strong dissenting notes of Bhandarkar,[15] Thibaut,[16] Hume[17] and others, whose analyses of the texts showed how palpably absurd it was. Both within and outside popular belief, however, it has become customary to talk of *the philosophy* of the Upaniṣads and the most widespread form in which it was propagated has been to identify the ultimate reality with pure spirit—called *Brahman* and *ātman* respectively—that is, some form of mystical and extreme idealism. The worst casualty was science and the scientific temper, or, perhaps more strictly, whatever promise there was of these in thinkers of the

Upaniṣadic age. Deussen, sharing the orthodox viewpoint,[18] came out with an open admiration of such a rejection of science in the Upaniṣads. As he observed:

> Very soon, however, it came to be realised that this knowledge of *Brahman* was essentially of a different nature from that which we call 'knowledge' in ordinary life.... The experimental knowledge which reveals to us a plurality, where in reality only *Brahman* exists, and a body where in reality there is only the soul, must be a mistaken knowledge, a delusion, a *māyā*.[19]

What concerns us most for our present discussion is how much we are deprived of understanding the real contributions of Uddālaka to the making of global science by this tenacious attempt to force his teachings into the general mould or the *Brahman-ātman* metaphysics alleged to be the exclusive philosophy of the Upaniṣads.

But let us leave fiction and turn to facts.

What needs to be noted at once is that Uddālaka was about the only prominent thinker in the Upaniṣads in whose discourse the word *Brahman* never occurs at all. Not that he was by any chance unaware of the concept; in fact, we find him engaged in a philosophical debate with Yājñavalkya,[20] the exponent *par excellence* of the *Brahman- ātman* metaphysics. His avoidance of it must have been deliberate, the reason for which was presumably the strong association of the word with the mystical metaphysics for which he had no taste. For the ultimate reality, therefore, he preferred to coin a new terminology, namely *sat*, meaning the bare existent or just being. The way in which he introduces this new concept is interesting.

In the *Chāndogya Upaniṣad*,[21] Uddālaka's account begins with a preamble, which already shows that he was going against the stream, though in his own way.

Once upon a time there lived Śvetaketu, the son of Uddālaka. According to the practice in those days, when he was twelve years old, his father sent him to thoroughly study Vedic lore, which already enjoyed the scriptural status.

Having studied the Vedas for twelve years under competent preceptors, Śvetaketu returned home at the age of twenty-four—conceited and proud of his learning. Uddālaka asked him, "Śvetaketu, my dear, you are conceited and proud of your learning. But did you also ask [your preceptors] about that teaching by which what has not been heard of [in ordinary discussions or even in scriptural lore] becomes heard of, what has not been thought of becomes thought of, what has not been understood becomes understood"?

The son failed to understand what his father was talking about, in spite of his thorough study of the scriptures for twelve years. Evidently, this was not because of his failure to learn, but because, as the text presently says, his preceptors themselves had no idea of what Uddālaka was questioning about. In any case, he requested his father to be clear about the question itself.

His father clarified that what he was talking about was the ultimate stuff of which everything in the universe was made. Significantly, Uddālaka wanted to explain his question with a series of commonplace observations:

> Just as, my dear, by knowing one piece of clay, everything made of clay may be known—the modifications (in the form of the varieties of the clay-objects) are mere matters of verbal distinction or simply names; the reality is just clay.
>
> Just as, my dear, by knowing one piece of golden ornament everything made of gold is known—the modifications (in the form of golden objects) are mere matters of verbal distinction, simply names; the reality is just gold.
>
> Just as, my dear, by knowing one nail-cutter, everything made of iron may be known; the modifications (in the form of all iron-objects) are mere matters of verbal distinction or simply names; the reality is just iron.
>
> So, my dear, that is what I am talking about.
>
> Śvetaketu said, 'Verily these learned men that taught me the scriptural lore have no notion of this; for if they had known it, why would they have not told me? So do you, Sir, tell it to me'.
>
> Uddālaka agreed to do so.

The possible significance of such a preamble cannot be glossed over. Nor can its main drift be in any way ignored. Without being blunt or strident, it was but a crafty way of showing the futility of scriptural lore. A full course of study in the Vedas stretched over a period of twelve years left the son quite in the dark even about the meaning of the quest for the ultimately real—the meaning of which Uddālaka hoped to clarify only with a series of actual observations or empirical data.

Aṣ far as I know, no one has so far commented on such implications of Uddālaka's emphasis on empirical data—an emphasis which, as we shall see, characterised practically every step of his discourse. What seems to be all the more important is that there was something extraordinarily audacious about it, that is, as judged in its actual context, inasmuch as this could be done only by flouting a favourite dictum of the scriptures and their custodians, the Vedic priests. We read this dictum repeated over and over again in the Brāhmaṇa literature, where it reads *parokṣa-priyāḥ iva hi devāḥ* or *parokṣa-kāmāḥ iva hi devāḥ*, usually translated by modern scholars as "the gods are fond of the mystic" or "the gods are fond of the obscure". Yājñavalkya, interested above all in the metaphysical mystification of reality, apparently felt that the full implications of the dictum were in need of some elaboration. Hence he restated it and said *parokṣa-priyāḥ iva hi devāḥ, pratyakṣadviṣaḥ:* "The gods are fond of the obscure and they *detest direct observation*".[22] It was in the teeth of such declarations concerning the divine distaste for empirical knowledge that Uddālaka—practically from the beginning to the end of his discourse—made empirical data or direct observation the sheet anchor of his own view. Not that we expect a thinker of the seventh or eight-century B.C. to be really meticulous about distinguishing between real observations and what we understand today as pseudo-observation: some of the empirical data on which he depended have for us the value only of the latter.

But that is beside the point. The point rather is the general direction of his thought and not the intrinsic worth of his conclusions in our standard. Thus judged, Uddālaka's position is really unique in the history of science, inasmuch as no one before him is known to have shown such a conscious enthusiasm for direct observation or empirical data as the basis of forming any view.

On this point it is imperative for us to digress into a brief comparison of Uddālaka with his junior contemporary, Thales.

As already mentioned, little of authentic value is known about him today. Still we are asked to look back at him as the founder of global science, mainly because he took the momentous step of scrapping the earlier religious view in defence of a natural principle being the first cause of the world or, as Farrington so lucidly says, Thales pushed out the water god Marduk of ancient Babylonian religion, retaining only water as the first cause or the original principle from which everything in the world originated.

If all this is accepted as the way of the transition from pre-science to science, we may return to our Uddālaka especially to compare his achievement to that of the generally acknowledged founder of scientific tradition in history. From the preamble to his account already quoted, it is evident that he, too, had to scrap all supernatural and mystical intervention with which the Vedas were teeming, and this for the purpose of arriving at a natural first cause of everything in the world. Compared to Thales, however, this must have been all the more formidable a task for him. Marduk of the Babylonians had for Thales been an alien god after all, while the gods and goddesses of the Vedas belonged to *the immediate intellectual context of Uddālaka in which they had already been invested with scriptural sanction*, and hence rejection of whom—tacit or otherwise—required a good deal of greater boldness.

Besides, for Uddālaka, it was not a mere question of introducing some sort of refinement of ancient cosmology by way of scrapping any old god. It was for him a question of making a new beginning altogether, taking for the purpose a number of observations of facts, behind which it is not difficult to see the common technicians of his time—the potter, the goldsmith and the ironsmith—that is, those who were then engaged in actually manipulating with nature as given in order to effect changes in it: clay into clay-pots, gold (or gold-ore?) into golden ornaments, iron (or iron-ore?) into iron implements. The observations with which Uddālaka chose to formulate the kind of quest he was interested in were *not just passive* observations of events taking place in nature but rather in matters in which *manual work was involved.*

Apparently, somebody with a contempt for the working hand would have chosen other examples to illustrate his point. Are we, thus, permitted to presume that in the sociology implicit in Uddālaka's understanding, the manual workers were not looked down upon as in the Dharmaśāstras? The question itself would not be considered irrelevant if we bear in mind two points. First, on the evidence of the *Uddālaka Jātaka*[23] of the Buddhists, B.M. Barua[24] has argued that caste contempt had actually no place in the sociology subscribed to by Uddālaka. Secondly, already in 1902-3, P.C. Ray[25] argued that by far the most important factor accounting for the eventual decline of the scientific spirit in India was the social degradation of the technicians and craftsmen—which, by implication, means that science draws its nourishment from the techniques—a point more elaborately argued these days by a section of the historians of science like J.D. Bernal, Joseph Needham, Benjamin Farrington and others. From this point of view, the very enthusiasm of Uddālaka to draw upon the experience of the manual workers or technicians could have more positive significance than simply the negative one of scrapping the early divinities.

But let us return to the way in which Uddālaka is reported to have explained his view. It is indeed a matter of considerable interest to note how systematically he unfolded it in the *Chāndogya Upaniṣad*.

Interested above all in the ultimate cause of the infinite multiplicity in nature, the first point he wanted to be clear about was the nature of causality itself. According to our text, with the preamble over, Uddālaka straightaway proceeded to the concept of causality. As he said to his son:

> In the beginning, my dear, this world was Being (*sat*), one only, without a second. To be sure, some people say, 'In the beginning this world was just non-Being (*asat*), one only, without a second; from the non-Being was produced Being'. But verily, my dear, how could this be? How from non-Being could Being be produced? On the contrary, my dear, in the beginning this world was just Being, one only, without a second.

A few points need to be clarified here.

First, in the intellectual climate to which Uddālaka belonged, there was a view sanctified by the scriptures which seems to have implied that the original cause of the world was so mysterious that it defied all descriptions either as Being or as non-Being. This was embodied in a cosmogonical hymn of the *Ṛgveda*,[26] according to which the creation of the world started from such a state of utter indescribability: "Then even nothingness was not, nor existence". Apparently, some of Uddālaka's contemporaries or near-contemporaries wanted to understand this as implying that in the beginning there was only non-Being—a view clearly formulated in some of the Upaniṣads.[27] Uddālaka found it necessary to reject it before proceeding to his own, arguing that from nothingness can originate only nothingness.[28] This made him the first seeker of truth wanting consciously to clarify the concept of causality.

Secondly, the view he himself defended cannot but be reminiscent of what in later Indian philosophy came to be known as *sat-kārya-vāda* or "the potential pre-existence of the effect in the cause". This was tenaciously defended by the Sāṃkhya philosophers who argued that, such being the case, the nature of the cause could be inferred from the nature of the effect. Hence, according to them, the effect being of the nature of the material world, the first cause could only be matter in some form. In their terminology, this was *prakṛti* or *pradhāna*—a principle of unconscious matter. Could it, then, be that Uddālaka laid the foundation of the philosophical view that later came down to us as the Sāṃkhya? If there is anything in such a possibility, it would prove disastrous for the later interpreters of the Upaniṣads, keen on reading an exclusively idealist-spiritualistic metaphysics throughout the corpus of the Upaniṣadic literature.

We are being tempted to add here some more points. Though the Sāṃkhya view, in the form in which it reaches us in the later period, is considered to be some sort of dualism—adding to this primeval matter or *pradhāna* some kind of a soul or spirit called the *puruṣa*—Sanskritists (as eminent as Sukhlalji Sanghvi[29] and S.N. Dasgupta[30]) argue that in its original version this soul or *puruṣa* was itself considered as evolving from the primeval principle of *pradhāna,* which, in other words, means that the original Sāṃkhya must have been some kind of archaic materialism or at least precariously near-materialism. Secondly, the great idealist Saṃkara frankly confessed in his *magnum opus* that the strongest rival of his own *Brahman-ātman* metaphysics was the Śaṃkhya one, so that by its refutation all other philosophies of comparatively minor significance were *de facto* refuted, just as in a wrestling arena one scored a victory over all the rivals by defeating the champion among them all (*pradhāna-malla-nivarhaṇa-nyāya*). But why did Śaṃkara consider Sāṃkhya such a strong rival? The answer is that he understood it frankly as *acetana-pradhāna-kāraṇa-vāda* or the doctrine of unconscious primeval matter, adding that he would have little resented Sāṃkhya if only it took the principle of the spirit or *puruṣa* with due seriousness.[31]

Thus the possibility of the Sāṃkhya originally having been a philosophy of the material first cause cannot be easily ruled out. Nor can the possibility of Uddālaka laying its real foundation, because of the simple fact that while trying to coerce into the entire Upaniṣadic literature what they considered the Upaniṣadic philosophy *par excellence*, one of the main headaches for both Śaṃkara[32] and Rāmānuja[33] was the possibility of Uddālaka's view being taken as the same as the Sāṃkhya.

Hence both of them argued their best to show that the original cause or primeval Being, mentioned by Uddālaka simply as *sat*, could by no means mean anything like the *pradhāna* of Sāṃkhya; what he could and did mean by the word was nothing but *Brahman*. But neither Śaṃkara nor Rāmānuja raised the question as to why Uddālaka ignored the word *Brahman* altogether if his real intention was to speak of it, especially in an age in which it was in wide circulation. Evidently, the question itself was too awkward to be raised at all. It may be worthwhile to remember in this connection what Uddālaka meant by *ātman* or soul, namely nothing else than this earth and not as viewed in the Vedānta as coeval to *Brahman*. Besides, the great anxiety of commentators like Śaṃkara and Rāmānuja to prove that by *sat* Uddālaka could not mean the *Pradhāna* or its prototype easily leads to the suspicion that there must have been some strong possibility for it: one does not need to negate a point elaborately that is *prima facie* impossible.

We do not have the scope here to reiterate all the arguments of Śaṃkara and Rāmānuja to make *Brahman* out of Uddālaka's *sat*. Nor is it necessary here; I have elsewhere tried to show that the arguments are flimsy.[34] Only one example should suffice for our present purpose.

After exploring various possibilities to show that Uddālaka's real position was but a way of putting traditional Vedānta, both Śaṃkara and Rāmānuja seemed to come out with their trump card as it were. The realisation of the *Brahman-ātman* view was assumed in the Vedānta to be the royal road to salvation or liberation (*mokṣa*). How, then, could Uddālaka deceive his dear son by preaching a material first cause, when his son approached him with the earnest desire for that knowledge which alone could lead to liberation?

But the difficulty about this line of argument is obvious. Nowhere is there even any hint in the Upaniṣads that the son Śvetaketu approached him with the desire of attaining liberation. In fact, the concept of liberation or *mokṣa* was completely ignored in what we are told about Śvetaketu, both in and outside the Upaniṣads. What we are told instead in the *Chāndogya Upaniṣad* is simply that Śvetaketu returned to his father with the conceit of learning the scriptural lore for twelve years and the first thing Uddālaka did was to show that the conceit was in vain after all: Vedic studies even for such a prolonged period gave the son no notion whatsoever of that which mattered most for Uddālaka. Indian cultural tradition outside the Upaniṣads is even worse for Śaṃkara-Rāmānuja's decisive argument: it pours just cold water on all their enthusiasm by simply proclaiming that Śvetaketu, the son of Uddālaka Āruṇi, was the actual founder of erotics or Kāmaśāstra.[35] *Kāma,* which means sex and sex only, is not mokṣa.

Speaking objectively, therefore, there is no chance of seeing in Uddālaka's view the same *Brahman-ātman* theory. Yet tradition is a great force and for about two thousand years a tradition is nourished in our philosophical circle that Uddālaka expounded the spiritualist-idealist view of liberation. In fact, this view is alleged to be expressed in four cryptic formulas—called *mahāvākyas* or "great sayings" —of the Upaniṣads. One of these simply means "That thou art"—*tat tvam asi.* This was oft-repeated in the teachings of Uddālaka. But what could the philosopher do other than remind his son that the latter was, in the ultimate analysis, nothing but the same primeval Being—that *sat*—from which originated everything in the universe, from the meanest creatures like the mosquito and worm to the great heavenly bodies like the sun and the moon, brushing aside the sun god, the moon god and in fact the whole host of deities that crowded the Veda? Evidently, as a human being Śvetaketu could not be outside all these. Not that Uddālaka dropped the word deity or *devatā* altogether. He used it while referring to not only his primeval Being but also to its three primary evolutes—*tejas* or heat, *ap* or water and *anna* or food—which, as we shall presently see, eventually went to the immediate making of everything in the universe. How, then, are we to understand this word in Uddālaka's discourse? B.M. Barua, who has gone into some detail of analysing the concept, answers: "Uddālaka's Deity (*devatā*)... is a most baffling term. But nothing is more certain than that it is on the whole a physical conception. We may suppose that in the realm of change the term applies to Matter or the Material".[36] In defence of such a possibility, it may not be irrelevant to mention here the ancient Greek parallel. Observes Burnet:

> The spirit of Ionian civilisation had been thoroughly secular, and this was, no doubt, one of the causes that favoured the rise of science... For our present purpose, it is of utmost importance to observe that it was just this non-religious use of the word 'god' which made it possible for the Milesians to apply it to their primary substance and their 'innumerable worlds'. That way of speaking does not bear witness to any theological origin of Greek science, but rather to its complete independence of the religious tradition.[37]

We have quoted B.M. Barua because he is almost the only notable Indian scholar who, in 1921, argued that Uddālaka represented a materialist or at least a near-materialist view. Apparently he is not aware that in 1916 Hermann Jacobi[38] was already trying to develop a similar line of argument, which is carried forward with greater vigour by Walter Ruben from 1954. Ruben proclaims Uddālaka also as the first philosopher. However, what seems to elude Barua, Jacobi and Ruben—or, at any rate, what is not adequately emphasised by them—is the circumstance that Uddālaka needs also to be recognised as the first nature scientist. Among the modern scholars Erich Fraüwallner[39] is about the only one who wants us to look back at Uddālaka as knocking —feebly though—at the gates of natural science to be opened:

"One would like to speak of it [Uddālaka's view] as an almost scientific attitude". But Fraüwallner himself seems to concentrate mainly on some stray conclusions of Uddālaka, bypassing what appears to us to be much more momentous about him, namely *the first formulation and application of the methodology of science—constantly drawing on empirical data and even using what cannot but be described as the experimental method.* In any case, Fraüwallner's assessment of Uddālaka is an isolated one, without making any dent on the prevalent understanding of the history of science and philosophy. The net result of all this is that Uddālaka remains totally unknown to the historians of science, who continue to look back at Thales as the real pioneer of science in history.

Since the present discussion is intended to focus mainly on this aspect of Uddālaka's contribution to the history of science, we propose to have here only a skeletal description of his general discourse, highlighting some outstanding points of his methodology.

Unlike Thales, Uddālaka refused to specify his original ground for everything as any gross element of our experience, like water. If any comparison with ancient Greek thought is at all permissible, the original Being of Uddālaka is reminiscent of the primitive matter of Anaximander, who is somewhat later than Thales. Anaximander viewed his primeval matter (sometimes conceived as the original "chaos") as the "eternal, infinite, indefinite ground, from which, in order of time, all arises, and into which all returns". But perhaps our comparison has to stop here. There are mainly two reasons for this. First, Uddālaka attempted to work out a systematic account of the evolution of everything in the world—both inorganic and organic—from his original *sat* or Being, though from what comes down to us as Anaximander's thought, he was also groping for some comparatively rudimentary explanation of this only in terms of the original contraries of heat and cold. Secondly, while Anaximander did not allow any quantitative or qualitative designation of this primal matter, in Uddālaka's teaching—

as the *Chāndogya Upaniṣad* wants us to believe—there seems to be a positive hint or the first foreshadowing of the atomic hypothesis, inasmuch as the finest essence of the Being which, in Uddālaka's view ultimately went to the making of everything, was made of minute entities—so minute that these could not be possibly seen and thus cut into minuter pieces. Significantly, the word actually used in the discourse for this "finest essence" of the Being is *aṇu* or atom, somewhat polished by the later Indian atomists as *parama-aṇu* or *paramāṇu*. The following forms part of the further dialogue between father and son in our Upaniṣad:

'Bring hither a fig from there'.

'Here it is, Sir'.

'Divide it'.

'It is divided, Sir'.

'What do you see there'?

'These rather fine seeds, Sir'.

'Of these, please divide one'.

'It is divided, Sir'.

'What do you see there'?

'Nothing at all, Sir'.

Then he said to him: 'Verily, my dear, that finest essence which you do not perceive—verily, my dear, from that finest essence this great fig tree arises. Believe me, my dear, that which is the finest essence—this whole world has that as its soul. That is Reality. That is soul. That thou art, Śvetaketu'.

'Do you, Sir, cause me to understand even more'.

'So be it, my dear', said he: 'Place this salt in water.

In the morning come unto me'.

Then he did so.

Then he said to him: 'That salt you placed in water last evening—please bring it hither'.

Then he grasped for it, but did not find it, as it was completely dissolved.

'Please take a sip of it from this end', he said. 'How is it'?

'Salt'.

'Take a sip from the middle', said he. 'How is it'?

'Salt'.

'Take a sip from that end', said he. 'How is it'?

'Salt'.

'Set it aside. Then come to me'.

He did so, saying, 'It is always the same'.

Then he said, 'Verily, indeed my dear, you do not perceive Being here. Verily, indeed, it is here. That which is the finest essence—this whole world has that as its soul.

That is Reality. That is soul. That thou art, Śvetaketu'.

Understandably, we do not expect a seeker of the ultimate constituent of Reality of the eighth or seventh century B.C. to use terminology sophisticated enough by our standard. Besides, though he used the word "soul" or *ātman*, we have already seen what precisely he meant by it, namely nothing more than the earth. In the present discourse, if the soul is identified with *sat* or original Being which it is difficult to understand as anything but Matter, Uddālaka's position cannot but be reminiscent of what comes down to us as the uncompromising materialism called Cārvāka or Lokāyata. What is significant about Uddālaka, at any rate, is that he wanted to conceive the basic stuff of the world as consisting of the finest essence, of invisible minute particles, which one comes across while dividing a seed of the fig into parts and further subdividing each part, or when one dissolves a lump of salt into water; that is, in our terminology, when its molecules get separated into invisible entities. It is because of this that B.M. Barua[40] boldly asserts, "Uddālaka anticipated the atomic theory of Kaṇāda". But there perhaps remains one point to be added to this. While for Kaṇāda—as for other early atomists like Democritus—the atomic hypothesis remained a speculative product after all, Uddālaka took the bold step of founding it on definite observation, however rudimentary that may appear by contemporary standards. While the other ancient atomists wanted us to *imagine the* process of cutting a thing into smaller and still smaller parts and argued that it had to stop somewhere (the further uncuttable or *atom*), Uddālaka seemed to demonstrate this by *actually cutting* the thing which, especially in the ancient context, was remarkable indeed. In any case, what appears to us as very remarkable about Uddālaka is that instead of just proclaiming some theory or seeking any scriptural declaration as its main prop, he wanted to demonstrate it on the strength of actual observation practically at every step of his discourse. Much more than his conclusion, thus, it was the methodology he followed that made him so important. For all that we know of his junior contemporary in ancient Greece, Thales, there survives not even a hint of any systematic methodology that led him to the view that water was the ultimate stuff of the whole world.

Assuming—what is sometimes doubted though—that a naturalistic understanding of nature made Thales the first nature scientist in global history, most of the histories of science are left only with the scope of conjecturing *how* he was led to such a view. Uddālaka, by contrast, left us with nothing vague about his own procedure or any conjecture about the methodology followed by him. With him, therefore, something genuinely new emerged in history.

We shall go here into a little more of the methodology followed by Uddālaka. To show that the primeval Being was made of minute particles, he depended mainly on two observations, the second of which in particular, if not an experiment in the later sense, shows at least the temper of loitering on its corridor. That the process of cutting something into smaller and smaller parts leads one to reach the invisible and hence further uncuttable particle may be taken as a matter of observation, though not simple observation in a passive sense, inasmuch as the active intervention of the observer is involved in the process. This becomes all the more obvious in the second example mentioned by Uddālaka. One is tempted to recall here the practice of the earlier chemists preparing in their laboratories some solution with the uniform distribution of the molecules of a dissolved substance, every part of the solution testifying to the presence of the substance before our sense organ. If one feels reluctant to call this an experiment, one is perhaps obliged to see in this procedure of demonstration an act of at least moving round its prototype, irrespective of the question of the atomic and molecular hypothesis being first foreshadowed in his understanding.

But the more important point about Uddālaka is that he was really not satisfied with just dabbling with the experimental method. On the contrary, he did formulate its essence in so many words and his formulation remained *de facto* accepted for centuries to come in the history of science. This is evidenced by way of demonstrating the thesis that the human mind (*manas*) is made of the finest particles of food (*anna*) consumed. Allowing other factors to remain the same, you can see that in the absence of food there is the absence of mind while in the presence of food there is the presence of mind. Let us review briefly how he developed the thesis, and then see how he proved it with definite experimental methods.

Uddālaka conceived his primeval Being as auto-dynamic or, in modern terminology, he viewed the multiplicity of the world evolving from motion inherent in matter. A thinker belonging to a hoary antiquity had evidently to grope for words to express such a profound idea. The word he actually used was *aikṣata*, literally" "desired": the primeval Being "desired" to become many, etc.

Śaṃkara and Rāmānuja, wanting to prove that the first cause conceived by him could not be anything of the nature of unconscious matter, wanted to make much of the use of such a word, arguing that the act of desiring could not be posited of anything unconscious. However, from the circumstance of Uddālaka using precisely the same word in connection with "heat" (*tejas*), water (*ap*) and food (*anna*), Rāmānuja[41] at any rate had to concede the possibility that this could be a metaphorical expression (*upacāra*) after all, like one saying that the scorched earth "cried" for water. It seems from the context that there is no escape from such an interpretation. Thus, notwithstanding the use of the word "desired", Uddālaka evidently meant that because of motion inherent in the primeval Being—that is, without the intervention of any external agency whatsoever—from it successively evolved *tejas* or "heat", from "heat" evolved *ap* or water and from *ap* evolved *anna* or food. Separated as we are from Uddālaka by over two thousand five hundred years, there may be some difficulty in understanding what precisely he meant by *tejas* or *"heat"*. But the way in which he tried to show how "water" originated from "heat" and "food" from "water" cannot but be evidence of his peculiar zeal for empirical evidence though, understandably enough, in his time superficial observation and even pseudo-observation could easily be mixed up with observation proper. Thus he argued that those tormented by heat shed tears and perspiration, while abundant food was produced in cases of abundance of water—observations intended to show that water was produced from heat and food from water. Judged by our standards, the first was only a pseudo-observation and the second at best an incomplete one. But, historically speaking, such a judgement would be an anachronism and in any case would prove nothing against Uddālaka's basic *zeal for* depending on observation practically at every step—a zeal the importance of which can by no means be underrated from the viewpoint of the history of science.

Thus equipped with the three principles successively evolving from the primeval Being, Uddālaka proceeded to show how everything in the universe—from the heavenly phenomena like the sun, moon and lightning to the meanest creatures on the earth like mosquitoes and worms—originated from heat, water and food, though in each of these one of the three principles predominated. Such an attempt at an all-comprehensive explanation of nature was evidently premature for his age. But it retains at least this much of interest for us that it was *de facto* an attempt to depopulate nature gods and goddesses—the sun-god, the moon-god, *et al.*—that crowded the Vedic pantheon. Besides, while talking of the making of all creatures from these three principles alone, he left hardly any room for the doctrine of transmigration of the soul as determined by *karma*—a doctrine that was already taking firm root in Indian culture in his time[42] and eventually became the basic justification of the caste-divided social norm of the Indian law-makers. At the same time, his discourse as recorded in the *Chāndogya Upaniṣad* gives us the impression that he talked of the origin of the heavenly bodies and so on, perhaps lured by the tendency to give some sort of completeness to his world-view, because he mentioned these in passing, as it were, that is, without trying to dilate into details.

On the contrary, as is evident from the subsequent discussion, the main focus of his interest seems to be to explain from the same three basic elements—and therefore ultimately from the primeval Being—the making of human beings, and this inclusive of what he evidently considered the three main peculiarities of man, namely life, mind and speech. In trying to offer a purely naturalistic explanation of all this Uddālaka—historically speaking—took a step towards nature science which, to say the least, was amazing.

First, none before him wanted—rationally and naturalistically—to explain the special peculiarities of man, namely life, mind and speech. The very fact that Uddālaka concentrated on the understanding of these three may be taken as an index of his scientific temper.

Secondly, as for "life", it is the differentia no doubt of organic matter. However, the very awareness of this differentia was something new in the history of ideas. For all that we know, the early Greek thinkers—inclusive of Thales, particularly with whom we propose to compare Uddālaka in the context of being recognised as the first scientist—were apparently unaware of this. They seem to have conceived matter itself as somehow endowed with life, or simply as something living. That is why in the history of philosophy the need is usually left for a new terminology appropriate for their real position. The term thus introduced is *hylozoism*, though the real advance of it from primitive animism appears to be somewhat marginal.

Thirdly, the fact is that no one before Uddālaka made any conscious attempt to pose the question of the origin of life. Uddālaka did it and it may be an error to denude his conclusion totally of any scientific interest, inasmuch as—when it comes to the basics—he somehow tried to understand the origin of life from water, or more strictly, from its finest essence.

Fourthly, none before him raised the question of the making of "mind" as Uddālaka did. What is perhaps more amazing is that he wanted us to view the "mind" as originating from the minutest constituents of the food consumed.

Fifthly—and there is no question of underrating its significance in the history of science—Uddālaka did not simply make this assertion on the basis of mere speculation, but offered an *experimental demonstration* in favour of the view. *All other considerations apart, it is this methodology of experimental demonstration that entitles him to be recognised as the first nature scientist in global history*. It is particularly on this point that he appears to be free from the need of any concession as belonging to the ancient period. The essentials of his mode of experimentation obviously contained a good deal of importance—or at least the potential thereof—of the experimental method for centuries to come. There is no doubt, as J.D. Bernal[43] wants us to remember, "The method of science is not a fixed thing, it is a growing process". Nevertheless, from the historical viewpoint, what matters most is the first step taken towards it. Uddālaka had not only taken this step in the eighth or seventh century B.C., but moreover essentials of the method suggested by him retain significance at least up to the time of John Stuart Mill.

Finally, Uddālaka somehow also wanted to explain the making of "speech"(*vāc*) from the minutest constituents of the *tejas* element, for which we have agreed to accept the translation "heat". What exactly he was referring to by the word is, however, a point that seems to require further investigation and as such his view of the origin of speech is not fully clear to us; this may not be because of anything in Uddālaka's statement itself but, rather, due to the present inadequacy in our understanding of one of his key terminologies. At the same time, the fact remains that he was undoubtedly the first in the history of science to have felt the need to offer a rational and essentially naturalistic explanation of the making of "speech", and this evidently because he felt that, like "mind", "speech" is a characteristic peculiarity of human beings.

In order to understand the way in which he put the points, it is necessary for us to quote in full the passage in which Uddālaka explained the making of man—a passage that seems to have unique importance as the earliest specimen of scientific literature we have. Here, again, it is necessary to note that, instead of depending on empty speculation, Uddālaka wanted to draw on the facts of actual observation, namely that of churning coagulated milk so that butter got separated from it. Do we not meet the technician—the milkmaid in this case—on whose experience Uddālaka drew in this connection? But let us first quote the passage:

> [Uddālaka explained to his son]: 'Food, when eaten, becomes divided into three parts. That which is its coarsest constituent becomes the faeces; that which is the medium, the flesh; that which is minutest, the mind (*manas*).
>
> 'Water, when drunk, becomes divided into three parts. That which is its coarsest constituent becomes the urine; that which is the medium, the blood; that which is the minutest, the life (*prāṇa*).
>
> Heat [which the later interpreters explain as oil, *ghee* or melted butter, etc., perhaps under the influence of the ancient medical view; cf. *Caraka-saṃhitā*, for example, I.13.14] when eaten, becomes divided into three parts. That which is its coarsest constituent becomes the bone; that which is the medium, the marrow; that which is the minutest, the speech (*vāc*).

'For, my dear, the mind consists of food; the life consists of water; the speech consists of heat'.

[The son said]: 'Do you, Sir, cause me to understand more'. [The father explained]: 'Of coagulated milk, my dear, when churned, that which is the minutest constituent all moves upward; it becomes butter.

'Even so, my dear, that which is the minutest constituent all moves upward; it becomes the mind.

'Of water, my dear, that which is the minutest constituent all moves upward; it becomes the life.

'Of heat [oil, *ghee*, etc.], my dear, when eaten, that which is the minutest constituent all moves upward; it becomes speech.

'For, my dear, the mind consists of food; the life consists of water; the speech consists of heat'.

[Then the son said]: 'Do you, Sir, cause me to understand more.'

'So be it, my dear', said he [and continued]: 'A person, my dear, consists of sixteen parts. For fifteen days do not eat; drink water at will. Life, which consists of water, will not be cut off from one who drinks water'.

Then for fifteen days he [the son] did not eat. So then he [the son] approached him [Uddālaka], saying, 'What shall I say, Sir'?

'The Ṛg [verses of the *Ṛgveda-saṃhitā*], my dear, the *Yajus* [the spell] of the *Yajurveda-saṃhitā*], the *Sāman* [the melodies of the *Sāmaveda-saṃhitā]'* [that is, in short, what the son was supposed to have gathered by his mental faculty for twelve long years].

The he [the son] said, 'Verily, they do not come to me, Sir'.

To him, he [Uddālaka] said, 'Just as, my dear, a single coal of the size of a fire-fly may be left over from a great kindled fire, but with it the fire would not thereafter burn much [here, again, the appeal to observation must not be overlooked]—so, my dear, of your sixteen parts a single sixteenth part may be left over, but with it you do not bring the Vedas to mind. Eat, then you will understand from me'.

Then he ate. So then he approached him. Then whatever he [Uddālaka] asked him, he answered everything. To him, he [Uddālaka] then said:

> 'Just as, my dear, one may by covering it with straw, make a single coal of the size of a fire-fly that has been left over from a great kindled fire blaze up, and with it the fire thereafter burns much [note the appeal to empirical data again]–so, my dear, of your sixteen parts a single sixteenth part has been left over. After having been covered with food, it has blazed up. With it you now apprehend the Vedas; for, my dear, the mind consists of food, the life consists of water, the speech consists of heat'. Then he understood from him—ye, he understood.

Before proceeding further, let us ask ourselves a simple question. What is, in essence, the method that Uddālaka was following? There can be only one answer to it. It is nothing but the method of observation and experiment.

It is sometimes suggested that some kind of observation formed the background of the view of Thales, too. It is the observation of land emerging from inundated areas. Even admitting this, we have to admit further that it is really a case of pseudo-observation or mal-observation—the land re-emerging being viewed as coming into being. Besides, the actual core of experience on which he builds his thesis is presumably borrowed from the ancient Egyptians and Babylonians. It is hinted, again, that his view of the earth as a flat disc floating on water could have been suggested by the observation of his homeland being but a tiny island surrounded by water.[44] As for the value of this observation for justifying his thesis, perhaps the less said the better. Leaving him, when we look back at Uddālaka, we cannot help feeling that we are entering a different realm of viewing things altogether. Though rudimentary by current standards, his zeal for observation is genuine and also relevant in defence of a thesis far more comprehensive than that of Thales.

And not simple observations alone. Especially in defence of the view that mind is made of the minutest particles of food digested, Uddālaka went in for a method which is nothing short of an experimental proof: other circumstances allowed to remain the same, in the presence of food there is the presence of mind, while in the absence of food there is the absence of mind.

Equipped with this methodology—and presumably drawn by the attraction of comprehensiveness, Uddālaka tried to explain other aspects of man, like sleep, hunger, thirst and death—the last as the gradual reversal of the evolutionary process, namely food returning back to water, water to heat and heat to the primeval Being again. It is not necessary for our present purpose to go into the details of this aspect of his view, much of which are formula-like repetitions and, in any case, without having anything more spectacular to add to what is already noted about him. But the way in which he summed up his main thesis more than once in his discourse may as well be quoted for a fuller understanding of his position. As the *Chāndogya Upaniṣad* records it:

> 'On this point, my dear, understand that this [body] is a sprout which has sprung up. It will not be without a root.
>
> 'What else can its root be than food? Even so, my dear, with food for a sprout, look for water as the root. With water, my dear, as a sprout, look for heat as the root.
>
> With heat, my dear, as a sprout, look for Being as the root.
>
> 'All creatures here, my dear, have Being as their root, have Being as their home, have Being as their support.....
>
> 'As the bees, my dear, prepare honey by collecting the essences of different trees and reducing the essences to a unity, and then the honey is not able to discriminate: "I am the essence of that tree"—even so, indeed, my dear, all creatures here, though they reach Being, know not: we have reached Being. [Note the appeal to observation again. Without exaggeration, we find in Uddālaka an observation-intoxicated man.]
>
> 'Whatever they are in this world, whether tiger, or lion, or wolf, or boar, or worm, or fly, or gnat, or mosquito, that they become.

> 'That which is the finest essence—this whole world has that as its soul. That is reality. That is *ātman* [soul]. That art thou, Śevetaketu'.

Lest, however, all this appear as but empty speculation, Uddālaka took the further step of proving it on the strength of an actual observation. As the text continues:

> [The son said]: 'Do you, Sir, cause me to understand even more'.
>
> 'So be it, my dear', said he [and continued].
>
> 'These rivers, my dear, flow: the eastern towards the east, the western towards the west. They go just from the ocean to the ocean. They become the ocean itself. [Observation again]! As they know not 'I am this one', 'I am that one'—even so, indeed, my dear, all creatures here, though they have come from Being, know not "we have come forth from Being". Whatever they are in this world, whether tiger, or lion, or wolf or boar, or worm, or fly, or mosquito, that they become.
>
> 'That which is the finest essence—this whole world has that as its soul. That is reality. That is *ātman* [soul]. That thou art, Śvetaketu'.

To sum up our discussion: Uddālaka Āruṇi, who could not presumably be later than the eighth or seventh century B.C., took the step from the magico-mythological view of the scriptures to a naturalistic understanding of nature. For this purpose, he—craftily enough—first showed the futility of the knowledge of scriptural lore and, clarifying the concept of causality, postulated as the original cause of the universe the primeval Being (*sat*), ignoring thereby the word *Brahman* (identified with pure spirit)—which was greatly in vogue in the general intellectual climate to which he belonged. Uddālaka showed no regard for a spiritualistic understanding of the soul or spirit, declaring that so far as he was obliged to use this concept of *ātman*, he was prepared to understand by it as nothing but the earth. With these preliminaries over, he proceeded to sketch a view of the evolution or development of everything in nature ultimately from the primeval Being or *sat*, with a dynamism or motion inherent in it. What strikes us as most remarkable about his procedure is that practically at every step of this sketch he drew upon empirical data of acts of direct observation, already censored by the priest class and other representatives of the *Brahman-ātman* philosophy, as distasteful for the gods—a trend lavishly patronised by the petty chiefs and nobles then consolidating their power in Āryāvarta. But indifferent to such philosophical fashions—and hence also to the patronage for it—Uddālaka stuck to direct observation and, at least while explaining the making of the mind or *manas* from the finest particle of the food consumed, took the momentous step forward to formulate the fundamentals of the experimental method.

This first step taken towards natural science in history awaits due recognition by the historians of science. Mostly under the influence of Eurocentrism they are inclined to assume that natural science began with some sort of "Greek miracle". In spite of the mounting protest against eurocentrism at least among a section of recent historians of science, Uddālaka's name remains totally unknown even to the historians of science with pronounced apathy to Eurocentrism, and this because of the tortuous effort stretched over two thousand years or more somehow to force his views into the general structure of the *Brahman-ātman* metaphysics of the Upaniṣads. This prevents us from seeing the real greatness of Uddālaka as the pioneer of conscious nature science.

What would have been the fate of the cultural history of the country only if objective conditions were created in it for an unbiased acceptance of the suggestions of Uddālaka Āruṇi? The answer can at best be conjectural, for the fact is that historical conditions were really not there for its acceptance. What is not a matter of conjecture, however, is that which actually happened in the country as a consequence of accepting the *Brahman-ātman* or Vedānta philosophy as the only official one, distorting for the purpose Uddālaka's real teachings beyond recognition. Let us allow Acharya P.C. Ray to describe the situation, who, while doing it, mentions the atomist Kaṇāda instead of Uddālaka as an example of science-oriented thought. This was evidently because the core of the scientific outlook of Uddālaka awaited in his time to be critically scaled off from the superimpositions of Vedānta on it. After showing how much of the contempt for manual work accounted for the decline of the spirit of science in India, Ray turned to the ideological situation and observed:

> The Vedānta philosophy, as modified and expanded by Śaṃkara, which teaches the unreality of the material world, is also to a large extent responsible for bringing the study of physical science into disrepute. Śaṃkara is unsparing in his strictures on Kaṇāda and his system. One or two extracts from Śaṃkara's Commentary on the *Vedānta Sūtras* will make the point clear: [Observed Śaṃkara] 'It thus appears that the atomic doctrine is supported by very weak arguments only, is opposed to those scriptural passages which declare the Lord to be the general cause, and is not accepted by any of the authorities taking their stand on scripture, such as Manu and others. Hence it is to be altogether disregarded by high-minded men who have a regard for their own spiritual welfare'.[45]
>
> Among a people ridden by caste and hide-bound by the authorities and injunctions of the Vedas, Purāṇas and Smṛtis and having their intellect thus cramped and paralysed, no Boyle could arise to lay down such sound principles for guidance as: 'And, truly, if men were willing to regard the advancement of philosophy, more than their own reputations, it were easy to make them sensible, that one of the most considerable services they could do the world is to set themselves diligently to make experiments, and collect observations without attempting to establish theories upon them before they have taken notice of all the phenomena that are to be solved'.[46]

The quotation from Boyle reminds us of Uddālaka, again, who collected observations as far as his historical conditions permitted him and even went on diligently to make experiments to understand nature and man. But the conditions that eventually developed in the country in which the law-makers[47] decreed the *Brahman-ātman* metaphysics as the only legitimate one prevent even the modern scholars form seeing Uddālaka's real contributions to the making of natural science.

REFERENCES

1. For such legends our best source is D.S. Kirk and J.E. Raven, *The Pre-Socratic Philosophers* (Cambridge, 1960), pp. 74-98.
2. J. Burnet, *Greek Philosophy* (London, 1924), Part I, p. 80.
3. Ibid., p. 20.
4. Ibid., pp. 20-21.
5. F.M. Cornford, *Principium Sapientiae* (Cambridge), p. 159.
6. For example, George Thomson, *The First Philosophers* (London, 1955), p. 158 f.
7. Burnet, op. cit., pp. 20-21.
8. B. Farrington, *Greek Science* (Harmondsworth, 1963), pp. 36-37.
9. Ibid., p. 41.
10. L. Renou, *Classical India*, Vol. III, English tr. (Calcutta, 1967), p. 29.
11. *Śatapatha Brāhmaṇa*, XI.I.1.1.ff.
12. *Bṛhadāraṇyaka Upaniṣad*, VI. 2.1 ff.; cf. *Chāndogya Upaniṣad*, V. 3.1 ff.
13. *Chāndogya Upaniṣad*, V.17.1.
14. M. Winternitz, *A History of Indian Literature*, Vol. I (Calcutta, 1927), p. 265.
15. D.R. Bhandarkar, *Vaiṣnavism, Śaivism and Minor Religious Systems* (Strassburg, 1913), p. 1.
16. G. Thibaut, tr., *Sacred Books of the East*, Vol. 34, reprint (Delhi, 1962), Introduction, p. ciii.
17. R.E. Hume *The Thirteen Principal Upanishads* (Oxford, 1951), p. 7.
18. Winternitz, op. cit., p. 265 f.
19. P. Deussen, *The Philosophy of the Upanishads*, pp. 74-75.
20. *Bṛhadāraṇyaka Upaniṣad*, II. 4. 12.
21. Subsequent quotations from Uddālaka's discourse are from chapter 6 of this Upaniṣad, separate references to which are not given here. The English translations used are generally from R.E. Hume, op. cit.
22. *Bṛhadāraṇyaka Upaniṣad*, IV. 2.4.

23. *Uddālaka Jātaka*. For an English translation, see E.B. Cowell, ed. *The Jātakas*, Vol. IV (Delhi, 1973), pp. 188-91.
24. B.M. Barua, *A History of Pre-Buddhist Indian Philosophy* (Calcutta, 1921), p. 126.
25. For extensive quotations from P.C. Ray on this point, see D. Chattopadhyaya, *History of Science and Technology in Ancient India* (Calcutta, 1986), p. 8f.
26. *Ṛgveda*, X.129.
27. See *Chāndogya Upaniṣad* III. 19.1 and *Taittirīya Upaniṣad*, II.7.
28. One is tempted to recall here the controversy on the question still going on among a section of scientists. Without commenting on it, it may not be irrelevant to mention that Uddāḷaka appears to have been the first to have posed the problem very succinctly.
29. Sukhlalji Sanghvi, *Adhyātma Vicāraṇa* (in Hindi), pp. 15-16.
30. S.N. Dasgupta, *A History of Indian Philosophy*, Vol. I (Cambridge, 1922-25), p. 218.
31. For an extensive discussion of Śaṃkara's refutation of the Sāṃkhya, see D. Chattopadhyaya, *Lokāyata* (Delhi, 1959), p. 372 f.
32. Śaṃkara on the *Brahmasūtra*, I.1.5 ff.
33. Rāmānuja on the *Brahmasūtra*, I. 1. 5 ff.
34. D. Chattopadhyaya, *What is Living and What is Dead in Indian Philosophy* (New Delhi, 1976), p. 481.
35. *Kāmasūtra*, Sādhāraṇa-adhikaraṇam 9.
36. Barua, op. cit., p. 132.
37. Burnet, op. cit., pp. 28-29.
38. See W. Ruben, *Studies in Ancient Indian Thought* (Calcutta, 1966), pp. 19-20: "In 1954, I started the theory that the first Indian philosopher was Uddālaka Āruṇi in *Chāndogya Upaniṣad*, VI. In 1961, I wrote finally a paper about the beginning of rational thinking in India, describing how the fight between materialism and idealism—between Uddālaka and Yājñavalkya—began in ancient India.... My revered teacher Hermann Jacobi (in *Festschrift Kuhn*, Breslau 1916) was the first to maintain that Uddālaka taught some materialistic elements".
39. E. Fraüwallner, *History of Indian Philosophy*, tr. V.M. Bedekar, Vol. I. (New Delhi, 1973), p. 70.
40. Barua, op. cit., p. 138.
41 Rāmānuja on the *Brahmasūtra*, I. 1.5.
42 Cf. *Chāndogya Upaniṣad*, V. 10.7: "accordingly, those who are of pleasant conduct here—the prospect is, indeed, that they will enter a pleasant womb, either the womb of a Brāhmaṇa, or the womb of a Kṣatriya, or the womb of a Vaiśya. But those who are

of stinking conduct here—the prospect is, indeed, that they will enter a stinking womb, either the womb of a dog, or the womb of a swine, or the womb of an outcast (Caṇḍāla)" (tr. Hume, p. 233).

43. J.D. Bernal, *Science in History,* Vol. I (Harmondsworth, 1969), p. 35.
44. Burnet, op. cit., pp. 20-21.
45. P.C. Ray, *History of Hindu Chemistry,* Vol. I (Calcutta, 1902/3), pp. 195-96.
46. Ibid., pp. 196-97.
47. See, for instance, *Manusmṛti,* IV. 49; and IV. 82-84.

2

The Maḳing of Mathematics in Ancient India

The subject I have chosen for discussion is the making of mathematics, geometry in particular, in the ancient Indian subcontinent. I shall later come to the questions of dating the event as well as of the peculiarities of the earliest texts that come down to us as incorporating this geometry. These questions are complex and even controversial.

One point nevertheless needs to be borne in mind. We have to move back to a hoary antiquity to see the first step being taken to geometry. The point is of material importance. I am braving to address here some of the front-rank scientists of India today. For them mathematics has become vastly sophisticated. Nevertheless, historically at any rate, the earliest step taken to science is usually considered the most prodigious one. Without it, science would not have been what it is today. It is thus not to be ignored because of being superseded by superior knowledge. Even contemporary science awaits to be superior knowledge. Even contemporary science awaits to be superseded in the future. As a matter of fact, if I am not mistaken, like the rest of the scientists all over the world, you are all working here with this purpose.

Thus in short, science is not born like Minerva fully attired. It has to proceed step by step. Of these, the earliest step is exceedingly important, for without it there is no beginning at all. Such a step had of course to be rather rudimentary.

As for geometry, to see this you have to move backward to a stage in which the simplest instrument box which your sons and grandsons pack up for their school kit was absolutely unimaginable. What the makers of geometry had at their disposal were only some strings and sticks. So they had to improvise. Looking back at them specially with the historians' eyes we cannot but be amazed by the simple fact that their improvisations did succeed. They made possible the making of geometry.

Take, for example, the first problem they were required to solve. How to make a perfect square the length of whose side is given? With the sticks firmly fixed on the ground and tying a string tightly to these, they can draw a straight line. They can also measure it, following some table of linear measurement on which they agree. Thus they come to the length of the side of the required square. Then, fixing sticks on the ground to serve as centres, they can draw with the string a number of intersecting circles, using this length as well as half of it as what we call the radius. This done, they simply join with the strings certain points of intersection of these circles. That gives them the result—a perfect square the length of whose side is specified. Here is a diagram illustrating how this is being done. (Diagram 1)

They in fact improvise two more methods of doing this, though for the purpose presumably using what we call arcs of circles instead of full ones. But we may as well skip over the details of these, for the time at our disposal is limited and we have too many questions to discuss. Still some initial clarifications are required.

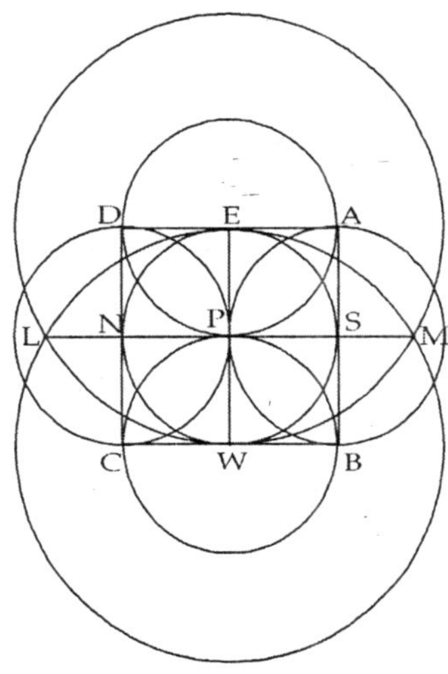

Diagram 1

The earliest texts that come down to us with geometrical knowledge are found to be composed in highly cryptic sentences—often even scraps of sentences—which in Sanskrit are called *sūtras*. Besides, as is perhaps only to be expected of genuine scientists, a whole host of novel terminologies had to be developed and used to ensure precision of what they are discussing. The texts—specially the hard core of geometry in these—are not easily understood. There are, of course, traditional commentaries on the texts, which, for the modern scholars, are pointers to the methods of the makers of this mathematics. Though highly helpful for modern understanding, these are not fully adequate. We had thus to await first-rate modern scholars like A. Burke, G. Thibaut, B.B. Datta and many others to salvage from these texts the mathematics they embody and this in terms with which we are familiar.

Depending on the texts and the commentaries on these, and basically taking the main clues from these pioneers among the modern scholars, my own colleague Professor Subinoy Kumar Ray has worked out the basic geometrical propositions embodied in the texts in an admirably simple form for modern understanding, verifying at the same time in modern terminologies the worthwhileness of the methods cryptically mentioned in the ancient texts. Following this simplified procedure, we give here some of the major propositions of the earliest evidence of geometry that we have, with diagrams illustrating each to facilitate our understanding.

Once the problem of constructing a perfect square is solved, our texts proceed to undertake progressively complicated ones. Thus:

How to construct a rectangle of given length and breadth?

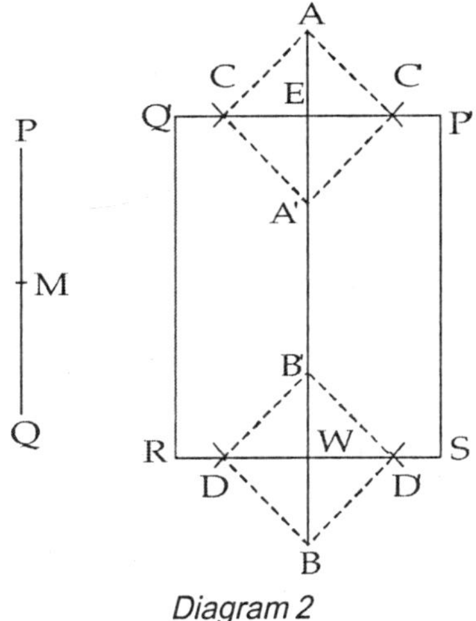

Diagram 2

How to construct a square whose area is equal to twice the area of a given square?

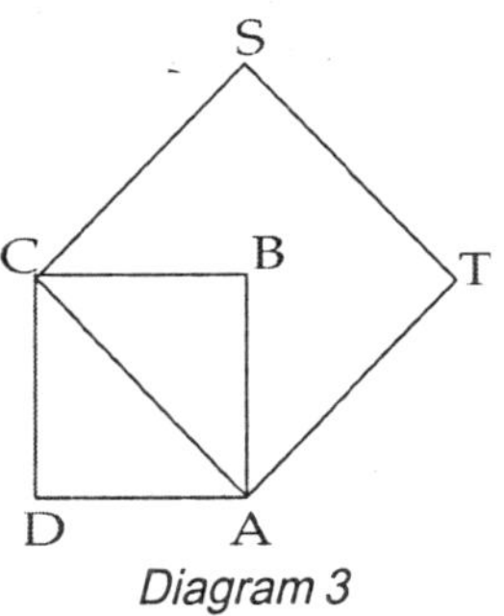

Diagram 3

How to construct a square whose area is three times the area of a given square?

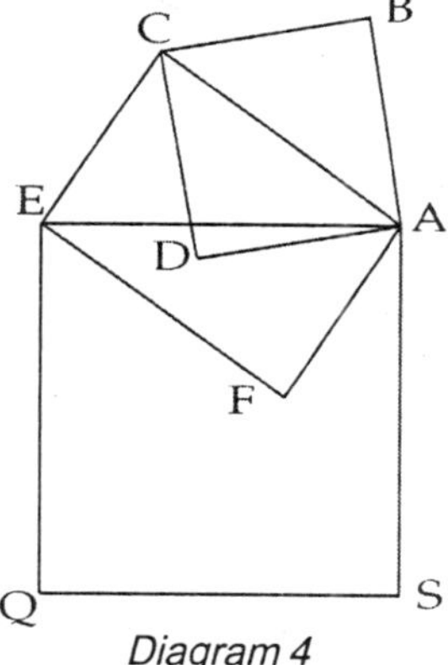

Diagram 4

How to construct a square whose area is equal to the sum of the areas of two given squares?

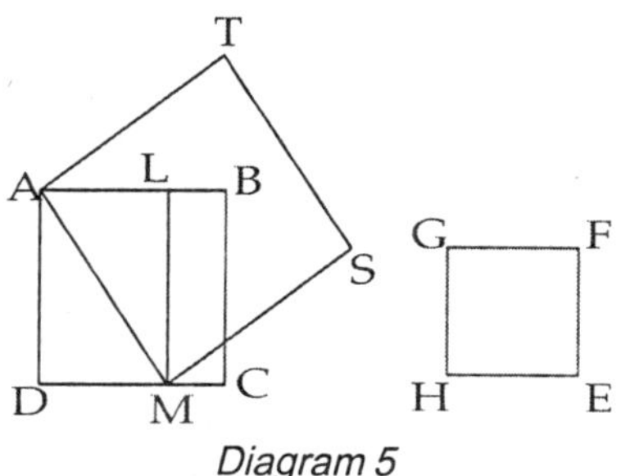

Diagram 5

How to construct a square whose area is equal to the difference of the areas of two given squares?

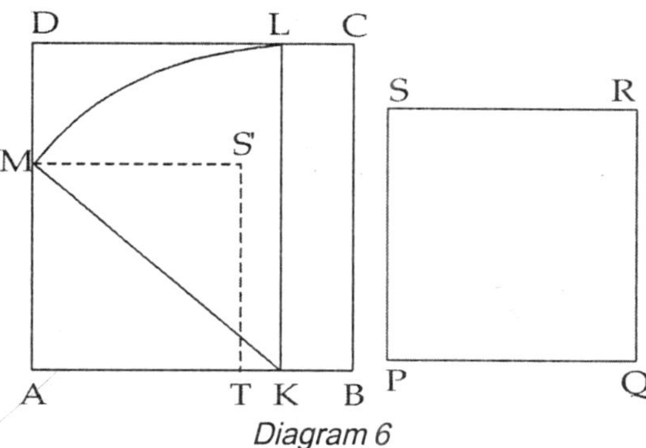

Diagram 6

How to transform a square into a rectangle whose length is equal to the diagonal of the square?

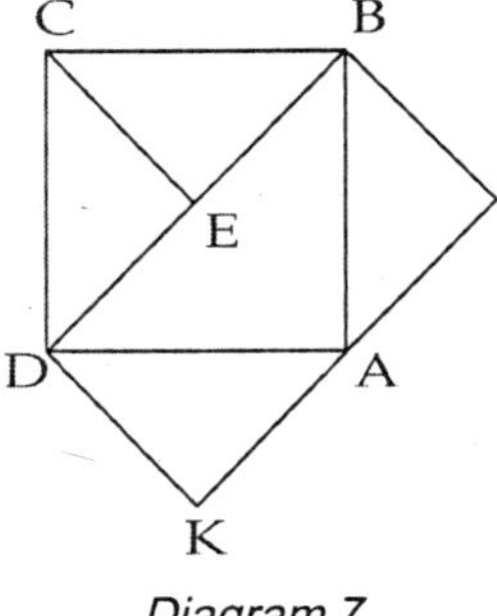

Diagram 7

How to draw a square equal in area of a given rectangle?

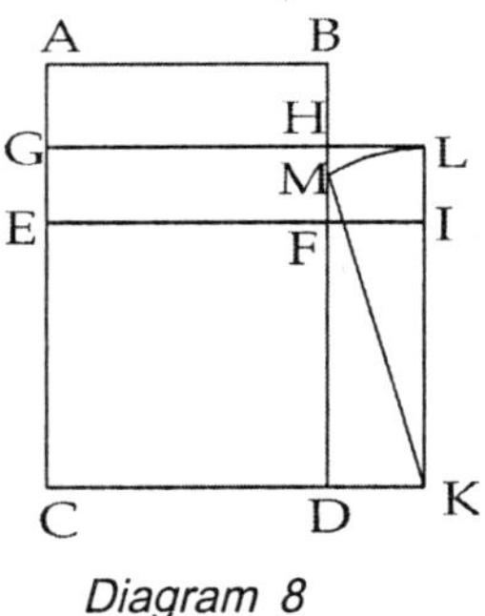

Diagram 8

How to draw an isosceles trapezium of a given side equal in area of a given square or rectangle, the given side of the trapezium being less than the side of the square?

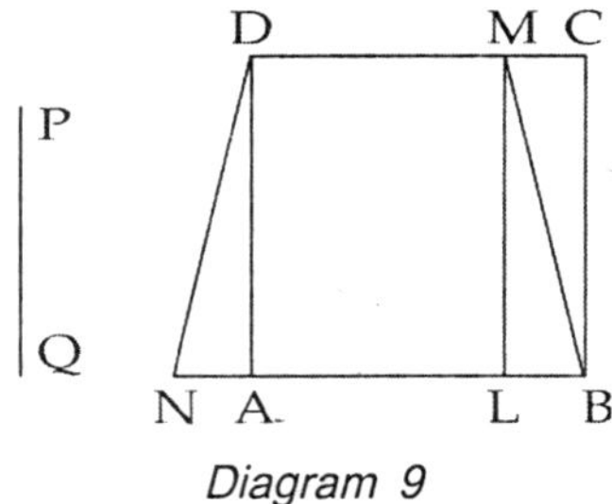

Diagram 9

How to construct a triangle whose area is equal to the area of a given square (or rectangle)?

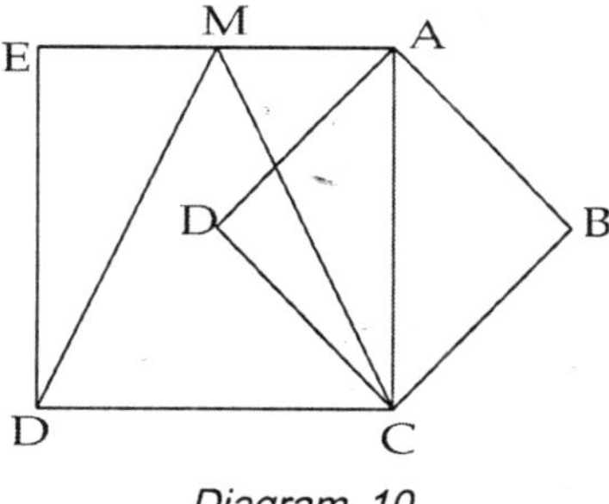

Diagram 10

How to construct a rhombus whose area is equal to the area of a given square (or a rectangle)?

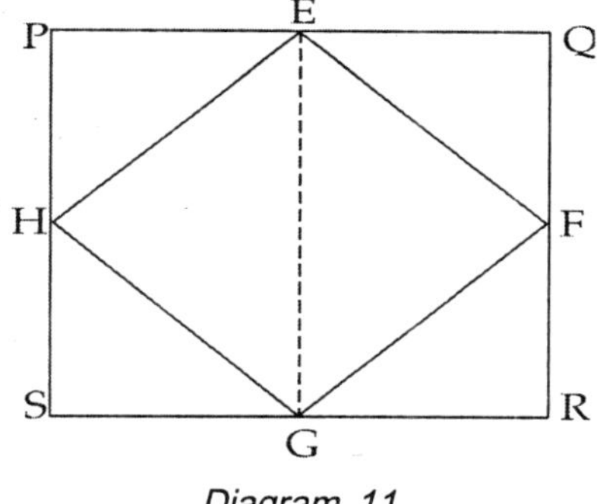

Diagram 11

How to construct a circle equal in area of a given square?

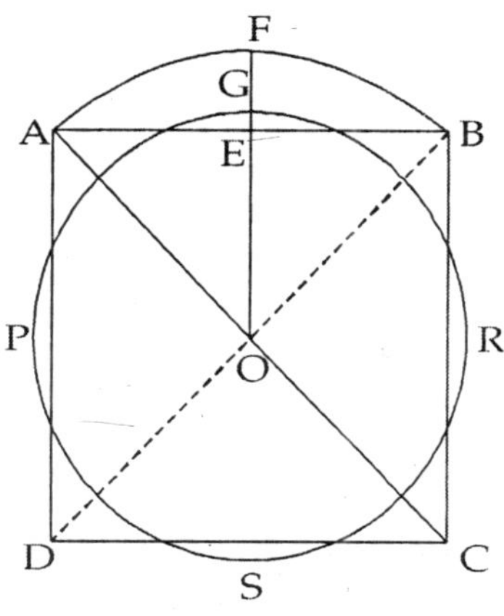

Diagram 12

How to construct a square equal in area of a given circle?

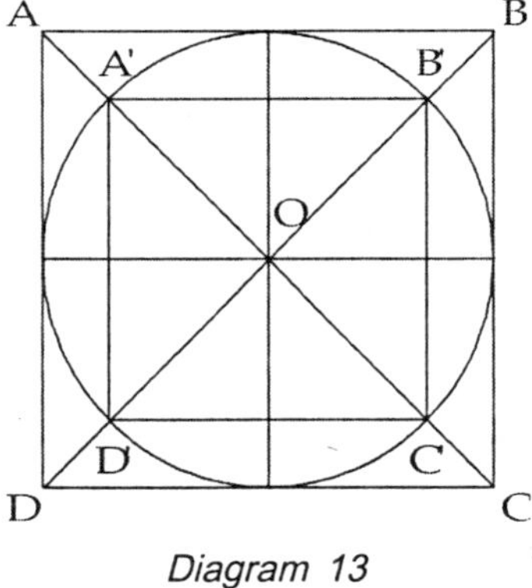

Diagram 13

Understandably they stumble over the last two problems, which in our terminology, are those of circling a square and squaring a circle. These problems, as you are aware, are insoluble. But both G. Thibaut and B.B. Datta, working diligently on the texts, point to something interesting in this connection. You can easily see why for solving these problems it is necessary to determine the value of what we call the *pi* (π). Our texts are groping for this and, following their rationale, Thibaut and Datta show that the alternatives suggested give us three possible values, namely 3.088321, 3.08811 and 3.0044. We know today that none of these is really accurate, in spite of the first two being somewhat better approximations. Historically, however, the more important point is that the need for raising this problem was felt after all, tacitly though it might have been.

Interesting appears to be that to which Thibaut and Datta draw our attention. The early geometricians raised in their own way the problem of determining the value of $\sqrt{2}$. Worked out by modern methods of calculation, it comes to 1.414215686, which agrees with the first five decimal figures of the accepted value today, namely 1.414213562.....

One is tempted to mention here that it was this question of $\sqrt{2}$ that created a crisis for the Pythagoreans. Here is how Farrington describes their crisis: "Inspired by their success in mathematics they were lured to construct a mathematical model of the world, though mixed up with their own theologico-mystical speculations. The model had to be essentially rational. It was based on the assumption that the world was made of points with magnitude, i.e. points with each one of which some definite magnitude can be associated, and hence a line is theoretically divisible into a finite number of points. Then, with the progress of their own mathematical science the foundation of their universe was suddenly swept away. It was discovered that the diagonal and the side of a square cannot at the same time be commensurable. $\sqrt{2}$ is an 'irrational number'. The term originated with them and indicates their shock when they, who held that number and reason were the same thing, found that they could not express $\sqrt{2}$ by any number. Their confusion was great. It follows that the lines are infinitely and immeasurably divisible. If lines are infinitely divisible the little points of which the Pythagoreans built their universe do not exist." (Farrington 52). Hence was the crisis for them.

But the mathematicians of the ancient Indian subcontinent did not have to face such a crisis for the simple reason that their interest was not that of building up a metaphysico-mathematical model of the universe. We shall presently see where exactly this interest is. Before passing on to it, we may as well mention another point. Talking of the Pythagoreans, it may as well be noted that in the Indian texts we are discussing is to be found the proposition concerning the so-called Pythagorean triangle stated in general terms along with a few specific cases of it, the sides of which are integral numbers. Thus we read (in Thibaut's translation): "The diagonal of an oblong produces by itself both areas which the two sides of the oblong produce separately (which simply means that the square of the diagonal is equal to the sum of the squares of the two sides). This is seen in those oblongs the sides of which are 3 and 4; 12 and 5; 15 and 8; 7 and 24; 12 and 35; 15 and 36".

All this is, of course, rendering the ancient Indian texts using geometrical terminologies with which we are familiar, that is the terminologies essentially Euclidean. But there was quite on the surface a world of difference between the geometry we are talking of with the one associated with the name of Euclid. The makers of geometry in ancient India do not at all follow the procedure of starting with certain so-called self-evident truths or axioms and go on deducing propositions after propositions from these. We do not have the scope here to enter into the problem of the pre-history of Euclidean geometry itself, i.e. the problem of how much Euclid himself depends on the essentially practical—or even manual—operations performed by the ancient Egyptians, from which Euclid showed the genius of soaring high into the realm of abstractions. But it is of material interest to note that, for all that we know, geometry in ancient India originates from meeting the requirements that are essentially practical in nature. To be specific, these were the requirements of brick-technology—the requirements, in other words, of constructing certain brick structures with specified shape and specified area, with bricks the number, size and shapes of which are very definitely specified again. This could not be at all done without first developing a substantial amount of geometrical knowledge. Hence was this geometry.

This leads us to see the genre of ancient Indian texts in which the geometry remains embodied. The texts are called the *Śulva-sūtras*. Several of these come down to us, of which two are considered most important. These are associated with two proper names, Baudhāyana and Āpastamba, which are supposed to be names of two important corporations of Vedic priests. What differentiates these texts from each other are points of minor importance and may as well be skipped over. What interests us is that which unites all the texts belonging to the same class.

Apparently at any rate the texts, in the form in which these reach us, are rather quaint. On their face value, as we shall see, these look like peculiar agglomerations of science and anti-science. The science-aspect of these constitutes the geometry we are talking of. The anti-science in these is a queer bundle of hoary magico-religious beliefs, connected with the former at best by a thin line of theological assumptions. We shall later see how overtly extrinsic and totally arbitrary the latter is for the former and how, failing to note this arbitrariness, the texts remain grossly misunderstood in most of the discussions on science in ancient India.

But the starting point of our own discussion is the texts taken at their face-value. The main theme of these is the technique of constructing certain brick-structures. The structures required vary in shape but are meticulously equal to one another in their areas. Here are diagrams of only a few of the major structures required to be constructed:

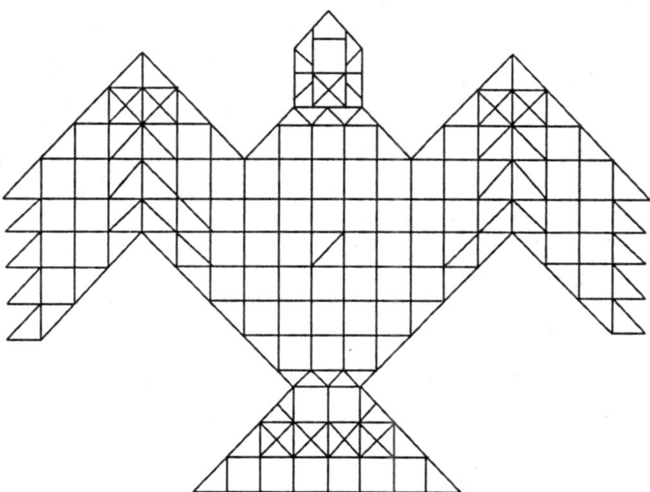

Figure 1: BŚSu BIRD SHAPED ŚYENA CITI
Type - I
Layers - 1, 3, 5

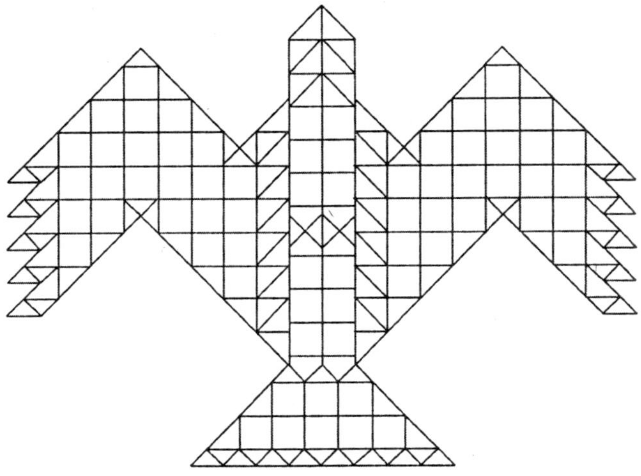

Figure 2: BŚSu BIRD SHAPED ŚYENA CITI
Type - I
Layers - 2, 4

This structure is called one having the form of a falcon with carved wings and extended tail : *Vakra-pakṣa-vyasta-puccha-śyena*. We shall presently return to the question of why we have projected two separate diagrams of the same structure.

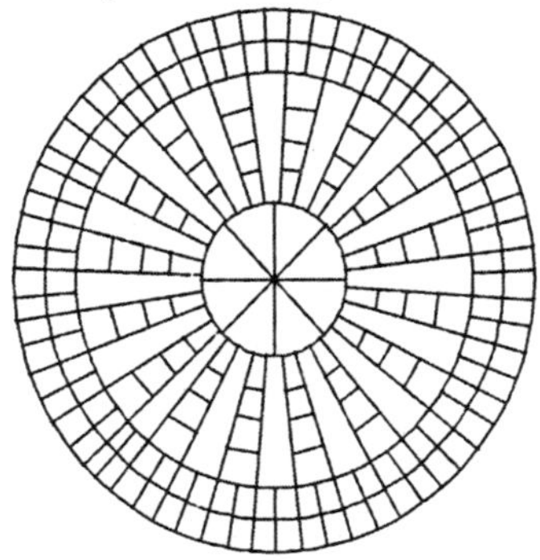

Figure 3

This structure is called one having the shape of the wheel of a chariot with spokes: *Sāraratha-cakra*. Here again two diagrams are visualised—one in full and the other only in part.

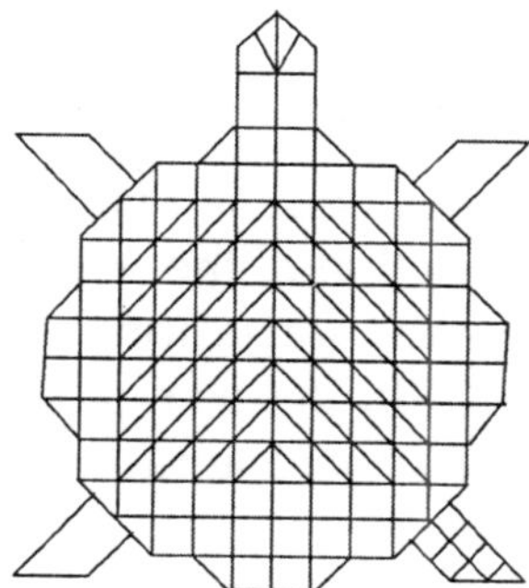

Figure 4: BŚSu Vakrāṅga Kūrma citi

This structure is called one having the shape of a tortoise—kūrma.

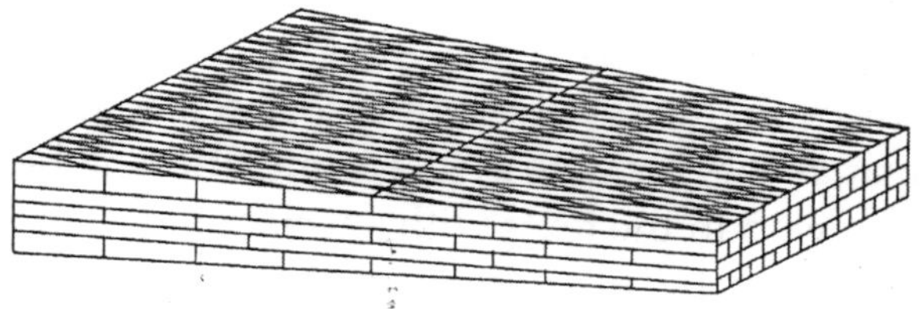

Figure 5: BŚSu Śmaśāna citi

This structure is called one having the shape of a cremation-pyre—*Śmaśāna*. Note that in this diagram there are five distinct layers.

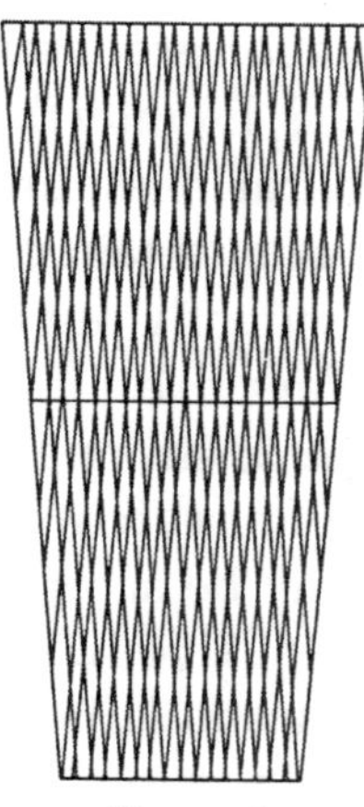

Figure 6

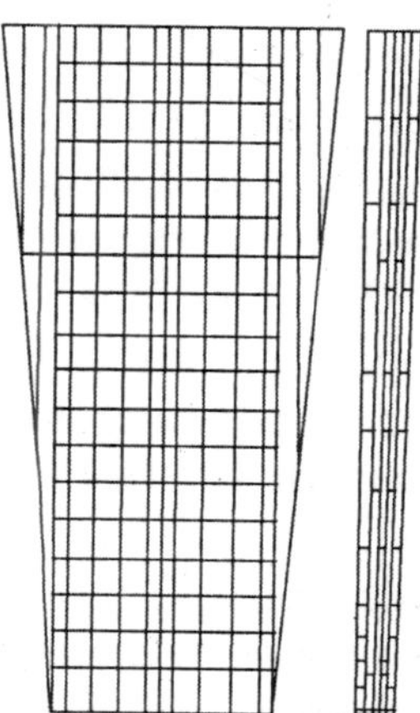

Figure 7

These are diagrams of the same structure. What is illustrated in these two is the difference in the layout of the bricks in the first and second layers—the third and the fifth layer of the previous structure repeating the same as that of the first, and the fourth that of the second.

Some other peculiar variations of the structure are discussed in the texts. But let us not go into these: what is already exemplified by the diagrams shown should serve our present purpose.

Before proceeding to see why geometry—and for that matter quite intricate geometrical calculations—are actually called for for the physical constructions of these various structures, it may be useful to have some clarification about the scale of linear measures followed in the texts. As a matter of fact, the *Śulva-sūtras* realise this, for we find the most important of the texts—the one associated with the name Baudhāyana—begins with a full enumeration of the units of length followed in the texts with special names and precise significance of each. This, once done, the texts can move freely with their calculations.

Of these units of linear measure specially two are essential for our present discussion. These are *puruṣa*, literally meaning the height of a man with uplifted hands. But since all men are not of equal height, such an understanding of the length remains arbitrary and hence useless for exact science. It is therefore more specified as 120 *aṅgulas*, literally the "finger". Lest, again, there remain any arbitrariness, an *aṅgula* is specified as the length of 14 grains of a certain plant called *aṇu* or 32 of some other called *tila*, evidently put in the form of a connected string. Earlier scholars like J.F. Fleet were satisfied by equating an *aṅgula* with 3/4th of an inch. But V.B. Mainkar, on the basis of years of research, calculates it to be equal to 17. 78 mm, which may be accepted for our present purpose. One *puruṣa* is thus equal to 120 × 17.78 mm = 2133.6 mm. One square *puruṣa* comes to 2133.6 × 2133.6 = 4.552 square metres. Seven and a half *puruṣas* thus equal to an area of 34.14 square metres or 367.48 sq. feet of our scale.

We have mentioned the area of 7.5 square *puruṣa*, because that is precisely the area to be covered by each brick structure discussed in our texts. Retaining this area absolutely in tact, one is asked to vary its shape—be it the shape of a falcon with stretched wings, a chariot wheel with spokes, a tortoise, a funeral pyre, and so on. Such a variation of shape of the brick structure with the area absolutely in tact as 34.14 sq. metres evidently requires ingenious calculations, specially when we remember that certain further conditions were made obligatory for the constructors. Thus:

1. Each structure must have five and only five layers of bricks.
2. The number of bricks to be used for each layer of each structure must be 200 and specifically so. Thus the total number of bricks to be used for each structure must be exactly 1000.
3. In height the structure must be exactly 32 *aṅgulas* and the thickness of the bricks in each layer must be equal. Thus, calculated according to our scale, the thickness of each brick has to be 113.792 mm or 4.48 inches. (Only in a few exceptional cases there is provision for using bricks of exactly half this thickness, without which the constructors cannot retain the exact height specified.)

Since there is no provision for the use of mortar, one peculiarity is to be followed for stacking the bricks to give the structure as a whole the temporary stability that it requires. This is done by arranging the bricks of the different layers in such a way that no brick in the lower layer should correspond exactly to another in the upper layer. In other words, the layout of the bricks in the first layer must differ from that of the second layer, though the layout of the first is repeated in the third and fifth layers, just as that of the second in the fourth one. That is why, while illustrating the structures in the form of diagrams, we found it expedient to use two for each, i.e. for showing the two different layouts of bricks required for each construction. Added to these are some stipulations which, though of comparatively less direct significance from the mathematical viewpoint, are nevertheless of interest for the architects, engineers and masons. These are:

"No brick, which has been formed by breaking is to be employed for the constructions of any structure (i.e. for example, a triangular brick which has been formed by breaking a square-shaped brick is forbidden).

No brick which is cleft (for example, square-shaped brick made out of two triangular bricks) is to be employed.

And no brick which is damaged in any way.

And no brick of black colour (presumably produced by over-burning, etc.)

And no brick is to be employed which has some mark (an impression of some foreign body, etc.)"

Bearing the above points in mind, let us return to have another look at the diagrams of some of the structures:

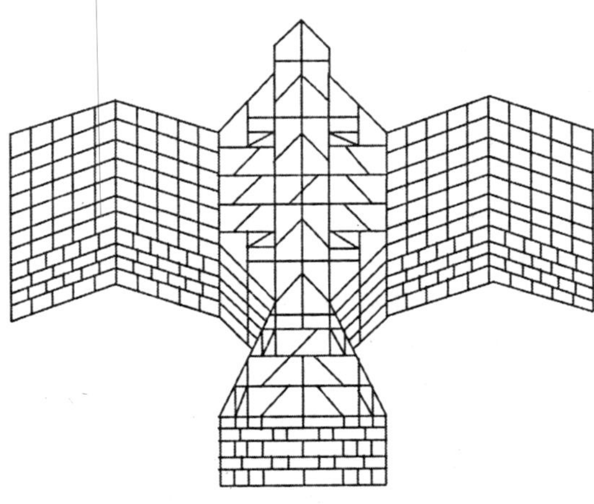

Figure 1(a)

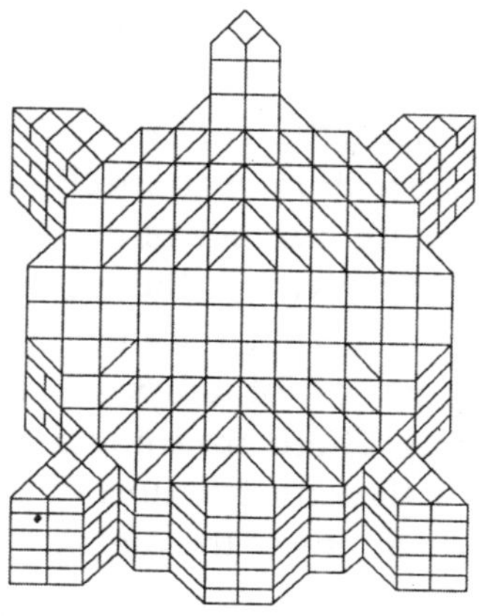

Figure 3 (a)

A few points about these immediately leap before our eyes.

First, constructing a bird-like brick structure in five layers with a specified number of bricks but covering an exact area of 7½ square *puruṣas* or , according to our scale, 34.14 square metres (= 367.48 square feet) is evidently not an easy proposition. More difficult is the proposition of constructing a circular structure resembling a chariot-wheel with spokes but covering precisely the same area and observing the same basic stipulations for construction. A good deal of mathematical calculations are bound to appear as all the more amazing when judged in the historical context of a hoary antiquity, when the constructors have nothing more at their disposal than just some strings and sticks.

Secondly, when we take a look at the diagrams even casually, we cannot ignore the point that the possibility of using any standardised brick-type is absolutely ruled out. Let us remember in this connection that breaking any brick or trimming one in any way to suit the construction purpose is forbidden. Each brick to be used must be a whole one. This, in other words, involves the problem of making a very large number of brick-types. Each brick-type has to have a specific geometrical shape with very specific measurement.

The texts tell us, for example, of ten different brick types—triangular, rectangular, square and what not in shape—required for the construction of the bird-like brick-structure. At the same time the texts have to specify the exact dimension of each brick-type, the number of each brick-type required for the construction as well as the modes of their layout in two different ways so that the chance of overlapping is eliminated and some sort of temporal stability of the entire structure is ensured. There are some diagrams of the brick-types required for the construction of the bird- like brick-structure with indications of the measurements required for their making that one may look up.

But this imposing list of brick-types becomes redundant when it comes to the question of constructing the circular structure imitating the chariot-wheel with spokes. Brick-types of different shapes altogether are required for the purpose. So also should be obvious from the other shapes of brick-structures discussed in the texts. Look back, for example, at the tortoise-shaped one or the one with the shape of the funeral pyre.

One is tempted to mention in this connection one more example of the geometrical excellence reached by the architects and masons whom we meet in the *Śulva-sūtras*. From one task undertaken by them, it is obvious that they somehow knew with precision—though we do not yet exactly know how—that the area covered by a parallelogram with an acute angle is less than that of a rectangle, both having sides of the same length, and how much this difference comes to depending on the measurement of the acute angle. To advanced mathematicians this knowledge may be elementary. To the historian, however, this cannot but appear as marvellous, because he is dealing here with people crawling to mathematical knowledge only with some strings and sticks at their disposal.

To sum up the discussion so far: Judged from the earliest texts that have come down to us with mathematical content it is absolutely indisputable that in the ancient Indian subcontinent mathematics came into being to meet the essentially practical requirements of the architects, engineers and masons, or, to put it in a more matter of fact manner, those of brick-makers and brick-layers. *If you take out of these texts—the Śulva-sūtras—the brick-technology as such, whatever you may be left with may have other interest, but no scrap of the mathematical knowledge worth its name.* We have to put special emphasis on this point because of reasons to be presently discussed.

Thus far we have perhaps no difficulty about the making of mathematics in the ancient Indian subcontinent. It is quite in accordance with the more advanced understanding of the origin of mathematics which has replaced the older one. The earlier view we often read in the histories of science is based on a statement of Herodotus. He said that geometry, literally meaning earth-measurement, originated among the Egyptians from their practice of measuring the land with ropes for administrative purposes: from the Egyptians the Greeks learnt it. This is reminiscent of what we read also in our *Jātaka* stories as well as the Aśokan edicts, which mention a class of officials called *rajju-gāhaka amaccas* or the rope-holding officials, entrusted with the work of land measurement for revenue collection, as was the case in ancient Egypt. Though significant, this however cannot be the whole truth. The more serious modern scientists like V. Gordon Childe and J.D. Bernal have shown that *geometry as an exact science* does not owe its origin to such a practice, a rough or approximate idea of the land measured being enough for taxation and other administrative purposes. For geometry acquiring the precision of a science, we have rather to turn to the architects, engineers and masons—the pyramid builders for example—for whom precision of measurement and calculation matters most. From this viewpoint, there is no difficulty about the *Śulva-sūtras*, in which geometry as an exact science is overtly intended to meet the practical requirements of the brick-makers and brick-layers.

Still, there is a great deal of difficulty about—and hence also a very widely prevalent misunderstanding of—the *Śulva-sūtras*. If the texts embody some astonishing achievements of ancient science, there is also a heap of magico-religious beliefs in these. These become obvious the moment we raise the question: Why was so much importance attached to the construction of brick structures that cannot but appear to be peculiarly quaint for us? Brick-technology is normally expected for construction of dwellings, granaries or such useful purposes. But then such constructions need not assume the weird forms of the falcon with stretched wings, or of the tortoise or of a chariot-wheel with spokes or of a funeral pyre, and so on. Yet, it is precisely such constructions that are found in our texts.

In short the question of *why* and *how* are entirely different. If the *Śulva-sūtras* strike us as answering the second question, the only answer we have of the first is that: "thus we are told" or "such is the authoritative instruction."

But who are those that tell the technicians to build such structures or issue the authoritative instructions? Essentially as manuals for the technicians, the *Śulva-sūtras* do not find it necessary to go much into this question beyond perhaps occasionally and cursorily mentioning them.

To the Vedic scholars, however, the answer to this is very well known. They are the Vedic priests for whom sacrificial rituals are the be-all and end-all and whose fabulously bulky literature comes down to us beginning with the *Yajurveda* and much more elaborated in a class of texts called the *Brāhmaṇas*. It is in this literature that we come across the answer to the question: *why* such structures at all? In other words, the instructions come from the Vedic priests and the makers of brick structures implicitly take these for granted. In the *Śulva-sūtras* the attempt is made to solve the problem of *how* best to execute these in practice.

But why do the Vedic priests dictate to the technicians terms to construct such peculiar structures? From the priestly view-point, the answer is quite simple. The structures are supposed to be used as fire-altars for the performance of the sacrificial rituals and are hence called *citis* or *agnis* in priestly terminology. Depending on the desire expected to be fulfilled for the *Yajamāna* or financier of the sacrificial rituals, the fire altars are supposed to have their specific shapes. Thus, for example, the financier wanting to fly to heaven quickly should have an altar built in the shape of a falcon, because the falcon is a fast flier. The same desire is also supposed to be fulfilled by way of changing the shape of the structure into that of some other birds, called *Kaṅka* and *Alaja*. For the fulfilment of the desire of the annihilation of enemies, the structure having the shape of the forepart of a cart (an isosceles triangle) is declared effective, though one with the shape of two such triangles joined at the base, of the one having the shape of a chariot wheel with spokes, is supposed to have the additional advantage of annihilating rivals of the future. The structure of the funeral pyre is effective for eventually going to the after-world inhabited by the departed forefathers. And so on.

Evidently, there must have once been rich patrons credulous enough to be attracted by such gambols of magico-religious fancies, and thus go in for the economic drainage which the sacrifices mean. Or else, we cannot explain the *Śulva-sūtras* in their present form, which come down to us as appendices to the priestly manuals. What motivates the priests to dictate terms to the technicians for making the sacrificial rituals as complicated as possible is not difficult to understand. That is a recognised way of adding awe and wonder to the sacrificial rituals—a need felt by priests practically all over the ancient world. The more one succeeds in doing this, the better is the prospect of attracting the financiers for sacrifice. Incidentally it is relevant to note here that the Vedic priests were under the necessary obligation of trying this trick. They depended *exclusively* on the professional fees or *dakṣiṇās* for performing the sacrifices, so much so that they do not hesitate even to declare that the professional fees for them constitute the essence of the sacrifices.

So the priests had their problems which they were trying to solve in their own ways. What concerns us, however, is another problem and that relates to the history of science. Practically all the modern scholars are inclined to accept the view that since in these texts geometry is found to meet the requirements of constructing the fire-altars, the makers of it must have been the priests or their corporations. This, if true, would lead to the paradox of superstition or anti-science giving birth to science. We are going to argue that such a paradox is not obligatory for us. What the *Śulva-sūtras* actually exemplify is anti-science being imposed on science and even the zeal of engulfing it. Still, if we agree to scratch the surface of the texts, we can easily see that science—in our case geometrical science—actually originates in technique: it is the technique of the architects, engineers and masons, superstition only wanting eventually to use it for its own purpose. Peculiar though it may sound, *the most decisive evidence for this is archaeological*. Before we pass on to it however, let us mention a few points of interest showing why it is impermissible to imagine that whatever may be the nature of the texts in which geometrical knowledge comes down to us, it could not have been created by the priests.

Let us have a look again at the Śulva texts. One point about these is quite on the surface. It is the difference between *what is to be done* and *how is this to be done*. The usual expression used in the texts to indicate the first is *vijñāyate, iti uktam*, etc. signifying 'such are the authoritative instructions'. The instructions are about the nature (shape, size, etc.) of the fire-altars required for sacrificial rituals. Their sources are, as Garbe and others have shown, the priestly texts, in strict sense—the *Yajurveda* and *Brāhmaṇas*. This means that what is to be done is dictated by Vedic priests.

Such instructions are simply taken for granted by the Śulva texts. But their distinctive content is of exclusive interest in the other question, viz. how is this to be done—the question of the know-how or technology. While discussing this, the texts mention no authority whatsoever. Significantly, Śulva mathematics is the direct outcome of the theoretical requirements of this. What is dictated by the priestly sources is only a body of magico-religious beliefs we have just mentioned. But the magico-religious beliefs are totally irrelevant for the mathematics required and worked out for the physical constructions of the brick-structure. The same mathematics would have been required had the rich patron desired this brick-structure for other purposes—say, for his pleasure—garden or playground for children. Thus, Śulva mathematics developed from technological requirements of the brick-makers, masons and architects rather than the magico-religious beliefs, which alone was characteristic of priest-craft in the real sense. Hence the Vedic priests are to be credited for the making of this mathematics at best in the sense in which the god-kings of ancient Egypt wanted the pyramids to be constructed, leaving the problem of their physical construction—and therefore also the mathematics required for the purpose—to the architects, engineers, and other technicians.

That, for the construction of the brick-structures, technicians outside the strict circle of the Vedic priests were required is virtually admitted by the Vedic tradition itself. In all the three appendices to the *Kātyāyana Śrauta-sūtra* we read that the Śulva technician is required to be —

śāstrabuddhyā vibhāgajñaḥ paraśāstra-kutūhalaḥ /
śilpibhyaḥ sthapatibhyaḥ ca ādadīta matiḥ sadā / /
(Khadilkar, *Kātyāyana Śulva-sūtra*, vii.6)

"One who is engrossed in the subject, knows the technique of divisions, has curiosity to know the science of the others and always pays proper attention to the work of the artisans and architects."

The mention of *śilpi* (artisan) and *sthapati* (architect) is clear and categorical. The expression *paraśāstra-kutūhalaḥ*—"having curiosity to know the science of others"—speaks volumes. How can the priest, with all his claim to great wisdom but equipped only with priest-craft in its strict sense, at all confront the problem of the actual construction of the brick-structures requiring above all whole-time specialisation of brick-makers, masons and architects?

Accordingly, the *Rāmāyaṇa* (Bāla. xiii. 6-9 & xiv. 26-28) tells us in so many words that for the sacrificial ritual—priests apart—are required the following classes of persons: manual worker (*karmāntika*), artisan (*śilpakāra*), carpenter (*vardhakī*), digger (*khanaka*) and mathematician (*gaṇaka*). The social status of such persons according to the Dharmaśāstra norm—which is characteristically priestly—is low; certainly far below that of the priests.

An enthusiast for Vedic culture may argue that a section of Vedic priests might have taken an all absorbing interest in brick-making and brick-laying; drawn by the theoretical needs for this, they contributed to the making of Śulva mathematics. Such a hypothesis, however, would necessitate the admission that they could do it not in the capacity of priests proper but that of technicians and craftsmen—flouting for the purpose the Dharmaśāstra norm, generally contemptuous of manual workers.

But an interesting evidence of the *Mahābhārata* (Ādi. lxi. 9ff) seems to pour cold water even on the enthusiasm for such a hypothesis. The king, wanting a sacrifice to be performed, got priests (*ṛtvij*) to measure the place for altar-construction and employed an expert Brahmin with specialised knowledge of priest-craft to construct the altar. But it was eventually found that there was some bungling about it and this bungling was detected by a mason (*sthapati*) well-versed in architectural technology (*vāstu-vidyā*). Thus something more than the knowledge of priest-craft was needed for altar-construction and that was the know-how of brick-makers and brick-layers.

But it is not easy to think that expert technicians were readily available in the Vedic settlements for the actual construction of the complicated brick-structures. The presumption is that the Vedic priests ware aware of the difficulty.

Hence the need was felt by them to bypass the whole problem of the physical construction of the structures. This is suggested by their recommendation of *chandaścit* and *manomaya* or *manaścit*. *Taittirīya Saṁhitā* (v. 4. 11. 1) says, "He who desires cattle should pile a piling with the meters (*chandaścit*); the meters are cattle; verily he becomes rich in cattle." But what is this *chandaścit*? B.B. Datta explains:

"In case of the *Chandaściti*, the *agnicit*, ('fire-altar builder') draws on the ground the Agni (altar) of the prescribed shape, ordinarily of the primitive shape of the falcon. He then goes through the whole prescribed process of construction, imagining all the while as if he were placing every brick in its proper place with the appropriate *mantras* (spells). The *mantras* are, indeed, muttered but the bricks are not actually laid. Hence the name *Chandaściti*, i.e. the *citi* or altar made up of *chandas* or Vedic *mantras* instead of bricks.

In his commentary on the *Brahma-sūtra* (iii. 3. 44. ff). Śaṃkara discusses at length the question of *manomaya* structures or *manaścit*, literally "mind-made altars". He speaks of thirty-six thousand varieties of these. They are *vākcit* (altar made of the organ of speech), *prāṇacit* (altar made of life-breath), *cakṣuścit* (altar made of visual organ), *śrotracit* (altar made of auditory organ), etc. All these are imaginary altars rather than physically constructed or actual brick-altars, but claimed by the priests magically to ensure precisely the same results as the real ones. What, indeed, could the priests do but recommend such imaginary or mind-made altars when the physical construction of actual brick-altars required highly specialised brick technologists not available in the Vedic settlements?

But all this also proves a point of crucial importance. There was no necessary connection between the physically constructed brick-structures and the magico-religious beliefs associated with these, as it is sometimes thought. Hence the know-how of brick constructions was not obligatory for the priest-craft, notwithstanding the circumstances of the Śulva texts coming down to us as appended to the manuals for practising priests.

As against the possibility of the Vedic priests themselves having been the real makers of the Śulva mathematics, one is tempted here to add some other points.

First, the general theoretical temper characterising the Śulva texts is not only different from but positively opposed to that of the priestly literature in its restricted sense. Eggeling (SBE. 43. p. xxii) discusses at some length what he calls the "sacrificial metaphysics" characteristic of the *Brāhmaṇa* texts. Without trying to go into its detail, it is permissible to note that the most prominent feature of it is some form of mystification necessarily required by the magico-religious beliefs.

Hence is the need felt for repeating the formula in the *Brāhmaṇas*: "the gods are fond of the obscure or of the mystic" (*parokṣa-kāmāḥ iva hi devāh*). The Upaniṣadic philosopher Yājñavalkya wants to make its real point more explicit by adding to it the expression *pratyakṣa-dviṣaḥ* (Br. Up. iv. 2.2), meaning that the gods detest direct knowledge.

Admitting this to be a pointer to the general theoretical temper of the priests, we have to note that the Śulva texts, putting the strongest emphasis on the accuracy of observed measurements, cannot but be viewed as indicative of a different theoretical temper altogether. As a matter of fact, the requirements for the accuracy lead the Śulva texts to create a whole host of precise mathematical terminologies which, judged in the ancient context, cannot but appear to be remarkable.

Philosophy apart, even the vocabulary of the Śulva texts is sometimes reminiscent more of the plebian craftsmen than the priestly élite. Śulva literally means the rope or cord or string. But the very word is so elitist-esoteric that it is difficult to come across it outside the titles or the texts. Within the texts, however, the word is never used; cord or rope being always referred to as *rajju*—a word so plebian that it is the same also in Pāli, the language of the people. For "body" again, the word invariably used in the texts is *ātman*—something not easily conceivable in the circle of Vedic élite and their philosophical inheritors. Specially after the *Upaniṣads*, the word *ātman* acquired the sense of Pure Spirit or Pure Soul with the most vigorous emphasis to distinguish it from the body. One is almost tempted to see in the Śulva texts the view equating *ātman* to body (*dehātmavāda*), characteristic of the Lokāyata, which according to philosophers like Śaṃkara and Mādhava, owes its name to the circumstance of being prevalent among the uncultured mob (*prākṛtajanāḥ*). This is a category to which the craftsmen and technicians unquestionably belong in Śaṃkara's understanding.

But let us return to the question of brick-technology to which Śulva mathematics owes its origin. It reached a high level of sophistication in the Indus Civilisation. But the word for it—*iṣṭakā*—is totally unknown to the *Ṛgveda*. It starts occurring from the *Yajurveda* onwards, and scholars like Przyluski (IHQ. vii. 735 f) have strongly argued that it is a Dravidian word, eventually borrowed by the Vedic people. It needs to be noted however that the *Yajurveda*, though using the word, usually looks at it as some kind of mysterious entity with tremendous magical potency. Thus we read in the *Taittirīya-saṃhitā* (iv. 4. 11):

"May these bricks, O Agni, be milch cows for me, one, and a hundred, and a thousand, and ten thousand, and a hundred thousand, and a million, and ten million, and a hundred million, and a thousand million, and ten thousand million, and a hundred thousand million: may these bricks, O Agni, be for me milch cows, sixty, a thousand, ten thousand, unperishing; Ye are standing on holy order, increasing holy order, dripping *ghee*, dripping honey, full of strength, full of power: may these bricks, O Agni, be for me milkers of desires named the glorious yonder in yon world".

In such gambols of pure fantasy it is difficult to see actual brick technology—a point corroborated by the random use of all sorts of fanciful brick-names in the text, inclusive of some typical names of Vedic meters and even 'grass brick', 'ghee bricks', etc. etc. Persons even with a semblance of the knowledge of what a real brick actually is would hardly talk of such ones.

At the same time the fact remains that the *Yajurveda* does speak of the bricks and even recommends the construction of various fire-altars with burnt bricks. For us it is difficult to view the whole thing as the outcome of pure fancy. If there was nothing whatsoever to answer to the concept of *iṣṭakā*, how could the priests possibly speak of it? Here, then, is some kind of paradox. How are we to resolve it?

Could it be that without really knowing what these things actually were—and certainly without the know-how of making these—the Yajurvedic priests were somehow acquainted with readymade bricks, i.e. bricks made by others and used many centuries ago, which they simply collect to add mysterious efficacy to their own rituals?

Such a possibility cannot be outright rejected from the standpoint of the Vedic literature. T. Burrow, in his paper *On the Significance of the term 'Arma—', 'Armaka—' in Early Sanskrit Literature*, convincingly argues that the Vedic people were acquainted with a considerable number of ruined cities, which, from the archaeological point of view, could only be the Harappan sites. The sites of the ruined cities presumably of the Harappan times were not only known to the Vedic people, their priests were moreover prescribing that *Kapāla* or 'potsherds' had actually to be collected from these sites to meet some of their ritual requirements. "From these references we gather that *arma*-s or ruined sites were a commonplace thing in the Vedic period, since these *arma-kapālāni* prescribed in the ritual appear to have been readily available." (FIH, xli. 161)

Incidentally, in an interesting article on *Potteries in Ancient India*, Shivaji Singh shows that the expression *arma-kapālāni* is interpreted by Sāyaṇa, by far the most important of the Vedic commentators, as: *cirakāla-śūnya-grāme bhūmau avasthitāni purātanāni*—ancient potsherds found lying on the grounds of 'eternally deserted' settlements. Since, however, no settlement can be 'eternally deserted', we have to follow Burrow in viewing these as but the Indus ruins.

If so, the possibility of these priests being acquainted with bricks in the same sites, though without knowing how actually to make these, may not appear to be so anomalous after all. If anything can be considered as most conspicuous about the ruins of the Indus cities, it must have been heaps of bricks, as is specially attested by the story of brickrobbery on a big scale told by Piggott: The entire railway line from Lahore to Multan was built by using as ballast the bricks collected from the ruined Harappan site. If so, it is easily conceivable that without knowing how actually to make the bricks—and therefore, what exactly these things were—the Vedic priests could as well collect these from the ruined Indus sites and persuade the financiers of the sacrifices to accept these as highly mysterious entities, the very use of which invested the ritual with wonderful magico-religious efficacy.

To one recension of the *Yajurveda* is appended the ritual text called the *Śatapatha Brāhmaṇa*. In this is extensively discussed again the question of the ritual with fire-altar and, along with it, that of various types of bricks for the construction of various types of fire-altars.

Being a ritual text after all, the *Śatapatha Brāhmaṇa* indulges in a good deal of mystification about the bricks and brick-altars, concocts fanciful names for the different kinds of bricks, imputes to these all sorts of magical potencies — all this for the purpose of validating the "sacrificial metaphysics" of the priests. At the same time, the way in which the text speaks of various types of bricks, their various sizes and the modes of using these in the altar-constructions cannot be viewed as outrightly fictitious. Presumably here must have been some technicians and craftsmen to answer to the requirements of the Vedic priests. We have already seen that the priestly tradition itself speaks of engaging skilled people recruited from outside the priestly circles to look after the technological requirements of altar-constructions. Who, then, could these people be? Could they be the stragglers of the Harappan craftsmen, among whom alone —as we are going to see—we expect the tradition of sophisticated brick technology?

From the internal evidences of the *Śatapatha Brāhmaṇa* itself the question may not appear to be irrelevant. In the section of the text discussing the sacrifices with fire-altars—and along with it matters concerning the making and using of burnt bricks—the authority mentioned is a certain Śāṇḍilya, while in the remaining portions of the texts this place of honour is assigned to one Yājñavalkya. Eggeling draws our attention to this, and along with it to certain other peculiarities of the text, which have interest for the point we have been trying to make.

The geographical and other references in those portions of the text which deal with the fire-altars of burnt bricks are unmistakable pointers to the extreme north-west of the ancient Indian subcontinent, or, in short, to the region where flourished the ancient Indus civilisation, often also called the Harappan culture. One of the most conspicuous features of this—as we shall presently see in some more detail—was the highly sophisticated brick technology.

This leads us to the consideration of archaeology which, as we have said, provides us with the most decisive proof against the possibility of the mathematics embodied in the Śulva texts originating in the circle of the Vedic priests. The point requires to be introduced with some preliminary clarification.

The pioneering works on the *Śulva-sūtras* by Thibaut and others were published in the nineteenth century. Since then, fundamental changes have taken place in the basic approach to ancient Indian history, thanks mainly to the work of the archaeologists. The turning point of this was 1921-1922, when preliminary diggings at Harappa by Daya Ram Sahni and at Mohenjo-daro by R.D. Banerjee yielded identical finds foreshadowing the discovery of the 'dumb outlines' of an imposing civilisation in the Indus Valley. The result in

Gordon Childe's words, is "the dramatic entry of India on the stage of oriental history", necessitating the admission that "India confronts Egypt and Babylonia by the third millennium with a thoroughly individual and independent civilisation of her own, technically the peer of the rest."

The discovery had a liberating effect for the serious scholars from the earlier but somewhat obligatory limitation of depending on the Vedic literature as virtually the only source of information for the earliest chapter of Indian history, inasmuch as following R.P. Chanda, B.C. Gupta, J. Marshall, Gordon Childe and many others, the Builders of the Indus Civilisation are viewed as pre-Aryans and non-Aryans. To this there is of course the dissenting note of T.N. Ramachandran and a few others, wanting the Aryans to be credited for it. Before putting much confidence on their claim, the readers may as well go through K.C. Chattopadhyaya's *Vedic and Indo-Iranian Religion, etc.* in which are to be found practically everything decisive against it from the viewpoint of Vedic scholarship.

Since the third decade of the twentieth century, considerable archaeological work has been done in India—and, from 1947, also in Pakistan—throwing new light on the cultural frontiers of the ancient Indian subcontinent and the need is felt for a serious revision in its periodisation from the archaeologists' standpoint. Thus:

I. Period of First Urbanisation culminating in Mature Indus Civilisation (which covered an area of about 500,000 sq. miles, having according to some, over 250 sites so far discovered) traced roughly to the middle of the third millennium B.C. A table prepared by D.K. Chakrabarti shows that at least 12 of these were inhabited by over 5000 people each, though the estimated population of the larger cities like Mohenjo-daro ranges from 33,469 (Datta) to 41,250 (Fairservis). There appears to be a a wilderness of conjectures concerning the cause of its final decline, though on the basis of radio-carbon dating it is now believed to have come to its end in *c.* 1750 B.C.

II. A "Dark Period" or "Dark Age" of over a thousand years following the final decline of the First Urbanisation.

III. Period of Second Urbanisation, the main archaeological index to which is a certain pottery type (NBP ware) and the early literary sources for our knowledge of which are mainly the *Upaniṣads* and the vast Pāli literature. This foreshadows the early historical period—the formation of the first historical cities roughly dating from 300 B.C.

The period intervening the two urbanisations was earlier the "Dark Period" or "Dark Age" because not much was known about it. Thanks, however, to the brisk field-work of Indian archaeologists since independence, we now possess a good deal of archaeological data about it. Notwithstanding this, the period continues to be "dark" after all. Compared to the spectacular achievements of the Harappan cities it was the period of reverting yet again to the pre-literate peasant communities. The use of script—an important trait of the First Urbanisation—is totally lost during this period, in spite of the unconvincing claim to see in the graffiti marks on the potteries excavated at Rangpur the survival of the Indus script. For the reintroduction of scripts proper (Kharoṣṭhī and Brāhmī) Indian history had to await the time of Aśoka. The technique of making excellent kiln-burnt bricks on a massive scale and used for constructing houses, drains, monumental structures in the big cities and even a "dock-yard" at Lothal—another imposing feature of the First Urbanisation—is forgotten in the intervening period, where we have only humble habitations of mud and mud-bricks. Archaeologically, the main index to the period is a pottery-type called Painted Grey Ware. Though excellent as pottery, its sites are not indicative of advanced material culture. In this general context of practically all-round technological regression, we are naturally discouraged to expect much scientific activity.

From the viewpoint of our present discussion, the point of decisive significance about the period is the total absence of the technology of making and using burnt brick in any form.

Yet this "dark" intervening period defines the chronological horizon within which are to be placed all that could be distinctive of the contributions of the Vedic people who called themselves *ārya*-s or Aryan and who gave to Indian culture the vast body of orally composed songs and hymns eventually compiled as the *Ṛgveda*. Without reopening the controversy concerning its date, we propose to proceed on the basis of the view (endorsed by a large number of serious scholars) preventing us from assuming that the Vedic people could have entered India long before the end of the First Urbanisation. As a matter of fact, notwithstanding the loud protests of our chauvinists, archaeologists as serious as V. Gordon Childe, think that the Indus cities, already in the grip of the most serious crisis because of various factors, could not stand the shock of the attack of the invading "Aryans" and thus come to their ultimate end. Be that what it may, there are overwhelming evidences to indicate that the Vedic people or self-styled Aryans could not retain much of their original ethnic identity by the time foreshadowing the Second Urbanisation. When they settled in the new sites (usually associated with the P.G. Ware) they got largely mixed up with the local people and often adopted the material culture of the latter. By the beginning of the Second Urbanisation, as A. Ghosh sums up, "the early Aryan society had made room for the Indian soceity, in which it is difficult to isolate Aryan and non-Aryan elements."

With this point in mind, let us return to the *Śulva-sūtra*-s. It is impossible, of course, to be exact about the date of the codification of the Śulva texts. Depending on circumstantial evidences, however, the modern scholars suggest various dates for this (ranging between the sixth and third century B.C.), none of which enables us to place the making of mathematics embodied in the texts outside the period awaiting reintroduction of the technology of making and using burnt-bricks worth noting. After the decline of Harappa, burnt-bricks reappear not before 300 B.C., though only in a rudimentary form. For the brick technology acquiring sophistication worth mentioning again, Indian history had to wait up to the medieval period. Here, therefore, we come across an apparent anomaly: the Śulva texts thriving on highly sophisticated brick technology belong to a period in which—archaeologically speaking—there is no such technology.

R.S. Sharma seems to suggest an easy way out of the difficulty: the bricks of the Śulva texts are not burnt-bricks but simply unbaked mud-bricks which are easily conceivable in the PGW sites viewed as Vedic settlements. But the view is not endorsed by the Vedic texts. Thus the *Śatapatha Brāhmaṇa* clearly declares that "they bake the bricks with fire; they thereby make them immortal." The text by using the expressions *agninā pacati* and *agninā apacat* leaves absolutely no scope for doubt that the bricks spoken of were burnt in fire.

The *Baudhāyana Śulva-sūtra*, too, while discouraging the use of over-burnt bricks (ii.55) and also by advising how to make up for "that which is lost by the heat and the burning (from the right size) of the bricks" (ii.60), is indicative of burnt rather than simple mud-bricks. Here again the word used is *pāka* which means firing. For unbaked brick the word would have been *āma*.

So the anomaly remains. We do come across burnt-bricks in the literature of a period in which these cannot be admitted. How, then, are we to explain this anomaly? The only way to try this at the present stage of knowledge at any rate is to move backward—indeed as far back as the Harappa period—from where the brick technology along with its concomitant mathematics could be transmitted to the later period and codified in the Śulva texts. With a few words on this, I should end the present lecture.

The literature produced on the ancient Harappan civilisation is already imposing and more is being added to it in our time. Yet many problems about the civilisation remain unsolved. Controversies about these are going on among the archaeologists. If, however, there is one point about which there is no scope for any controversy, it is about the imposing brick technology developed in the ancient period. There has no doubt been brick robbery on a massive scale. To the story told by Piggot of how bricks from the ruined Harappan site were used as ballasts for laying the railway line from Lahore to Multan, B.K. Thapar adds the account of bricks from another ruined city we know as Kalibangan that were used for constructing the railway line from Hanumangarh to Suratgarh. What still survives in the sites excavated is profoundly impressive. In the first full-length report on the Indus Valley civilisation edited by Marshall, Mackay gives us the description of at least fifteen varieties of bricks found, ranging in size from 9.5 x 4.35 x 2 to 20.25 x 10.5 x 3.5 inches.

These bricks are so well-burnt that he describes them as "practically indestructible and can be used over and over again". In the Indus cities these were used for various constructive pruposes; the building of houses, granaries with platforms, the citadel, the "great bath" lining the inner walls of the wells and underground drains, the dockyard and so on. In short, the Harappan culture presupposed the tradition of developing highly sophisticated technology of brick-making and brick-laying. Evidently enough, this could not be possible without also developing a substantial amount of mathematical knowledge. It is actually being proved by the archaeologists by digging up some broken scales as well as instruments presumed to have been used for mathematical purposes. To all this may be added the evidence of certain designs on the Harappan ceramic unquestionably of geometrical interest.

R.P. Kulkarni of Maharashtra Engineering Research Institute, on the basis of the examination of the "seals" with design as corroborated by some structural remains at Mohenjodaro and Harappa, has proposed to reconstruct a number of geometrical propositions presumably known and applied in the Indus cities. His interesting article *Geometry as Known to the People of Indus Civilisation* is evidently in need of being followed by working engineers to enrich our knowledge of the subject. Other points of mathematical interest are worked out by modern scholars like Mainkar by painstaking examination of the weights and measures used in the Indus civilisation. Specially interesting appears to be his attempt to correlate the standard brick-sizes of the Indus ruin with the linear measures of the broken scales, in terms of which he proposes to explain the construction plan of the "great bath" and other Indus structures that survive for us only in ruins.

All this brings us back to the Śulva texts in which geometry is inextricably interlinked with brick technology and in fact is the outcome of the works of the engineers, architects and masons. It is not at all necessary to try to connect this geometry with the magico-religious claims of the Vedic priests.

3

Making of Astronomy in Ancient India

A masterly analysis of global archaeological data led Gordon Childe to the concept of the 'Urban Revolution'. Urban revolution refers to the profound socio-economic transformation that ushered in the earliest cities in human history. Childe recognised three primary centres of this in the ancient world, viz. Egypt, Mesopotamia (the present-day Iraq) and India (primarily the Indus Basin). One of the profoundest achievements of this revolution, in Childe's view, was the birth and growth, in these cultures, of 'exact and predictive sciences'. Both the Egyptian and Mesopotamian civilisations had established traditions in mathematics and astronomy and had evolved suitable calendrical systems. These are well documented since papyri and clay tablets of these civilisations have been successfully deciphered. In contrast, the Indus Valley Civilisation (also called Harappan Civilisation) has been notorious for the difficulties it has presented to the historian in the deciphering of its records. In spite of numerous claims to the contrary, the Harappan 'seals' remain undeciphered and hence inaccessible to date. Thus we lack direct documentary evidence of the development of astronomy in this civilisation. Yet the main purpose of this essay is to argue in favour of the view that astronomy started in India in the pre-Vedic era with the Indus Civilisation.

The earliest Indian literary compositions are called the Vedas—the *Ṛgveda, Sāmaveda, Atharvaveda* and *Yajurveda*—

which in total bulk are literally staggering. Though it is impossible to be exact about their dates, it is generally believed that these were orally composed by a branch of the Indo-European language speaking people, who called themselves Aryans and who entered India roughly in the sixteenth century B.C. as predominantiy pastoral nomads. Of the four Vedas we shall be referring particularly to the *Yajurveda* which was later than the *Ṛgveda* and which took a sharp turn to discuss the rituals. It appears that there were once over a hundred recensions of the text, of which only a few have reached us. These are roughly dated as 1000 B.C. Apart from the detailed prescriptions for the performance of the rituals, the *Yajurveda* contains theological or quasi-theological discussions that foreshadow the next phase of development of the Vedic literature, which are called the *Brāhmaṇas*. According to the modern scholars, the *Brāhmaṇas* date from somewhere between the tenth and seventh centuries B.C., when the Aryans moved from the north-west where they had entered India and started settling in the Indo-Gangetic divide and the Upper Gangetic Basin—geographically somewhat below the latitude 28°N. Of the *Brāhmaṇas* we shall be referring mainly to one, which is known as the *Śatapatha Brāhmaṇa*.

Specially in these ritual texts we come across glimpses of some calendrical system and, therefore, also of some astronomical views on which it is based since these texts proposed to specify the time, day, season or some observed celestial phenomenon appropriate for the performance of the rituals. Among the modern scholars, B.G. Tilak and H. Jacobi, independently, proposed to revise the generally accepted date of the Vedic literature on the basis of these astronomical data. They recovered from the Vedic literature certain references to basic astronomical observations. Analysis of these by modern methods indicated a hoary antiquity—the third or fourth millennium B.C., for their actual occurrence. According to Tilak the period could be even earlier. These two scholars, then, argued that the Vedic literature itself was of the same antiquity since they assumed that the observations referred to in the literature were from the same period as the literature itself. Such an assumption is generally questionable and particularly so in the present case for a number of reasons.

First, the astronomical data found in these Vedic texts are so desultory and so deeply embedded in discussions concerning ritual trivialities and theological disputations that it is nearly impossible to locate them and then disentangle the data from the framework of highly quaint logic which sought support in these. It is indeed difficult to imagine that the authors of these texts had any genuine interest in astronomy which they seem to have used for sheer mystery-mongering. The priests, whom we meet in the *Yajurveda* and the *Brāhmaṇas*, interested as they were above all in their *dakṣiṇā* or the sacrificial fee, could, quite conceivably, be trying to use every scrap of astronomical data they had inherited from antiquity, to add to their own rituals an awe-inspiring appearance without ever bothering to verify these by direct observations. This belief is strengthened when one sees that the astronomical observations referred to in the *Brāhmaṇas* do not quite fit in with the spatial and temporal contexts of these texts. Secondly, there are other sounder ways of dating the Vedic literature (e.g. philological considerations) and these disagree with Tilak and Jacobi on pushing back the dates of the Vedas to the hoary antiquity. It is outside the scope of the present discussion to consider the technicalities of the question of dating the Vedas but we can still quote some authoritative opinions on this. R.S. Sharma, the noted Indian historian states that 'The French scholar Louis Renou, a lifelong student of the Vedic texts, accepted the view of Max Müller that the Aryans appeared in India around the fifteenth and sixteenth centuries B.C. and placed the hymns of the *Ṛgveda* around this date.' The *Yajurveda* texts are of much later origin. Sharma continues: 'On the present showing the use of iron in the Indo-Gangetic divide and the Upper Gangetic basin, in which the *Yajus* texts and the *Brāhmaṇas* and *Upaniṣads* were compiled, cannot be taken back earlier than 1000 B.C., for this metal is known to several texts. Renou thinks that the *Brāhmaṇas* should be placed between the tenth and seventh centuries B.C.'

Keeping these views in mind, we may now examine some of the data of interest found in the Vedic literature. One of these concerns a certain asterism—*Nakṣatra* (usually rendered as 'lunar mansion' or 'lunar station')—called *Kṛttikā*. The Vedas as well as the different recensions of the *Yajurveda,* e.g. the *Taittirīya saṃhitā, Kāṭhaka-saṃhitā* and *Maitrāyaṇī-saṃhitā* give a list of twenty-seven *nakṣatras* beginning invariably with *Kṛttikā*. Jacobi argued that *Kṛttikā* was assigned the first position because during the period of these texts, its position coincided with the vernal equinox. This led him to conclude that the Vedic culture was already in existence by 3000-2000 B.C. While his last inference is open to question, Jacobi was certainly right about the position of *Kṛttikā*, as some further remarks made about the asterism in these texts show.

One such remark is to be found in a section of the *Śatapatha Brāhmaṇa* where it forms part of a theological controversy. The controversy is concerning the setting up of the two fires—called Gārhapatya and Āhavanīya under the *nakṣatra* considered most auspicious for the purpose. The opposing views are regarding whether the fires were to be set up or not under the *Kṛttikās*. The dispute itself is of little interest to the historian of science. However, the following fact mentioned in the course of the argument is of scientific relevance—it states the *Kṛttikās* do not move away from the eastern quarter while the other asterisms do so. To quote the text

> *etā ha vai prācyai diśo na cyavante sarvāṇi ha vā anyāni nakṣatrāṇi prācyai diśas cyavante.*

Commenting on the words *prācyai diśo na cyavante* (does not swerve from the east), Sāyaṇa, by far the most authentic commentator of the Vedic texts, observed *niyamena śuddhaprācyām eva udyanti,* i.e. 'rises invariably in the due east'. Scholars have accepted this distinctive property of the *Kṛttikās* as observed then.

Based on astronomical treatises like the (modern) *Sūryasiddhānta, Kṛttikās* are identified with Pleiades in Taurus, with Eta Tauri (Alcyone) as its determinative star. If, therefore, we accept this as an actual piece of observation codified in the *Śatapatha Brāhmaṇa*, it is possible to determine, with the help of the methods of spherical astronomy, the date when this observation was made since the present position of Eta Tauri in the sky as well as the precessional rate of the Earth's axis are also known to us. It turns out that the date when the position of Eta Tauri coincided with vernal equinox is as early as 2334 B.C. On the same basis in 1000 B.C., the earliest time that could be assigned to the *Śatapatha Brāhmaṇa* by responsible Vedic scholars, the celestial longitude of Eta Tauri would be 18°30′. Thus the statement that the *Kṛttikas* rose exactly in the east could by no means be based on an actual observation from the period of the *Śatapatha Brāhmaṇa.* On the other hand, it is entirely possible that the piece of observation that the *Kṛttikas* rose exactly in the east formed part of the astronomical knowledge of a much earlier period and came down to the authors of the *Śatapatha Brāhmaṇa* who accepted and codified it without verification. The priests whom we encounter in the *Brāhmaṇas* show such utter lack of genuine scientific interest that it is not surprising they never bothered to find out if during their time the *Kṛttikas* rose in the due east or not.

Once we accept this historical interpretation we are led to speculations with far-reaching consequences. A people, genuinely interested in astronomical observations, would not be satisfied with noting just an isolated phenomenon like the rising of *Kṛttika* in the east; it is more logical to presume that they would have a whole system of astronomy, of which this observation formed a part. If such a system were from a culture antedating the period of the Vedas, it is possible that the Vedic priests used scraps of knowledge from it whenever the need arose, mainly to settle their non-scientific disputes. Could it be then that the entire *nakṣatra* system which we find in the *Saṃhitās* and the *Brāhmaṇas* had its real roots in the astronomy of a culture which preceded the Vedic?

In fact it is the analysis of the astronomical data found in the Vedas which led Tilak and Jacobi to the conclusion that the Vedas actually far antedated their then accepted date of birth. What they ignored was the possibility that the actual observations were not contemporaneous with their codification, that they possibly formed part of a tradition which came down from a hoary antiquity only to be used in codified form at a much later period by a people who had little enthusiasm for direct observation or lacked an adequate scientific temper to verify what they inherited. That the Vedic priests generally encouraged speculation rather than direct observation is amply evident in their writings. As they put it

parokṣa-priyāḥ iva hi devāḥ pratyakṣa-dviṣaḥ

i.e. 'the gods are fond of deliberate mystification, and they detest direct observation.'

It would be unfair on Tilak and Jacobi to not mention here that during their time nothing was known about any Indian civilisation predating the Vedas; for them the Vedas were the necessary starting point of understanding Indian culture. Jacobi understood this limitation in his own way when he said in 1909 that if 'we are quite sure that Vedic culture was no older than 1200 or 1500 B.C.' we would be obliged to seek other explanations of the astronomical data contained in these. Referring to the usually accepted date of the Vedas he added: 'As long as this fact remains in suspense, either my arguments or these three subversive interpretations given to them by my opponents will appear plausible in accordance with the estimated age which critics assign to Vedic culture. When the new theory on the antiquity of the Vedas was first discussed, I made this same statement to Mr Tilak, who wished to enter upon a campaign against all opponents. I told him that the discussion would have no definite result unless excavations in ancient sites in India should bring forth unmistakable evidence of the enormous antiquity of Indian civilisation.'

The discovery of the Indus Valley Civilisation within a decade and a half of Jacobi's prescient remarks settled this question once for all. The story of this discovery, though well known, does deserve a few lines here. It was in 1921 and 1922 that preliminary diggings at Harappa by Daya Ram Sahni and at Mohenjodaro by R.D. Banerjee yielded identical finds including exotic seals and soon the potential of the sites came to be realised and the elements of a forgotten civilisation identified. After examining the collection of antiquities from these two widely separated sites and being convinced that they were totally distinct from anything previously known in India, John Marshall announced the discovery in 1924. This took the archaeological world by surprise, for the excavations at Ur by Leonard Woolley, almost during the same period, had already created a great sensation. Marshall remarked that the discoveries had 'at a single bound taken our knowledge of Indian civilisation some 3000 years earlier'.

The relics of the Indus Valley Civilisation are found over a vast area covering roughly 80,000 square miles, with at least fifteen cities, so far unearthed, each containing a population of about 5000. The estimated population of the bigger ones like Mohenjodaro varies between 35,000 to over 40,000. There is no doubt that the civilisation thrived mainly on agricultural surplus and the recent discovery of a ploughed field at Kalibangan, with marks of ploughed furrows, leaves us with little doubt about the advanced agricultural technique then in use. Such advanced agriculture specially in a region always confronted with the problems of flood and inundation makes a strong case for the knowledge of some calendrical system, and, hence, of astronomy in a certain form. 'Another remarkable feature of the civilisation is the meticulous town-planning uniformly followed in all the cities unearthed and this is evident in the rigid north-south and east-west orientation of the streets and lanes'. In addition, in the burials the dead were placed with their heads pointing to the north and the feet pointing to the south. Both these features indicate that the people had knowledge of stars in some form. It is further claimed that this civilisation was in communication with Mesopotamia through maritime trade and this would imply, once more, knowledge of the sky for purposes of navigation specially in default of the discovery of any compass or its prototype.

Highly sketchy and stray, such are some of the material evidences of the existence of astronomical knowledge in the Indus Valley Civilisation. To these may be added the findings from another line of research which is increasingly gaining prominence. Two teams of scientists, one in the Soviet Union and the other in Scandinavia, have been involved in efforts to decipher the Indus script using computers. Their results converge on the claim that the inscriptions on the seals are pointers to a calendrical system. The Indian scholar I. Mahadevan has been trying laboriously to work out the same thing in his own way. Though it is somewhat premature to report on the final outcome of these efforts, it is proper to mention at least one point here. The calendrical system claimed to have been revealed in the inscriptions is same as or similar to what is called the 'sixty-year cycle (the cycle of Jupiter)'—a cycle of five twelve-year periods with some zoomorphic symbol to indicate each year. Among the neighbouring countries, Tibet had borrowed this calendrical system. The Tibetan scholars persistently claim that the system originated in some place called Sambhala, which remains to be identified but which could be somewhere within the cultural zone of the Indus Civilisation.

An alternative way of dealing with historical problems of the kind posed by the Indus Civilisation, where the lack or inaccessibility of the direct records makes any analysis sketchy and conjectural, is to apply the 'method of retrospective probing' on which I propose to put special emphasis. The assumption on which this is based may first be mentioned. When we come across some data codified in the literature of a period, which on various considerations, seems to be much later than the period of the data itself, the possibility of moving backward to some period, when such data are logically conceivable, should be seriously considered. The presumption then is that although the data were contained in the literature of a later period, their origin is to be traced to an earlier period where they were generated. Jacobi and Tilak followed such a procedure unconsciously and somewhat erroneously when they analysed the astronomical data found in the Vedas and opened for us the possibility of determining the antiquity of Indian astronomy. In the present article we have already given an example of this method when we discussed the possibility that the *Kṛttikās* rising in the due east far antedated the codification of it in the *Brāhmaṇas*. To continue further with this, we note that if the later Vedic literature contained data, which appear to be a chronological pointer to the Harappan period, they also contain data which may be taken as a geographical pointer to the Harappan region as the place where the astronomy in question began. In the following we shall concentrate on one such datum. This is to be found in *Vedānga Jyotiṣa*, meaning literally, 'astronomy as a limb of the Vedas', which claims to codify the views of a certain Lagaḍha, about whom nothing is known other than the fact that the name is clearly non-Vedic. The datum in question is part of a description of the annual motion of the sun. According to *Vedāṅga Jyotiṣa*, one solar year consists of 336 civil days, a civil day being the time from one sunrise to the next, i.e. nychthmeron of the Greek. The solar year was divided into two equal *ayanas*, each consisting of 183 civil days. They were *uttarāyaṇa* and *dakṣiṇāyana*. *Uttarāyaṇa* defined the period of the northward movement of the sun from its southern-most declination, i.e. beginning with the winter solstice to the summer solstice and *dakṣiṇāyana* defined the period of its reverse movement (southward) beginning with the summer solstice to the winter solstice. The text asserts that during the *uttarāyaṇa* the day increases by one *prastha* and the night decreases by the same amount while during the *dakṣiṇāyana* just the opposite takes place. Finally it states that the maximum time difference between a day and a night is 6 *muhūrtas* which is also the time difference between the shortest and the longest day in a year. The *Vedāṇga Jyotiṣa* goes on to describe the various units of time mentioned above. A certain contraption called *jala-yantra* was used for time measurement. Nothing but a vessel with a hole, the water discharged from it was measured in units called *prastha.* Without going into the details of the measurement and the definition of the various units of time, it should suffice for us to know that one *muhūrta* equals our 48 minutes and one civil day is thirty *muhūrtas* long, to be exact. Thus according to *Vedāṅga Jyotiṣa,* on summer solstice when the day is the longest and the night the shortest, the time difference between them is six *muhūrtas* or 288 minutes. That is, the day is 18 *muhūrtas* long (our 14 hours 24 minutes) and the night lasts 12 *muhūrtas* (our 9 hours 36 minutes). Having described the crucial datum, we can now state our inference. Since the relation between the shortest and the longest day of the year is a function of the geographical latitude of the place of observation, the particular time difference between the two mentioned in the *Vedāṅga Jyotiṣa* should immediately tell us the latitude of the place where the observation was made. A simple exercise in spherical astronomy leads to the answer that the latitude is 34°5′ N. Since the Vedic people eventually settled and produced their literature much further south (approximately 28° N), the astronomical contents of the *Vedāṅga Jyotiṣa* could not be based on their own observation. The northern latitude inferred for the place of observation falls within the cultural frontier of the Indus Valley Civilisation. Thus we have here another example of the astronomical data of the Harappans which came down to the Vedic priests and were codified in their literature and perhaps used by them without verification.

The observation under discussion of the longest and shortest day specifies only the latitude of the place of observation but not the longitude. As a result it could also be that the datum was from the Mesopotamian Civilisation, whose southern capital Babylonia was located at $32^{0}5'$ N. This perhaps is one of the many reasons why it has often been suggested that Indians borrowed their astronomy from the Mesopotamians. I differ from this point of view. Apart from the possibility of independent and parallel developments in two different cultures, we should also note that the *Vedāṅga Jyotiṣa* view is based on detailed calculation and also on the use of a certain apparatus for measuring the time-unit. We do not find parallel calculations, nor the relevant instrument for measuring time-unit in the Mesopotamian culture. Mere coincidence in the geographical latitude and the recognition of the fact that Mesopotamians also had developed their system of astronomy do not justify such a sweeping conclusion. Both Whitney and Thibaut dealt with this point. Although their remarks were made long before the discovery of the Indus Valley Civilisation and therefore quite obsolete in the light of our present knowledge, it is worth considering them since by these remarks they may have inadvertently perpetuated certain misconceptions about the achievements of the Aryans. Thus Thibaut wrote in 1877: 'Regarding the disputed point whether the rule fixing the length of the shortest and longest day of the year has been borrowed by the Indians from some foreign source, for instance from Babylon, or sprung up independently on Indian soil, I am entirely of the opinion of Prof. Whitney who sees no sufficient reason for supposing the rule to be an imported one. It is true that the rule agrees with the facts only for the extreme north-west corner of India; but it is approximately true for a much greater part of India, and that an ancient rule—which the rule in question doubtless is—agrees best with the actual circumstances existing in the north-west of India is after all just what we should expect.' Since for Thibaut the only valid starting point of Indian history was the *Ṛgveda* and since it was unanimously assumed that the Vedic people entered India from the north-west, he seems to have tacitly assumed that while entering India from the north-west, these people actually observed that the longest day consisted of *18 muhūrtas* and the shortest of 12 *muhūrtas*. However, there are a number of reasons why we cannot agree with Thibaut's assumptions. If the Vedic people actually observed such a phenomenon while they were entering India from the north-west, it is only reasonable for us to expect some reference to it in the earliest stratum of the *Ṛgveda*. But there is nothing in the entire *Ṛgveda* even remotely suggesting this. Secondly, when the Aryans entered India, they were on the whole nomadic pastoral people whose socio-economic life did not need astronomical knowledge. When they settled down many centuries later in the *'Āryavarta'* (or *'Madhyadeśa'*) and converted to agriculturists, astronomical knowledge perhaps did become indispensable for them though from what we have said it appears that they depended for this purpose more on surviving heresay than on actual observations. Thirdly, from what we read about the technological development of the Vedic people in the *Ṛgveda* itself, it is difficult to imagine that during the period of the oral composition of this vast literature they could improvise the time-measuring instrument which was so central to the determination of the lengths of the day and night.

With the benefit of hindsight we could now say that the Harappan Civilisation, which flourished in north-west India at least a thousand years before the arrival of the Aryans, did require and depend upon astronomical knowledge for its socio-economic development producing the vast agricultural surplus for which evidence exists. It is left to the future historians to decipher the records of this civilisation and confirm what we have asserted here about the existence of a system of astronomy in this civilisation. In the absence of direct documentary evidence we had to follow the 'method of retrospective probing' and have tried to show that the literature of the Vedic people does contain data which in all probability originated in the astronomy of this earlier culture.

REFERENCE

1 *Editor's note:* That Pleiades are among the first stars mentioned, appearing in the Chinese annals of 2357 B.C., Alcyone then being near the vernal equinox (see *Star Names—Their Lore and Meaning* by R.H. Allen, Dover, 1963), is in remarkable agreement with the view expressed in this article.

4

Tradition of Rationalist Medicine in Ancient India

CASE FOR A CRITICAL ANALYSIS OF THE *CARAKA-SAṂHITĀ*

The form in which the source-books of ancient Indian medicine reach us, is, to say the least, most queer. It is the form of a strange amalgam of science and its opposite, or more specifically, of natural science and regimented religion. In spite of this peculiarity of the medical compilations in their extant versions it is possible to identify the hard core of natural science in these, on which were imposed—evidently later—an assorted heap of religious ideas and attitudes.

To begin with, let us note some examples of the flat inconsistencies as found particularly in the *Caraka-saṃhitā*. The inconsistencies are both theoretical and practical. I shall choose some examples of the latter, because heated controversies are still going on in India about these.

In full conformity with what is called the orthodox view of life, the text expresses great religious reverence for the cow. But it also shows a frankly medical interest in the animal, prescribing its flesh as diet or drug. In short, it wants people to worship the cow as well as to eat it to satisfy the purely physical requirements.

Nothing is more pleasing than the former for the orthodox religious sentiment. However, though most revolting for the same, the latter also remains embodied in the same text obviously as a feature of the medical conscience. Many times the *Caraka-saṃhitā* recommends the worship of the cow.[1]

In this the text is acceptable to the Brahmins who propagate the view that the cow is as holy as they are themselves. Strangely, however, the same text also shows a clearly medical interest in the same animal, i.e. an interest in its flesh etc. from the therapeutic point of view.

In Chapter 27 of the *Sūtra-sthāna,* the cow is found no longer in the venerable company of the gods and Brahmins, but where it actually belongs according to the general zoological understanding of the text. It is the class of animals called *prasaha,* i.e. those that grab and tear off their food. To this class belong twenty-nine varieties of animals—cow, ass, mule, camel, horse, panther, lion, bear, monkey, wolf, tiger, hyena, dog, crow, eagle, vulture, etc.[2] The main theme of this chapter is dietetics, from the point of view of which it mentions the flesh of all these animals and also of a large variety of other animals belonging to other classes. The food value of the cow's flesh is discussed in this chapter in two forms. First, as the general food value of the general class of animals to which the cow belongs. Secondly, as the specific food value of the specific variety of animal, though belonging to a general class.

The flesh of animals belonging to the five general classes called *prasaha, bhūmiśaya, anūpa, vāriśaya* and *ambucārin* "are heavy, hot, unctuous, sweet and promotive of strength and plumpness. They are aphrodisiac and highly curative of *vāyu* and great provokers of *kapha* and *pitta.* They are wholesome to those who take daily exercise and whose digestive fire is strong."[3] Thus the flesh of the cow, as an animal belonging to the *prasaha* class, is understood to have certain general food values also possessed by other animals belonging to the same class—say, the ass, mule, camel, horse, monkey, vulture, owl, and so on.

But all this is not to be misunderstood. To the five broad classes of animals just mentioned belong ninety varieties of animals. The text is not so naive as to suggest that the flesh of all these animals have the same or identical food value. What is just quoted simply means that the flesh of all these animals have some very broad qualities in common. But the text immediately adds that it is not enough for the physician's purpose to know only these general qualities.[4]

What, then, are the specific qualities of the cow's flesh? Ātreya answers: "The flesh of the cow is beneficial for those suffering from loss of flesh due to disorders caused by an excess of *vāyu*, rhinitis, irregular fever, dry cough, fatigue, and also in cases of excessive appetite resulting from hard manual work."[5]

For patients suffering from emaciation due to pectoral lesions is recommended barley-meal with either the milk or meat-juice of the cow, buffalo, horse, elephant, and goat.[6] Some diseases are viewed as due to the excess of *vāyu* in the body and since the cow's flesh is considered greatly beneficial in disorders due to excess of *vāyu*, the meat-juice of the cow—like that of various other animals—is recommended as a cure for these.[7]

Since persons suffering from consumption are badly in need of adding flesh to their bodies and since the physicians think that the cow's flesh—like that of the other animals belonging to the *prasaha class*—is promotive of flesh and plumpness, they freely recommend it for the consumptive patients, along with a number of alternatives to it.[8]

To say all this in ancient India is risky. There is a strong religious sentiment for the cow, and hence also a strong religious taboo against beef-eating. The origin of these may form the subject of serious socio-historical investigation. But the risk faced by the physicians is obvious. For the purpose of ruling the people effectively, the law-givers and statesmen found a cluster of superstitions extremely useful, which therefore they wanted systematically to enforce. The religious reverence for the cows and Brahmins belongs to this cluster. Here is how Kane compiles some of the evidences for this: "Manu xi. 79 says that if one sacrifices one's life in defence of *Brāhmaṇas* and cows, one becomes free from the sin of even

Brāhmaṇa murder. Viṣṇu xvi. 18 declares that even an untouchable (*bāhya*) went to heaven by giving his life in defence of *Brāhmaṇas*, cows, women, children. . ."[9]

Thus notwithstanding the systematic effort of the law-givers and politicians to boost veneration for the cow—to declare that slaughtering the cow is a sin causing the loss of caste[10] and therefore demanding a prolonged penance[11]– the genuine physicians in our medical compilation appear to remain unconcerned. What interests them is a different point altogether. It is only the food-value of the cow's flesh, like that of the flesh of various other animals, for they think that the most important factor determining health is food.[12]

In such a view of food, there is obviously no scope for the intrusion of any religious or extra-medical consideration.

The physician's view of food is summed up in a recapitulatory verse: "The body is the product of food, the disease is born of food, the distinction of happiness and sorrow resulting from the distinction of wholesome and unwholesome diet..."[13]

To assume the appearance of extreme piety, the text even goes to the extent of asserting that those with medical knowledge proper declare celibacy as the best road leading to liberation.[14]

Still the question is: Can one with real medical knowledge actually declare this? Or, is it one among hundreds of concessions to the counter-ideology in the extant *Caraka-saṃhitā*—concessions with which the ancient doctors try somehow to save their science from the continuous condemnation of it by the law-givers?[15]

Two absolute preconditions for the observance of celibacy are, as explained by the law-codes, total abstention from sex and alcohol. Of these two let us discuss here the latter.[16]

As a matter of fact, the question of celibacy apart, the Indian law-givers express very strong disapproval for alcoholic drinks as such.[17]

To the genuine physicians of the *Caraka-saṃhitā* any absolute view of the desirability or otherwise of alcohol is impermissible, because real medical knowledge allows no absolute view of any substance. Hence they declare:

"Wine is prepared from various substances and possesses various qualities. It has various actions on the body. It is intoxicating in nature. Hence it should be viewed from the point of view of both its good as well as evil effects.... If a person takes it in right manner, in right dose, in right time and along with wholesome food, in keeping with his vitality and with a cheerful mind, to him wine is like ambrosia. While to a person who drinks whatever kind comes in hand to him and whenever he gets an opportunity and whose body is dry on account of constant exertion, this very wine acts as a poison."[18]

Following their dialectical approach, therefore, they proceed to explain some detail of their understanding of alcohol. This discussion of the *Caraka-saṃhitā* seems to retain interest even for our times. We quote it at some length:

"Three stages of intoxication are observed in a person who drinks wine: the first the middle or the second, and the last or the third. We shall describe the characteristics of each of them. It promotes exhilaration, delight, a finer discrimination of the qualities of food and drink, desire for music, songs, jokes, and stories. It does not impair the intellect or memory, and causes no incapacity for sense-pleasures. It promotes sound sleep as well as happy awakening. This is the first or happy stage of alcoholic effects.

Fitful recollection, fitful forgetfulness, frequent indistinct, thick and larynged speech, indiscriminate talk, unsteady gait, impropriety in sitting, drinking, eating and conversation—these are to be known as the symptoms of the second stage of alcoholic effects.

After transcending the second stage and before reaching the last stage, there is no impropriety which persons of *rājasic* and *tāmasic* nature will not commit.

Having reached the third stage of intoxication, he becomes paralysed like a felled tree with his mind submerged in intoxication and stupor, and though alive resembles a dead man.

....On account of his addiction, he is condemned and censured by all people and is regarded an unworthy man by them, and he later on develops painful diseases as a result of his addiction."[19]

The *Caraka-saṃhitā* is indeed very keenly aware of the undesirable consequences of excessive drinking. It prescribes certain remedies for alcoholism, inclusive of the controlled use of alcohol itself,[20] and—reckless again to the orthodox ethico religious norm—"the aid of affectionate embraces of women's bodies full of the warmth of youth, the warm clasp of their waist, thighs and full grown breasts."[21] What is remarkable about the physicians, however, is that they refuse to judge alcohol by the alcoholic behaviour or the intrinsic nature of the drinks by the consequences of morbid drinking. On this point, the *Caraka-saṃhitā* sums up its attitude as follows: "But wine, by nature, is regarded similar to food in its effects. It is productive of disease if taken in an improper manner, and is like ambrosia if taken in a proper manner..."[22]

More examples of flat contradictions in practical precepts are not necessary, though it is important to remember that the extant *Caraka-saṃhitā* is full of examples of similar contradictions in basic theoretical attitudes also.[23] Which of the two contradictory attitudes and ideas embodied in the *Caraka-saṃhitā* represents the standpoint of the hard scientific core of ancient Indian medicine? Before trying to answer this, let us first note some of the rather well-known facts about this compilation and about the history of its formation.

The *Caraka-saṃhitā* is an enormous medical compilation, parts of which are entirely in verse, parts in prose alternating with verse, parts simply in prose usually concluding with mnemonic verses. Its language, as Filliozat says, "is classical and does not correspond to a definite epoch."[24] On a rough calculation, it is about three times in bulk of what survives as the medical literature of ancient Greece, the so-called Hippocratic corpus.

A great deal of rigour is not maintained in the arrangement of the main subjects discussed in the eight books of the text. The text as a whole is full of repetitions and digressions. It also describes debates and disputes among various authorities on questions of basic theoretical importance and what is highly interesting, the text insists that such debates are extremely useful for expanding the mental horizon of the doctors.[25] In any case, the *Caraka-saṃhitā* is fully aware of the differences of opinion among practising doctors and even tells us of the works of different medical schools having been in circulation.[26] Though it is not easy for us to guess today what precisely is being referred to by these, there is no doubt that the *Caraka-saṃhitā* wants to specify certain conclusions as characteristic of the medical school different from the other medical schools having conclusions characteristic of their own. What is remarkable, however, is that, in spite of the awareness of the differences among the different schools of medicine, the text insists that there are certain conclusions essential for medical science as such. In other words, there are propositions which—instead of being characteristic only of this or that school of medicine—are necessarily shared by all schools of medicine. These constitute the absolutely minimum body of postulates without which medicine is not at all possible. The text calls these *sarva-tantra-siddhānta* or conclusions unanimously shared by all schools of medicine, and says:

"Among these (conclusions) those are called the unanimously admitted ones which have a reputation in each and every treatise on the subject (viz. medicine). Such are: there are causes; there are diseases; there are ways of curing the curable diseases".[27]

That means there are three minimum propositions for medical science as such. These are: 1. the principle of causality, 2. the recognition of the fact of disease, which seems to mean the acceptance of disease *as* a disease rather than any supernatural phenomenon and 3. the self-assurance of the doctor that there must be techniques of actually curing the disease coming under those that are not incurable.

It is appropriate here to note some points about the formation of the *Caraka-saṃhitā.*

As for its possible date, modern scholars have proposed various views. These range from the sixth century B.C. or much earlier to the first century A.D. or much later. I have elsewhere tried to show that though any tendency at absolute dating of the text is bound to be fallacious, there are important evidences suggesting what Filliozat calls "the epoch of the creation of the doctrine contained therein" being very likely to be pre-Buddha.[28]

In any case, the medical tradition embodied in the text is admittedly ancient. But the only form in which it reaches us is quite later. It is not improbable that the *Caraka-saṃhitā* retains in its own way the memory of the earliest theoretician of the medical school.

It is hard to believe that the vast compilation with all its inner complexities is based on the oral instructions of a single person codified by only one of his students. The simple fact on the contrary seems to be that besides many religious and metaphysical elements introduced in course of time it contains the total pool of medical knowledge of a considerable number of ancient doctors and, what is also most important for our understanding of it, it passes through various hands before reaching us in its present form.

For understanding the history of Indian science it is as important to identify what are alien additions to the text as to see what survives as positive achievements of ancient Indian medicine.

But what is the criterion on the basis of which we can possibly identify the scientific core of the *Caraka-saṃhitā* and the alien ideas superimposed on it? Fortunately, we need not go outside the compilation for determining it.

To begin with, let us recall the account of a medical colloquium we have in the text. In this, Vāryovida expounds an anthropomorphic view of wind as the ultimate principle governing everything. But another medical authority, Marīci, leaps to the attack: "Even if all these were true, what is the point in saying or knowing these in the medical discipline? Whatever is said here must be said strictly in accordance with the requirements of medicine."[29] Thus, in short, what interests the physician is medicine and medicine alone.

We have in this bold protest of Marīci against Vāryovida's metaphysics a formulation of the criterion by which to judge what is intrinsic and what is extrinsic to medical science in our extant medical compilations.

One peculiarity of the *Caraka-saṃhitā* as already noted, is that it is aware of considerable differences of opinion among different medical authorities. It also mentions theoretical conclusions characteristic of the other systems of medicine, i.e. differing from the one supposed to be codified in the text.

We are told: "Among the people are current various treatises on medicine". Hence, after making up the mind for going in for medical studies, one has first of all to select the right treatise for oneself. Thus is the need felt for describing the model medical treatise. For our present purpose, the most relevant point about this model is that a medical treatise must confine itself exclusively to topics having strict relevance for medical science, that it must not contain anything extrinsic to or irrelevant for its subject matter, or as the text puts it, it must not mix up (*asaṃkula*) its actual theme with anything else.[30]

This chapter of the *Caraka-saṃhitā* which formulates the model of medical treatise, finds it necessary to go also into much detail or the methodology of medical discussion. In the course of this, it explains certain fallacies resulting from the violation of the norm of right discussion.

The physician is interested only in safeguarding the integrity of his science . For this purpose, he is formulating the general rule that in medical science no proposition is to be allowed which does not belong to the strictly medical context.

Still, the way in which the fallacy of contradiction resulting from the confusion of contexts, as illustrated in the text, has its own interest. It is the way in which the physician is trying to defend the integrity of his science against the possible intrusion of it by the counter-ideology. No proposition belonging to the context of *yajña* and that of *mokṣa* is to be allowed in medicine. To resist the invasion of medical science by Vedic orthodoxy, the physicians require the general rule of excluding the possible confusion of contexts. Thus the way in which the physicians illustrate this amounts to the assertion that, for the sake of self-consistency, medical science has to avoid Vedic orthodoxy as a whole. Significantly, apart from the context of strict medical science, the text speaks only of two other contexts— the ritual context and liberation-context, i.e. *karma-kāṇḍa* and *jñānakāṇḍa*. Propositions belonging to either of these two is not to be allowed in medicine.

The physicians seem to reiterate the dictum, in the course of which they find it necessary also to come out with a defence of the essentially rationalist attitude. "The propositions and counter propositions on all the topics covered by it are to be clearly and cogently worked out. Every statement made must be based on a clear and careful understanding of these. Medical discussion is to allow no proposition which is irrelevant, unauthoritative, uninvestigated, without any practical significance (*asādhaka*), confused and without a general applicability (*avyāpaka*). Every proposition must be substantiated by reason (*sarvaṃ hetumat brūyāt*). Only those propositions that are substantiated by reason and are untainted by any other consideration, prove useful for therapeutic purposes, because such propositions alone help the intellect to be broadened and only uninhibited intellect to the successful culmination of an undertaking."[31]

What exactly is the nature of their own specific context— that of the medical science—the integrity of which the physicians want to preserve and therefore the possible confusion of which with anything else they want to avoid?

This is briefly answered: there are four and only four factors on which medicine depends. This view of medicine as depending on four factors retains considerable importance in the *Caraka-saṃhitā*. In the Āyurvedic view, successful medical treatment depends on four factors. These are: the physician, substances (drugs or diets), nurse and patient. Accordingly, a chapter of the *Caraka-saṃhitā* is designed to explain these four factors, or more properly, the desirable qualities or qualifications of each of these four, the combined operation of which leads to therapeutic success. The text mentions in this connection four such qualities of each of these four factors. We quote these not only to see how remarkably free the medical view is from supernaturalism and scriptural cant but moreover because some of the things said by the ancient doctors retain profound significance even for our times.

The four essential qualifications of the physician are: 1. clear grasp of the theoretical content of the science, 2. a wide range of experience, 3. practical skill, and 4. cleanliness.[32]

The four essential qualities of the drugs or substances are: 1. abundance, 2. applicability, 3. multiple use (or, what is perhaps called "broad spectrum" in modern medical jargon) and 4. richness in efficacy.[33]

The four essential qualifications of the nursing attendant are: 1. knowledge of the nursing technique, 2. practical skill, 3. attachment for the patient, and 4. cleanliness.[34]

The four essential qualifications of the patient are: 1. good memory, 2. obedience to the instructions (of the doctor), 3. courage, and 4. ability to describe the symptoms.[35]

Something is so striking about this enumeration of the qualities of the "four factors" ensuring medical success that it is impossible for us to overlook it. While enumerating the desirable qualities of the patient, the medical compilation is absolutely silent about the accumulated merits of his past actions contributing to his recovery. In other words, it is totally silent about *Karman* and *adṛṣṭa*. How are we to account for this silence? Could it be that the ancient physicians were unaware of the importance attached to this view in the officially boosted world-outlook of ancient India? It is obviously impossible to take such a possibility seriously. Could it then be that the doctors believed in *karman* and yet forgot to mention it in this context? This again is inconceivable, because the discussion of the merits of the patient is about the surest context of mentioning the *adṛṣṭa* of the patient on the part of those who believed in it. The silence of the *Caraka-saṃhitā* about *karman* and *adṛṣṭa* of the patient, even in this context of discussing the qualities essential for his recovery, can thus have only one significance for us. From the medical viewpoint, *karman* is considered a redundant hypothesis. So the physicians prefer to ignore it altogether. They have far more serious things to discuss instead, namely the real merits of the patient really contributing to his recovery. The ancient doctors lived in a world in which the law-givers declared that any indifference to the law of *karman*—which this assertion obviously entails—is nothing short of heresy. The ancient Indian doctors, however, cannot help this. Their science and the law of *karman* do not go together. This becomes all the more obvious when they defend the intrinsic efficacy of medical science.

The fact is that in spite of receiving medical treatment characterised by these four factors a patient is often found to die, just as a patient is often found to be cured in spite of the absence of these four factors.

There is a theory widely circulated in ancient India with the powerful backing of the priests and law-givers according to which both recovery and death are being determined by some omnipotent law other than the one the physicians speak of. That is the law of *karman*. While answering the objection raised against the efficacy of medical science, the physicians do in fact completely ignore the law of *karman*. They seem to brush aside the officially boosted view that life and death, health and disease—in fact all that a man enjoys or suffers—are being determined by the "unseen" hangovers of actions performed by him in his past life. They argue, on the contrary, that the knowledge and technique which they represented have by themselves the efficacy of ensuring long life, of effecting actual cure.

Not that they make the absurd claim that they can cure all diseases. Like the modern doctors the ancient doctors are also aware of the fact that medicine notwithstanding, certain diseases remain incurable, though of course the range of incurable diseases for them is much wider than it is for the modern doctors. But they very strongly assert that a right doctor rightly applying the therapeutic technique can never fail to cure a curable disease. It is not enough to observe whether a patient gets cured by medical treatment or not. It is essential to note moreover the nature of the disease he suffers from. If the disease is incurable by nature, the patient dies in spite of full medical care, or, according to the Āyurvedic way of putting it, in spite of all the four factors of medicine along with their sixteen qualities being present. But this cannot be true when the disease is a curable one.[36]

The physicians of the *Caraka-saṃhitā* feel that the vast empirical data before them help them to develop insight into certain laws of nature, which rightly followed enable the doctors to cure the curable diseases without fail. What makes the medical technique infallible is that it is based on some well-defined principles justified by empirical data: "We follow the following principles because all these are well-established by our direct observation. We cure the sick by sickness-removing drugs, the emaciated persons with nourishment, just as we prescribe restrictions of food for the flabby and fat persons. We treat with 'cold' those who are afflicted with 'hot' and with 'hot' those who are afflicted with 'cold'. When some body-element becomes diminished we prescribe for its increment, just as when some body-element becomes excessive we prescribe for its diminution."[37]

But what about the incurable diseases? The *Caraka-saṃhitā* says, "The incurable diseases also fall into two categories: those that respond to palliatives and those that are not even so."[38]

Something really remarkable about this is not to be overlooked. It is the claim that even in some cases of incurable disease, the doctors can prescribe effective palliatives, and thereby relieve the patients of the inevitability of suffering caused by the diseases. Is this not another way of disowning the law of *karman,* according to which—like the disease itself—the suffering caused by it is completely determined by the bad actions performed in the past?

It remains for us to discuss another point in this connection. The objection raised against the intrinsic efficacy of medicine is based on two main grounds. First, patients are observed to die in spite of receiving full medical treatment. Secondly, patients are found to recover even without any medical treatment. We have seen how, in refutation of the first ground, the *Caraka-saṃhitā* insists on determining the nature of the disease. But what about the second ground of the objection? The text says, "And, again, as regards those who recover without the aid of any treatment—even in their case there is a special reason for giving them a complete course of treatment. Just as a man, by lifting another who has fallen—although the latter is able to rise by himself—gives him support, in consequence of which he rises sooner and without difficulty; in like manner do patients receiving the aid of a complete treatment recover more easily and without difficulty."[39]

Thus the ancient doctors do not deny the natural power of the organism helping it to get cured of certain diseases, though their actual knowledge of this natural endowment of the body—compared to that of the modern doctors—is understandably limited. But medicine ensures quicker and surer recovery even for those that may eventually get cured by the natural endowment of the body.

To sum up the discussion: Anything found in the extant *Caraka-saṃhitā* not discussing the four factors essential for medicine—specially the ideas and attitudes belonging to the contexts of ritual performance and of liberation—is to be considered as "irrelevant" for medical science and, as a matter of fact, in flat contradiction to the genuine scientific core of the work. If we depend on this criterion, we can easily see how much of the extant *Caraka saṃhitā*—the tedious discussions contained in it on soul, rebirth, *mokṣa* and all the theoretical correlates of such ideas—have to be scrapped for our real understanding of the tradition of ancient Indian medicine.

REFERENCES

1. Caraka-saṃhitā, Gulabkunverva edition, Jamnagar 1949; see, e.g. I.18.18; I.8. 25; II. 7.11; III.3.7; III.8.13; V.12.71; V.12.18; VI.14.23; VI.9.94; VII.1.10.
2. I.27.35–37.
3. I.27.56–58.
4. I.27.63–64.
5. I.27.79–80.
6. VI.1.183.
7. VI.14.126–127.
8. VI.8.158.
9. Kane, *History of Dharmaśāstra II*, 775.
10. Manu XI. 60.
11. Manu XI. 109–117.
12. I.25.36.
13. I.28.45.
14. I.30.15.
15. Āpastamba I.6.19.14; Gautama XVII.17; Vasiṣṭha. XIV.1–10; Manu IV.220; Viṣṇu LXXI.66; etc. etc.
16. See Kane II, 796.
17. Gautama II.25; Āpastamba 1.7.21.8; Vasiṣṭha.I.20; Manu XI 54; Viṣṇu XXXV.1.
18. VI.24.26–28.
19. VI.24.41–51.
20. VI.24.113.
21. VI.24.134.
22. VI.24.59–67.
23. Chattopadhyaya, *Science and Society in Ancient India* 372ff.
24. Filliozat, *Classical Doctrine of Indian Medicine* 50.
25. III.8.15.
26. III.8.3.
27. III.8.37.

28. The crucial evidence for this seems to be the long section on *bheṣajjaka* in *Mahāvagga* of the *Vinaya-piṭaka*, the whole of which presupposes the *yukti-vyapāśraya bheṣaja* or "rationalist therapeutics" of the *Caraka-saṃhitā*.
29. I.12.9.
30. III.8.3.
31. III.8.67.
32. I.9.6.
33. I.9.7.
34. I.9.8.
35. I.9.9.
36. I.10.5.
37. I.10.6.
38. I.10.9.
39. I.10.5.

5

A Critical Analysis of the Medical Compilations*

By far the most extraordinary phenomenon in the situation of science in ancient India remains at best cursorily discussed by the modern scholars. While steps were being taken by the ancient physicians and surgeons to move towards remarkable results, the most intense contempt was shown for them in the legal literature, called Dharmaśāstra. This contempt was already pronounced when the law-codes were taking distinct shape in the sixth or fifth century B.C.

There was nothing subtle about it. It was sheer raw hatred. Nor was any reason mentioned for it. The damnation of the doctors was simply decreed. It was declared over and over again that they were inherently impure—so impure indeed that their very presence pollutes a place; food received or given to them was said to be as filthy as blood and pus; in social status they were considered no better than the whores, hunters and followers of other despicable professions.[1] The obvious need of their services for society was acknowledged of course,[2] as was that of the followers of other so called mean professions. Because, however, the healers were supposed to be absolutely shorn of respectability it was prescribed that

* Taken from *History of Science and Technology in Ancient India*, II, *Formation of Theoretical Fundamentals of Natural Science* by Debiprasad Chattopadhyaya. Copyright: National Institute of Science, Technology and Development Studies.

medical practice should better remain restricted to a caste which the law-makers were pleased to call the Ambaṣṭhas.[3] The low status of these Ambaṣṭhas was sought to be established by imputing to them a fanciful origin—the mating of Brahmin males with Vaisya females, which therefore simply meant that they were bastards of some sort (*varna-saṃkaras*) in the caste norm.

The earliest law-codes are associated with such names as Āpastamba, Gautama, Vasiṣṭha and a few others. Modern authorities like P.V. Kane[4] propose the date sixth or fifth century B.C. for them. And practically all of them can be quoted to illustrate the legal contempt for medical practitioners. But it will be tiring to quote them—the almost endless repetition of the arrogant assertion that a doctor cannot but be a dirty man. It may be refreshing instead to quote the doctors, for whom personal cleanliness is an essential requirement of their own profession. Here is how the *Caraka-saṃhitā* describes one fit for medical education:

> He should be peaceful (*praśānta*) noble in disposition, incapable of any mean act (*a-kṣudra-karman*), with straight eyes, face and nose, with slim body, having a clean and red tongue, without distortion of teeth and lips, with clear voice (i.e. with voice neither indistinct nor nasal), persevering, without egotism, intelligent, endowed with powers of reasoning and good memory (*vitarka-smṛti-sampanna*), with broad mind (*udāra-sattva*), inclined to medical study either because of being born in the family of physicians or by natural aptitude, with eagerness to have the knowledge of truth (*tattva-abhiniveśin*), with no deformity of body and no defect of sense-organs, by nature modest and gentle, contemplating on the true nature of things (*artha-tattva-bhāvaka*), without anger and without addiction, endowed with good conduct, cleanliness, good habits, love, skill and courtesy (*śīla-śauca-ācāra-anurāga-dakṣya-pradākṣiṇya-upapanna*), desirous of the welfare of all living beings, devoid of greed and laziness (*alubdham analasam sarvabhūtahitaṣiṇam*) and having full loyalty and attachment to the teacher. (iii. 8.8)

To this may be added from the *Suśruta-saṃhitā* the following description of the norm of the doctors:

> He should be clean in his habits and well shaved, and should not allow his nails to grow. He should wear white garments, put on a pair of shoes, carry a stick and an umbrella in his hands, and walk about with a mild and benign look as a friend of all created beings, ready to help all, and frank and friendly in his talk and demeanour, and never allowing the full control of his reason or intellectual powers to be in any way disturbed or interfered with. (i. 10.2.B)

It is thus not at least in the norm of the medical man that one is allowed to sense so much filth which the law-givers impute to them. Evidently the filth is sensed elsewhere. From the legal point of view it is in their commitment to natural science. Here is an interesting evidence from Manu (x. 116) who is placed sometime between 200 B.C. and A.D. 200 and whose codification of the laws enjoyed the most widespread authority in the country.

According to Manu, certain modes of obtaining the livelihood are too derogatory to be normally allowed to the *dvijas* or members of the privileged classes. Only under exceptional conditions causing dire distress, the law-giver grudgingly allows the *dvijas* to go in for these. Their list, as given by the law-giver, is: *vidyā śilpam bhṛtiḥ sevā gorakṣam vipaṇiḥ kṛṣiḥ*, i.e. learning, crafts, wage-earning, servitude, cattleraising, shopkeeping, agriculture. Specially puzzling about this list is the item mentioned first, viz. *vidyā*, which means learning or cultivating some branch of knowledge. There is not much difficulty to understand why wage-earning, servitude, etc. are to be considered normally incompatible with noble birth. But what possibly is wrong about *vidyā* or learning, so that a *dvija* should be advised to avoid it normally, or to accept it only under conditions of dire distress? The commentators Medhātithi and Kullūka Bhaṭṭa naturally feel that some clarification is necessary about this point. The clarification offered by both is quite striking. The word *vidyā* or learning is to be understood here in a specific sense. It is learning or 'discipline' in its non-scriptural or anti-scriptural form, i.e. in the form in which the physicians, logicians, poison-removers, etc. understand it. As Kullūka Bhaṭṭa very pointedly says: *vidyā vedavidyā-vyatirikta-vaidyatarka viṣāpanayana-ādi-vidyā*–" by learning is meant here those specific forms of learning which are different from the learning of the Vedas, as for example the kind of learning cultivated by the physicians, logicians, poison-removers, etc."

Two points about this clarification need specially to be noted. First, the kind of learning the physicians cultivate is not only characteristically different from scriptural learning but also derogatory from the standpoint of the latter. Hence, though people of noble birth are encouraged to cultivate learning in the scriptural sense, they are under normal conditions forbidden to study medicine. This is in full agreement with what the law-givers elsewhere declare: persons with noble birth must not go in for medicine. Secondly, to the general class of learning considered derogatory from the scriptural standpoint belong—along with medicine—certain other disciplines, two of which are specially prominent. These are learnings or *vidyas* in the sense in which the logicians and poison-removers are specially concerned. There may not be anything odd in the mention of the poison-removers along with the physicians, because poison-removing is considered an important part of the ancient medical technique. But why is the mention of the logicians in the same context? There is only one answer to this. In the law-giver's understanding, medicine and logic are very closely related. Here, at any rate, the law-giver's thesis is not fanciful. The physicians themselves fully approve of it. Accomplishment in logic is a necessary prerequisite for medical studies. At the same time where the law-givers differ from the physicians must not be overlooked. The former detest logic and this for the simple reason that an excessive indulgence in logic encourages heresy or the tendency to question the scriptures. Assuming therefore that the commentators like Medhātithi and Kullūka Bhaṭṭa do not misunderstand Manu, we may see in the law-giver's declaration some indication of ideological considerations involved in the otherwise unexplained contempt for the physicians.

Precisely because it is apparently so quaint that the contempt for the healers is in need of fuller exploration. The main clue to it is to be found in the nature and source of the Dharmaśāstras. Though professing to have absolute authority in matters concerning the law of the land, this literature originates in the priestly corporations and has the primary purpose of validating the ideal of the hierarchical society—an ideal of which the priests are the main theoretical custodians. The requirements felt for the purpose go flatly against those considered indispensable by the physicians for the defence and development of natural science. Hence is the tension between Dharmaśāstra and Āyurveda.

Let us try to have a fuller idea of the former first.

In these works, as Kane[5] shows, the word *dharma* already acquires the sense of "the privileges, duties and obligations of a man, his standard of conduct as a member of the Aryan community, as a member of the castes, as a person in a particular stage of life." The discussion of all these necessitates the clarification of many topics that belong to law in the later restricted sense. Some of these are: "the peculiar duties of the four castes, the responsibilities of the king, taxation, sources of ownership, treasure-trove, guardianship of minor's wealth, punishments for libel, abuse, assault, hurt, adultery and rape, theft in the case of several *varṇas* and rules about moneylending and usury and adverse possession, special privileges of Brāhmaṇas as to punishments, payments of debts, deposits, rules about witnesses, falsehoods when excusable," etc.

Had the *Dharmasūtras* been concerned only with topics like these, they could have been considered "law literature" in our sense. But the fact is that over and above the discussion of all these, the texts also prescribe—usually with greater zeal—rules about many practices which more properly belong to the context of the religio- ritual techniques in which the ancient priests are most keenly interested.

Therefore, though in the course of time the *Dharmasūtras* acquire absolute authority in legal matters, they actually represent Indian law still bound by the umbilical cord as it were with the ancient priest-craft from which these are born. As Winternitz puts it,

> The Dharmasūtras originated in the closest association with the literature of rituals (Vedāṅgakalpa). This association with the literature of rituals is still wholly manifest in the Dharmasūtras. Hence they are neither mere collections of rules, nor pure lectures on jurisprudence; but they, with predilection, deal with the religious duties of man. They form the constituent elements of religious and Vedic literature. They, exactly as the old manuals, had sprung up in the Vedic schools and were written by Brahmins, priests and scholars for the purpose of imparting instruction and were not written as codes for practical use in the courts of law.[6]

Thus, what comes down to us as law- codes of ancient India does not embody laws in the secular sense. These have their origin in the priestly manuals concerned mainly with ritual techniques and come down to us as completely dominated by the aims and aspirations of the ancient priest-class. Indian legal literature retains this character throughout its subsequent career. Much that is discussed in it are frankly the components of the religio-ritualistic complex and even what are declared in these as laws in the comparatively later sense remain under the commanding influence of this complex. Thus, in short, beginning from its earliest career of incomplete emancipation from the religio-ritualistic complex, Indian law-codes remain throughout their subsequent career under the spell of the ideology or manner of viewing things characteristic of the ancient priests.

Since the science policy of the Indian law-givers is the direct outcome of this ideology, we shall have to take note of some of its prominent features for a proper understanding of the law-givers' contempt for the physicians. For this purpose, we shall have to move backwards from the law-codes to the vast prose literature called the *Brāhmaṇas* and also to the *Yajurveda*, which are the earliest literary records of the class-conscious priests formulating their ideological requirements.

The earliest priestly manual par excellence is the *Yajurveda*. It takes an all-absorbing interest in the priestly rituals, called *Yajña*. In doing this it shows a very decisive turn in the Vedic tradition itself. However strongly it may be contested by the Brahmanical orthodoxy, this decisive shift in the Vedic tradition is so palpable that it can be questioned only by totally disregarding the actual Vedic texts. For our present discussion we are interested in this shift mainly in so far as it concerns the attitude towards the doctors.

For understanding the nature of this changed attitude, we have to begin with a few words on the place of the healers and healing technique in the *Ṛgveda*.

An entire hymn of the *Ṛgveda*[7] is in praise of the healing herb or *oṣadhi*. The poet to whom it is attributed is mentioned as "the seer called physician, son of the Atharvans"—*atharvaṇaḥ putrasya bhiṣaknāma ārṣam*. *We* quote in rough rendering only two verses from it:

> Oh bright herbs, you are like the mothers. In your presence I promise to offer to the physician cows, horses, clothes and even myself...
>
> The wise physician is one round whom the herbs gather, in the way in which the chiefs gather round the king in the war-council. He wages war on sickness in all forms.

Can this "seer" of the Veda, remembered in the Vedic tradition by the name physician, really see a distant future in which the law-giver like Manu, while pretending to have the highest reverence for the *Ṛgveda*, goes to the extent of declaring that the physician is so impure that even food offered to him becomes filthy as pus and blood? Evidently, whatever may be the source of this contempt for the physician, it has no sanction in the ancient poetry of the *Ṛgveda*. There is in other words something palpably dishonest about the law-givers in so far as they want to justify their laws on the authority of the *Ṛgveda*. The fact on the contrary is, as I have elsewhere tried to show in some detail,[8] that the really ancient songs that remain compiled in the *Ṛgveda* are totally unaware of the hierarchical society and therefore also of any ideological need to justify it with the contempt for the techniques and the technicians, to which healing and the class of healers belong.

The analogy used in the hymn just quoted is undoubtedly archaic. So also is the mythological imagination in terms of which medical practice is often eulogised in the *Ṛgveda*. What concerns our present discussion, however, is *the fact of eulogising it* rather than the *way in which that is done.*

Some of the famous Vedic gods are specially praised in the *Ṛgveda* because of their skill in medical practice, or more simply for being outstanding physicians.

Rudra is invoked as the ablest of the physicians. "I have heard that you are the ablest of the physicians": *bhisaktamaṁ tvā bhiṣajāṁ śṛṇomi.* [9] The same hymn specially praises the hands of Rudra with which he prepares medicines for all: *Kva sya te rudra mṛḷāyakuḥ hastaḥ yaḥ astibheṣajaḥ jalāsaḥ*—"Oh Rudra, where are your beautiful hands with which you prepare medicines benefiting all?"[10] In another hymn, the same god is praised as lording over all the medicines that exist on earth: *yaḥ viśvasya kṣayati bheṣajasya.*[11]

Among the physician-deities of the *Ṛgveda* is included Soma, who treats the ailing ones on earth: *bhiṣakti viśvam yat uram.*[12]

Varuṇa is eulogised as possessing a hundred *bhiṣajaḥ*, which, as interpreted by Sāyaṇa, means either a hundred medicines or a hundred physicians: *śatasamkhyāni auṣadhāni vaidyā vā santi.*[13] Along with Mitra, Varuṇa is connected with Soma and this in the sense of medicine of the ailing.[14]

Water—deified in Vedic imagination—is specially praised as containing remedies or medicines: "In the waters exists ambrosia, in the waters exist all medicines (*apsu bheṣajam*). Let the sages be prompt in praise of waters. I am told by Soma that all the remedies exist in the waters (*apsu me somaḥ abravīt antaḥ viśvāni bheṣajā*).[15] In the custody of the All-gods (*Viśvadeva*), water becomes the healing agent or medicine: *āpaḥ it vā u bheṣajiḥ āpaḥ amīvacātanaḥ/āpaḥ sarvasya bheṣajiḥ tāḥ te kṛṇvantu bheṣajam*—"Water itself is medicine: water causes the cure of diseases; water is medicine for all diseases. Let that water act as medicine as administered to you."[16] In the same song wind or air is also eulogised as blowing in beneficial medicines.[17]

A song in praise of the Maruts says, "Oh dancing Maruts, with bright plates decorating your chests, men are moving towards you desiring your friendship... Oh Maruts, you are beautiful and magnanimous friends of ours, bring your medicines for us... Oh Maruts with beneficial rituals, aware as you are of medicines that exist in the Sindhu, in the Asiknī, in the oceans and mountains—bring all these for the welfare of our bodies and instruct us in their use for curing sickness. Oh Maruts, cure those that are sick among us and remove their physical imperfections."[18]

Many more examples like these may be easily quoted from the *Ṛgveda.* But that is not necessary. It is necessary only to note that all these do not represent any trend of stray thought in this vast collection of ancient hymns. These represent instead an important feature of the general theoretical temperament of the ancient poets which they express by way of eulogising their deities for the superb skill in medical practice or for being directly or indirectly connected with the healing agents. There is no doubt that this poetry is basically of the nature of wish-fulfilment on the part of the people with only rudimentary control over nature and as such it will be wrong to expect from it any impression of a sophisticated medical science. Indian medicine has indeed to develop a great deal in order to reach the stage represented by the *Caraka-saṃhitā* and *Suśruta-saṃhitā.* But that is a different point. What we are concerned with at present is not the stage of development of medicine but *the attitude to it*. If the ancient hymns show that medicine has yet to cover a long course to be anywhere near the stage it attains in the classical compilations, these also show that the contempt for it characteristic of the law-codes of later times is not even remotely foreshadowed in these early songs. The reason for this seems to be that these songs or hymns are not the products of the hierarchical society and are hence without the need of an ideology more interested in controlling man than struggling with nature, an ideology of which the science-policy of the law-givers—specially their damnation of medicine—is the outcome.

If the earlier strata of the Vedic literature want us to correlate the absence of the hierarchical aspiration with the absence of an attitude that proves hostile to medicine, the comparatively later development of the same literature indicates a positive correlation between the presence of the two. When we move forward from the ancient hymns of the *Ṛgveda* to the comparatively later works belonging to the same literature, we see one of the most amazing transformations in ancient Indian history. Just as there emerges the hierarchical norm on the ruins of the early Vedic one still full of the memory of the collective tribal life, so also there emerges a new theoretical temper on the ruins of that of the early poets—a theoretical temper completely under the grip of the hierarchical aspirations, or, in the language of the *Brāhmaṇa* texts, the aspirations of the "lordly power" in collusion with the "holy power". From these aspirations follow the contempt for medicine and its practitioners. This contempt assumes indeed a very dramatic form, inasmuch as the priests of the later Vedic literature find it obligatory for themselves to degrade and denounce some of the ancient gods, and this on the specific ground of their medical past.

The gods thus degraded and denounced are the Aśvins, who are physicians par excellence in the ancient Vedic mythology. We begin with some idea of their status in the *Ṛgveda*.

"Next to Indra, Agni and Soma," observes Macdonell, "the twin deities named the Aśvins are the most prominent in the *Ṛgveda* judged by the frequency with which they are invoked. They are celebrated in more than fifty entire hymns and in parts of several others, while their name occurs more than four hundred times."[19]

Of their prominent qualities in the *Ṛgveda*, it is impossible to miss two. They are most "wonderful" and they are by nature "opposed to falsehood". The two most distinctive and frequent epithets of the Aśvins are *dasra, 'wondrous'*, which is almost entirely limited to them and *nāsatya*, which is generally explained to mean 'not untrue' *(na-asatya).*[20] Their aversion for untruth is indeed so fundamental that in the *Ṛgveda*, Nāsatyas is freely used as an alternative proper name for them. Like many other gods, they are frequently described to have very great wisdom.[21] But the distinctive feature of this wisdom—like their wonder-works—appears to be their great knowledge and skill in medicine.

This is crucial for understanding the special glory of the Aśvins in the mythological imagination of the early poets. We have just seen how in this mythology various gods are praised as superb physicians. Rudra, Soma, Varuṇa, Mitra, Ap, Maruts, Dyāvāpṛthivī, Viśvadevas and others are variously connected with medicine and its practice. Compared to the Aśvins, however, their connection with healing appears to be secondary. In Vedic mythology, the Aśvins are the greatest of the physicians. When the gods themselves are in need of medical help, they have to rush to the Aśvins. And so do the mortals, for whom the Aśvins are dearest specially in the capacity of healers.

The Aśvins are addressed as the physicians of gods—*daivya bhiṣaja*, which Sāyaṇa interprets as *deveṣu bhavantau cikitsakau*, "You two, who are the doctors of gods."[22] They also cure the diseases of all the suffering mortals.[23] It is because of this that they are so dear to the gods and men, in fact to everybody. As the refrain of one of the songs in praise of these "wonderful physicians" (*dasra bhiṣaja*) puts it, "May our friendship with you be never snapped; may we be freed from diseases": *mā naḥ vi yauṣṭam sakhya mumocatam.*[24] The grand physicians, as the poets so intensely feel, are also the dearest friends of all.

A number of hymns of the *Ṛgveda*[25] describe the most "wonderful" feats of the Aśvins. They rejuvenate the old, effect safe and painless delivery, give an artificial limb to one who has lost it, cure the burns, heal the wounds caused by leopards, etc. Along with all these, the poets tell us how compassionate they are. "The story most often referred to is that of the rescue of Bhujyu, son of Tugra, who was abandoned in the midst of the ocean... The sage Rebha, stabbed, bound, hidden by the malignant, overwhelmed in the waters for ten nights and nine days, abandoned as dead, was by the Aśvins revived... They delivered Vandana from calamity and restored him to the light of the sun, raising him up from a pit in which he lay hidden away as one dead... They succoured the sage Atri Saptavadhri who along with his companions was plunged in a burning pit by the wiles of a demon... The Aśvins even rescued from the jaws of a wolf a quail which invoked their aid... They befriended Ghoṣā when she was growing old in her father's house by giving her a husband."[26] And so on.

The details of all these legends—like those of the obviously legendary accounts of the surgical and medical feats of the Aśvins—need not be taken at their face value. This is mythology, not history. Still, historically speaking, all these are not irrelevant, because they are undoubtedly indicative of a historical fact, viz. the general trend of the ancient Vedic thought. The poets dream of the model physicians as endowed not merely with the most wonderful medical skill and knowledge but also with a very strong compassion for all—a compassion that makes them the friendliest of all friends. To these the poets add that they have the firmest commitment of truth (*nāsatya*).

The level of medical knowledge and technique in the *Caraka-saṃhitā* and *Suśruta-saṃhitā* is understandably much higher than we can possibly expect in the ancient Vedic period. But at least a section of the later doctors seem to remain inspired by the image of the ancient Aśvins—a composite image of skill and wisdom combined with the commitment to truth and compassion for all.

In the *Yajurveda,* however, it is all different. The Aśvins are censured precisely for the reason for which the ancient poets of the *Ṛgveda* go ecstatic over their glory. The gods have to atone for their medical past in order to regain a place in the holy order approved of by the later priests. These priests moreover leave nothing vague about the need felt for censuring them. It follows clearly from their hierarchical aspirations. Medical practice demands of the ancient Aśvins far more commitment to democratic values than can possibly be tolerated by the social norm which the priests are so anxious to validate. Bloomfield is about the only modern scholar to note this point. As he puts it, medicine is condemned in the *Yajurveda* because "the practice entails promiscuous, unaristocratic mingling with men".[27]

Accordingly, the *Yajurveda* formulates the rule in so many words that a Brahmin must never practise medicine. If therefore the later law-givers have any Vedic sanction for their condemnation of the physicians and their science, it is to be found in the *Yajurveda*. But the point is that the *Yajurveda* itself has to flout the more ancient Vedic values for the new purpose of condemning the physicians. In short, compared to the ancient times, the priests have a different ideological temper altogether. This temper proves inimical to medicine, i.e. to the ancient discipline with the greatest science-potentials because of its commitment to certain values found irreconcilable with the hierarchical norm.

Of the two main versions of the *Yajurveda—viz. the White Yajurveda and Black Yajurveda*—the second one is preserved for us in a number of recensions. One of these is called the *Taittirīyā-saṃhitā.* We shall quote this first, because the priestly contempt for medicine and its practitioners is very clearly expressed in it. The context in which it is expressed is an apparently peculiar legend, according to which *Yajña* or the sacrifical ritual was itself once in need of medical attention, because "its head was cut". The legend occurs also elsewhere in the Vedic literature and some of the modern scholars have tried to discuss its possible significance.[28] More important for our purpose than this legend is the sacrifical formulas in the context of which the *Taittirīya-saṃhitā* reiterates this legend. As one of these sacrifical formulas, the text[29] quotes a scrap of a *Ṛgvedic* verse[30] though, as Keith[31] shows, in a somewhat corrupt form. It invokes the Aśvins:" ...Oh Aśvins, come hither to drink this *soma*". The *Yajurveda* prescribes that this *Ṛgvedic* scrap is to be recited as an appropriate incantation at a certain stage of performing the Soma sacrifice. But the texts of the *Black Yajurveda* give us not merely sacrifical incantations or formulas; to these are also added explanatory comments, which eventually become the special theme of the *Brāhmaṇa* texts. As an explanatory comment like this on the ritual use of the *Ṛgvedic* scrap, what the *Taittirīya-saṃhitā* says is startling. In rough rendering, it is as follows:

> The head of the sacrifice was cut.
>
> The gods said to the Aśvins: 'You are the physicians. Repair (replace) the head of the sacrifice. (The Aśvins seem to bargain for the medical service requisitioned).
>
> They replied, 'Let us choose a boon. Let there be a libation for us also herein. (The implication evidently is that in this Soma sacrifice the Aśvins are normally supposed to be denied of any share.)
>
> (The gods agreed to this.) They drew this libation for them—for the Aśvins.
>
> Then indeed did they (the Aśvins) repair the head of the sacrifice. In that (the libation) for the Aśvins is drawn; (it is) to restore the sacrifice.
>
> The gods said of these two: 'Impure are they, wandering among men as physicians.'
>
> Therefore, a Brahmin must not practise medicine, for the physician is impure—unfit for the sacrifice.

> Having purified them (the Aśvins) by the Bahiṣpavamāna (stotra), they drew for them this libation for the Aśvins. Therefore, the libation for the Aśvins is drawn when (the purifying) Bahiṣpavamāna (stotra) has been sung. Therefore, by one who knows thus the Bahiṣpavamāna should be performed; verily he purifies himself.[32]

Let us first try to be clear about the implications of this remarkable passage.

It is of the nature of a didactic or theological discourse on the ritual use of a morsel of a Ṛgvedic text. Read in its actual context, it gives us the obvious impression of a simple and unqualified admiration for the Aśvins, which is characteristic of all the Ṛgvedic hymns mentioning them. But the theological discourse of the *Taittirīya-saṃhitā* proposes to amend it. The reason for this proposed amendment is not that the Aśvins suffer any loss of their wonderful medical skill; the real reason on the contrary is that they are supposed to retain it. In other words, in the later priestly view, the Aśvins remain excellent physicians—so excellent indeed that the gods have to approach them for healing the injured *yajña*. In this, the later priestly view continues to be the same as that of the ancient poets or "seers" of the *Ṛgveda*. Where the priestly view breaks away from the older one is another point. There is obviously something wrong—something polluting —about the Aśvins, because of which they do not normally qualify themselves to receive the sacrificial share, as do the other gods. In the priestly way of thinking, bargaining is the normal thing to do. In accordance with this, in the priestly theology the Aśvins are made to make a bargain, flouting again the Ṛgvedic spirit in which they cure the sick, moved only by the compassion and love for all. In the *Yajurveda*, the Aśvins agree to render the medical service only on condition of being allowed a sacrifical portion. The other gods have to agree to this, though with some obvious reluctance. They are allowed the sacrifical share only after undergoing some process of ritual purification, i.e. after what the text calls purification by the Bahiṣpavamāna-*stotra*.

But what exactly is so wrong about these two ancient gods, so that they can be entitled to the normal status of the other gods only after being properly purified? This question is crucial for our present discussion. So also it is for the *Yajurveda* priests, who want to leave nothing vague about their answer to it.

The text says:

> The gods said of these two: Impure are they, wandering among men as physicians (*tau devā abruvan apūtau vā imau manuṣyacarau bhiṣajau iti*).

To remove any possible uncertainty about the priestly norm, the text adds:

> The physician is impure, unfit for sacrifice. Therefore, a Brahmin must not practise medicine (*tasmāt brāhmaṇena bheṣajam na kāryam, apūtaḥ hi eṣaḥ amedhyaḥ yaḥ bhiṣak*).

All this is most astounding. I am not aware of anything comparable to it anywhere else in world literature. The twin-gods, once eulogised in the mythological imagination of the Vedic people for their medical skill, are later declared as degraded precisely on the same ground. Such has been the calamitous consequence for natural science of the development of the hierarchical society and the zeal to eulogise its aspirations.

The same contempt for the ancient twin-gods, the Aśvins, runs through the *Brāhmaṇa* literature and—evidently for mass consumption—reiterated in the *Mahābhārata*. In the Dharmaśāstras it was unnecessary to reiterate the mythology of the gods. What was retained in these is only the crude contempt for medicine and its practitioners, senseless though it may appear to us.

Already in the passage quoted from the *Yajurveda*, we have some hint of why the priests were so annoyed with the healers—an annoyance which it knew to express mainly in terms of impurity and pollution. The healers were supposed to be intrinsically impure because their practice required of them the commitment to the democratic norm. Or, as

Bloomfield puts it, to that of the unaristocratic mingling with men. Democracy was understandably the limit that the spokesmen of hierarchical aspirations could tolerate.

But there was more in the law-makers' denunciation of the physicians and surgeons. There were a number of reasons that prompted the law-makers, to take such a negative attitude to the medical science and its practitioners. We may note here some of these that are quite on the surface. Thus:

For the safety of the hierarchical society the law-makers felt that a number of restrictions were better enforced on the behaviour-pattern of the masses which, irrespective of their intrinsic worth, could keep them under the spell of superstition. Superstition had the acknowledged efficacy of keeping men under control. Of such superstitions, one of the most widely known is the reverence for the gods and Brahmins along with the allegedly holy animal, the cow (*deva-go-Brāhmaṇa*)

The makers of rationalist medicine, by contrast, were much too committed to their ideal of curing the sick to remain crippled by such injunctions. From this point of view they could perhaps be somewhat indifferent to the questions of having any reverence for the deities and Brahmins. But the question of the cow was a different one altogether. They observe with as much rigour as is possible for them that it has very definite medical efficacy. The beef, like certain other varieties of meat, is thus a must in their medical prescription for certain diseases. In doing this they are however confronted with a problem no doubt. Being fully aware of the fact that the religious, aesthetic and other considerations of the patient are likely to make him so intensely averse to these meats that even if he is forced to take them he was only likely to vomit these out.

What then is to be done? The answer suggested in the *Caraka-saṃhitā* is remarkable. To be a successful physician, one had to be a really good cook—so good indeed as to make the meat preparation to be passed as a vegetable one. This is bluffing the patient no doubt or telling him a lie. But that does not matter. The only concern of the doctor is to cure the patient. That is the medical ethics for rationalist medicine. The question of truth and falsehood in their abstraction is one outside the interest of rationalist medicine.

All this appears to be quite extraordinary specially in the ancient Indian context. We may thus go in for some textual data showing how the *Caraka-saṃhitā* puts the points. The first question obviously is:

What are the specific qualities of the cow's flesh? Ātreya answers: "The flesh of the cow is beneficial for those suffering from loss of flesh due to disorders caused by an excess of *vāyu*, rhinitis, irregular fever, dry cough, fatigue, and also in cases of excessive appetite resulting from hard manual work."[33]

For patients suffering from emaciation due to pectoral lesions is recommended barley-meal with either the milk or meat-juice of the cow, buffalo, horse, elephant and goat (*go-mahiṣi-aśva-nāga-ajaiḥ kṣiraiḥ māmsarasaiḥ tathā*).[34] Some diseases are viewed as due to the excess of *vāyu* in the body and since the cow's flesh is considered greatly beneficial in disorders due to excess of *vāyu*,[35] the meat-juice of the cow—like that of various other animals—is recommended as a cure for these. "The meat-juices of iguana, fox, cat, porcupine, camel, cow, tortoise and pangoline should be prepared like vegetables and cooked *sali*-rice may be given with meat-juices for the relief of *vāyu*."[36]

Since those suffering from consumption are badly in need of adding flesh to their bodies and since the physicians think that the cow's flesh—like that of the other animals belonging to the *prasaha* class—is promotive of flesh and plumpness,[37] they freely recommend it for the consumptive patients, along with a number of alternatives to it. "The flesh of peacock, partridge, cock, swan, hog, camel, ass, cow and buffalo are greatly promotive of flesh."[38]

Thus notwithstanding the systematic effort of the law-givers to boost veneration for the cow—to declare that slaughtering the cow is a sin causing the loss of caste[39] and therefore demanding a prolonged penance[40]—the genuine physicians in our medical compilation appear to remain unconcerned. What interests them is a different point altogether: it is only the food-value of the cow's flesh, like that of the flesh of various other animals, for they think that the most important factor determining health is food.

This being a fundamental proposition for the physician, he has no scope to introduce any religious or other consideration into his view of food.

But there is a problem for the physician in recommending for the patients all sorts of flesh, their medical efficacy notwithstanding. He is fully aware of the possible strong disgust in the patient for at least some of these, provoked by the patient's religious, aesthetic or other sentiments. The revulsion for such flesh may be strong enough in the patient to lead him either to stubbornly refusing these or even to vomiting these out if forcibly administered. What, then, is to be done by the physician?

The answer given in the *Cikitsā-sthāna* immediately before what is already quoted—i.e. the recommendation of the flesh of swan, hog, camel, ass, cow, buffalo, etc.—is remarkable. The physician as physician is interested only in one thing, and that is the cure of the patient. If, therefore, it is essential for the patient to eat some flesh, the physician has to work out a certain tactical method by which to lead the patient to overcome his religious or aesthetic revulsion against these. When necessary, such a tactical method may include deliberate deception or sheer fluff. It is thus not any absolute fidelity to traditional morality that makes one a model physician. What makes one so is also the occasional capacity to lie—though obviously in the patient's interest.

The entire discussion of this in the *Cikitsā-sthāna* needs to be quoted here, for it has considerable theoretical interest for understanding the position of the real physician in the *Caraka-saṃhitā*. What concerns him is medicine and medicine alone. If therefore there is any direct clash between medicine and morality in its abstract sense, the physician as physician cannot help choosing the former. For him there is no clash between scruple and medicine, for the real scruple that he is aware of is that of curing the patient. As the *Caraka-saṃhitā*[41] puts it:

> For the emaciated consumptives continuing to lose flesh, the physician skilled in dietetics should prepare well-cooked dishes of meats of carnivorous animals. To the consumptives must be given the peacock's flesh and—in the name of the peacock's flesh—the flesh of vultures, owls and blue jays properly cooked in prescribed manner. In the name of partridge, give the flesh of crows; in the name of the snake-fish, give the flesh of snakes; in the name of intestines of fish, give fried earth-worms. In the name of rabbit-flesh the physician may give dressed meats of fox, large mongoose, cat and jackal-cubs. For increasing the flesh in the consumptive patient, the flesh of lion, bear, hyena, tiger and similar carnivorous animals may be given in the name of the flesh of deer. For promoting the flesh of the patient, the meats of elephant, rhinoceros and horse—well–seasoned with spices—should be given. The flesh of birds and animals that have grown plump on flesh diet is an excellent flesh-increasing food. Being acute (*tīkṣṇa*), hot (*uṣṇa*) and light (*laghu*) it is specially beneficial. Those fleshes that are considered unpleasant by the patient because he is not used to them should be given to him with deceptive names. Then he readily takes these. But if their real nature be known, these will either not be eaten at all out of revulsion, or, even if eaten, will be vomited out. Hence these must be disguised and given under a false name.

Can a physician—with a medical scruple as strong as to declare all this—be prevented by religious or other scruples to recommend the flesh of the cow in cases where he is convinced of its medical efficacy? The fact is that the real physician in the *Caraka-saṃhitā* shows no such inhibition. Immediately after the discourse on the need of occasionally deceiving the patient with false names of the meats served to him, we read the recommendation of the cow's flesh to the consumptive patient, along with the suggestion of various alternatives to it, like the flesh of the hog, camel, ass, buffalo, etc.

All this does not mean that the *Caraka-saṃhitā* shows any special fad for beef-eating, as some of the social reformers of nineteenth-century Bengal wanted deliberately to cultivate it as part of their struggle against superstition. From the medical view-point such a fad would be as a-scientific as the taboo against beef. Though without any inhibition against it, the text is also without any unscientific enthusiasm for it. As far as the ancient doctors understand, beef is not easily digested and, in this sense, undesirable among meats, just as wild barley is among grains furnished with awns, black gram among pulses, river water of the rainy season among waters, etc., etc.[42] But this is a medical view of undesirability and has nothing to do with the religious taboo against beef. When medically necessary, therefore, the doctors consider it a must for certain patients.

We have mentioned here only one example of how the medical ethics of the *Caraka-saṃhitā* came into open confrontation with the demands of the law-makers. Many more examples like this can be quoted from the medical compilation.

But the confrontation of rationalist medicine with the political requirements of the law-makers seems to become sharpest when the former argues in defence of the intrinsic efficacy of medicine. This has been argued at length in the *Caraka-saṃhitā*, and in the course of this argument, our medical compilation speaks of four and just four factors of medicine: the physician, the substances (used as drugs and diets), the nursing attendant and the patient. While explaining the essential qualifications of these, what rationalist medicine completely scraps by overt implications is the law of *karma*. This, from the viewpoint of the Dharmaśāstra is the limit of audacity, because the law of *karma* forms the indispensible assumption for justifying the hierarchical society which the entire corpus of the legal literature is intended to justify.

Here therefore was the real rub. The Dharmaśāstra is nothing if not a defence of the hierarchical society. Rationalist medicine, again, is nothing if not a defence of medical science. What then can the law-makers do but to condemn rationalist medicine and its practitioners?

To sum up the discussion so far: Judged in its ancient context the step towards rationalist medicine was about the most spectacular one in the history of science in ancient India. In the same context, however, it was a very risky step. The risk involved was frankly political. In defence of their own political philosophy supposed to ensure safety of the caste-divided society the law-makers cannot but come out sharply against the doctors.

What then do the doctors do in defence of their science? From the medical compilations in their present form the presumption is that they—or at least those through whose hands the compilations eventually passed—tried to evade the censorship of the law-makers by way of paying heavy ransom to the demands of the latter. Thus we read today in the *Caraka-saṃhitā* of the absolute validity of the Vedas, the defence of the theory of *karma*, the damnation of the heretics, long eulogy to the ideal of *mokṣa*, not to speak of sundry superstitions like the reverence of deity-cow-Brahmin and what not. It would be tiresome to quote passages of the *Caraka-saṃhitā* to illustrate all these. To any reader of the text the points are obvious. These leave us to wonder as to why such concepts should at all be there in a work on medical science, particularly when there are innumerable other works specialising in the discussion of all this. At the same time these cannot be purposeless. The purpose cannot obviously be medical which is motivated exclusively by the cure of the patients. It can thus be only extra-medical. But what kind of extra-medical purpose can all these ideas and attitudes possibly serve, specially when we find them embodied in the medical text? The answer seems to be that in spite of going flatly against rationalist medicine these do help rationalist medicine by way of being used as a protective crust for the science.

It follows from what is argued that everything embodied in the extant compilations cannot be taken as indicative of genuine rationalist medicine. As a matter of fact, it is impossible to have a coherent idea of Āyurveda if all that we read in the medical compilations are taken at their face value. On the contrary, any proper understanding of rationalist medicine requires of us the discrimination between what is intrinsic and what is extrinsic to it in the compilations as finally codified.

However, what is at once necessary for such a discrimination is the criterion for the purpose. Lest however the criterion accepted should run the risk of being subjective—or motivated by the personal preference of the modern investigator—it is safe to seek for it within the *Caraka-saṃhitā* itself. When we do so, we cannot but feel surprised by the extraordinary circumstance that with all the alien grafts of ideas and attitudes on the compilation, it somehow retains a clear pointer to a very sound criterion for distinguishing what is extrinsic and what is intrinsic to rationalist medicine in it.

To begin with, let us note the account of a medical colloquium in the *Caraka-saṃhitā* (i.12.9f). In this, a certain Vāryovida expounds an anthropomorphic view of wind as the ultimate principle governing everything. But another medical authority, Marīci, leaps to the attack: "Even if all these were true, what is the point in saying or knowing these in the medical discipline? Whatever is said here must be said strictly in accordance with the requirements of medicine." Thus, in short, what interests the physician is medicine and medicine alone. Anything without strict relevance for medicine is to be rejected as irrelevant for medical science, irrespective of the question of its truth or otherwise from the non-medical standpoint. We have in this bold protest of Marīci against Vāryovida's metaphysics a glimpse of the criterion by which to judge what is intrinsic and what is extrinsic to medical science in our extant medical compilations. Lest this should be ignored as being based on a mere isolated statement of an individual doctor, we shall note here how his point is being variously reiterated in the *Caraka-saṃhitā*.

One chapter of the *Caraka-saṃhitā* (iii.8) which formulates the model of a medical treatise, finds it necessary to go also into great detail of the methodology of medical discussion. In the course of this, it explains certain fallacies resulting from the violation of the norm of right discussion. Two of these are specially relevant for our present purpose. One is called *adhika* or redundance a form of which is irrelevance. The other is a particular form of the fallacy of contradiction or *viruddha*. Both these fallacies are included in the final list of what is technically called *nigrahasthāna* or "point of defeat" (iii.8.65). One committing any such fallacy forfeits one's right to medical discussion.

What, then, are the two fallacies?

The fallacy of irrelevance (*adhika* in one form) is illustrated as follows: *yat vā āyurvede bhāṣyamāne bārhaspatyam auśanasam anyat vā yat kiñcit apratisambandhārtham ucyate.* "Thus, for example, while discussing medical science, to quote the authority of Bṛhaspati, Uśanas, or to cite anything which is not strictly relevant to the subject-matter of medicine" (iii.8.54). Uśanas—like Bṛhaspati in this particular context—is supposed to be a renowned authority of political science and jurisprudence in ancient India. But though considered authoritative in their own fields, it is only by committing the fallacy of irrelevance that one can quote them in a medical discussion, for the simple reason that such a discussion is supposed to be restricted to medicine and medicine alone. A statement, even though authenticated by some otherwise exalted persons, is not to be allowed in medicine unless it has positive medical significance. Let Uśanas and Bṛhaspati enjoy their authority in their own fields. Since, however, what they say is medically irrelevant, a doctor is not allowed to cite their authority in the medical discussion. Such a dictum can be formulated only by those who have strict fidelity to their own science.

The fallacy of contradiction or *viruddha*, as the *Caraka-saṃhitā* wants us to understand it, has three forms, resulting from a statement contradicting any of the following: (1) the instance (*dṛṣṭānta*) cited in favour of it, (2) the conclusion (*siddhānta*) which it intends to establish, and (3) the specific context (*samaya*) in which it is made: *viruddham nāma dṛṣṭānta-siddhānta-samayaiḥ viruddham* (Ib.). Of these three, we are specially interested here in the last, viz. the fallacy of contradiction resulting from a statement going against its own context or *samaya*. The *Caraka-saṃhitā* wants to be quite specific about it:

> Context, again, is threefold. These are: (1) the context of medical science, (2) the context of ritual sacrifice, and (3) the context of the doctrine of liberation.
>
> Among these, the context of medical science. (A statement relevant for it, is:) 'Medical science depends on four factors, (viz. the physician, substances used as drugs, etc. nursing attendant and the patient).
>
> The context of ritual sacrifice. (A statement relevant for it is:) 'The sacrificial animal is to be slaughtered by the yajamāna' (or one who gets the sacrifice performed).
>
> The context of the doctrine of liberation. (A statement relevant for it is:) '(One must practise) non-violence to all living beings.'
>
> A statement becomes contradictory when it is made in violation of its own specific context. (Ib.)

The examples are carefully chosen. It is essential for the sacrifical context to state that the sacrificer must slaughter the sacrificial animal. It is equally essential for the context of the doctrine of liberation to state that one must practise total non-violence. Thus the essential proposition of one context, if allowed to be mentioned in that of another, results in flat contradiction. However, the genuine physician is interested in neither of these two contexts. He is interested only in safeguarding the integrity of his science. For this purpose, he is formulating the general rule that in medical science no proposition is to be allowed which does not belong to the strictly medical context.

Still, the way in which the fallacy of contradiction resulting from the confusion of contexts, as illustrated in the text, has its own interest. It is the way in which the physician is trying to defend the integrity of his science against the possible intrusion of it by counter ideology. *No proposition belonging to the context of ritual or that of mokṣa is to be allowed in medicine.* But these two contexts of ritual and liberation represent the two branches of Vedic orthodoxy, generally called its *karma-kāṇḍa* and *jñāna-kāṇḍa*. Sacrificial ritual is the be-all and end-all of the former, liberation that of the latter. To resist the invasion of medical science by Vedic orthodoxy, the physicians require the general rule of excluding the possible confusion of contexts. In substantiation of the rule, they remind the doctors of the two main branches of Vedic orthodoxy and of the fatal consequence of confusing these with medicine. Thus the way in which the physicians illustrate this amounts to the assertion that, for the sake of self-consistency, medical science has to avoid Vedic orthodoxy as a whole. Significantly, apart from the context of strict medical science, the text speaks only of two other contexts—the ritual-context and liberation-context, i.e. *karma-kāṇḍa* and *jñāna-kāṇḍa*. Propositions belonging to either of these two are not to be allowed in medicine.

The physicians seem to reiterate the dictum, in the course of which they find it necessary also to come out with a defence of the essentially rationalist attitude. As it is put in the *Caraka-saṃhitā*:

> In a colloquium (*vāda*, meaning 'debate') of the physicians, they must move strictly within the limits of medical science and must not digress to anything else (*vādastu khalu bhiṣajām pravartamāno pravarteta āyurveda eva, na anyatra*). The propositions and counter-propositions on all the topics covered by it are to be clearly and cogently worked out. Every

> statement made must be based on a clear and careful understanding of these. Medical discussion is to allow no proposition which is irrelevant, unauthoritative, uninvestigated, without any practical significance (*asādhaka*), confused and without a general applicability (*avyāpaka*). Every proposition must be substantiated by reason (*sarvam hetumat brūyāt*). Only those propositions that are substantiated by reason and are untainted by any other consideration, prove useful for therapeutic purpose, because such propositions alone help intellect to be broadened (*praśasta-buddhi-vardhakatvāt*) and only uninhibited intellect (*anupahata-buddhi*) leads to the successful culmination of an undertaking. (iii.8.67)

Here then we have a definite criterion for determining what is intrinsic and what is extrinsic to rationalist medicine in the two grand compilations in their present form. Medical science is concerned with four and specifically four factors: the doctor, the substances used (as drug or diet), the nursing attendant and the patient. The qualifications essential for each are also specified. The discussion of something connected with these are intrinsic to medical science. By contrast, any topic unconnected with these—however much may be their importance in philosophy, religion and traditional morality—are extrinsic to medicine. One has therefore to scrap all these for the purpose of forming an idea of the real theoretical fundamentals of rationalist medicine.

With this clarification of the contents of the *Caraka-saṃhitā*, we may now pass on to the question of its possible dating.

We have already seen why any hope to date the text by accepting an individual authority bearing the proper name Charaka is at best questionable. For the purpose of dating the formation of the essential doctrinal content of our compilation, we have to look elsewhere. It is perhaps to be found in the *Vinaya-piṭaka* of the Buddhists which the Buddhists themselves "place at the head of the canon."[43] An entire section of it, called *bhesajjaka*, is devoted to the discussion of medicaments. The way in which this discussion is introduced is extremely relevant. The Buddha is reported that certain monks of his order (*samgha*) have fallen sick, are advised by the doctor to take some substances as curative agents and the Buddha is asked if the taking of such substances would be consistent with the codes of conduct of the monastic order. Except for human flesh, the Buddha allows everything, though specifically for medical purposes. The entire discussion is remarkable, specially when we note that the wide range of curative agents recommended are only natural substances which is strongly reminiscent of the essential point of *yukti-vyapāśraya bheṣaja* of the *Caraka-saṃhitā*—i.e. therapy based on the use of natural substances as diet or drugs rather than resorting to spells, charms, amulets, etc., the characteristic of *daiva-vyapāśraya bheṣaja*. The entire section of the *Vinaya-piṭaka* is totally unaware of spells, amulets, etc.

It needs to be noted in this connection that the Buddha, having as he did scant respect for the Brahmanical law-makers, was not in the least influenced by their contempt for medicine. On the contrary, many passages in the early Buddhist literature shows his pronounced enthusiasm for medicine. Besides, there are extensive legends about his close friend Jīvaka, the grand physician of Buddhist India, the whole of which could hardly grow out of nothing.

We do not have the scope here to go into the detail of all these. The question of the Buddha and medical science seems to form the theme of comprehensive research. There is already a view according to which the Buddha was profoundly influenced by the medical science while formulating the fundamentals of his own teachings. Such a possibility cannot be rejected outright.

What we have been discussing here is, however, a different point. It is the possible dating of the theoretical fundamentals of rationalist medicine. Early Buddhist sources indicate that this took place sometime before the Buddha. Whatever may be the date of the codification of the early Buddhist canons, it would obviously be impermissible to question the basic fact that these do embody the Buddha's teachings. Thus, in short, the steps to rationalist medicine were presumably taken sometime before the Buddha.

REFERENCES

1. *Āpastamba* i. 6.19.14 ff. *Gautama* xvii.7;&17; *Vasiṣṭha* xiv.1-10;19; etc., etc.
2. *Viṣṇu* 1xxi.66.
3. *Manu* x. 46-7.
4. P.V. Kane i.2.
5. *Ib. i.14.*
6. M. Winternitz iii. 538.
7. *RV*. x. 97.
8. D. Chattopadhyaya WLWD 139 ff.
9. *RV*. ii. 33.4.
10. *RV*. ii. 33.7.
11. v. 42.11.
12. viii. 79.2.
13. i. 24.9.
14. iii. 72.17.
15. i. 29.19-20.
16. x. 137.6.
17. x. 137.3.
18. viii. 20.20-6.
19. A. Macdonell VM. 49.
20. *Ib.*
21. *RV*. vi. 63.5; viii. 8.2; x. 93.7 etc.
22. *RV*. viii. 18.8.
23. *RV*. viii. 22.10.
24. viii. 86. 1-5.
25. i.116; viii.22; x.39.
26. A. Macdonell VM 52.
27. M. Bloomfield in SBE XLII. Intro. XL.
28. *Śat. Br.* xiv.1.1.8ff. cf. Muir OST iv. 124.
29. *Tait. Sam.*147.
30. i. 22.1.
31. A.B. Keith VYS 1. 54n.
32. *Tait. Sam.*vi. 4.9.
33. i.27. 79-80.
34. vi.11.83.

35. i.27.79.
36. vi.14.126-27.
37. i.27.56-7.
38. vi.8.158.
39. *Manu* xi.60.
40. *Manu* xi. 109-17.
41. vi. 8. 149-57.
42. i. 25.39.
43. M. Winternitz ii. 21.

6

Sources of Indian Idealism

In an important sense the perennial source of Indian idealism is a trend of speculation recorded in the *Upaniṣads*. It is by no means the only trend of Upaniṣadic thinking, as Śaṃkara and his followers want us to believe. But already in the *Upaniṣads* it is more or less the predominant trend and has the potential of developing into a very influential philosophy of the later times.

1. UPANIṢAD *OR* VEDA-*END*

The *Upaniṣads* are traditionally viewed as the end portions of the *Veda*. The word *veda* means knowledge, though to the followers of Vedic orthodoxy it means the most infallible knowledge which has been directly revealed. Concretely the name stands for the literary product of those people who call themselves Aryans and who, it is usually assumed, migrated into northern India as pastoral nomad tribes, without the art of writing but with considerable literary gifts combined with skill in warfare. How they gradually lose their racial identity while spreading over India, settle down and move from barbarism to civilisation is a story that will interest us mainly in so far as it throws light on their ideological development.

The earlier portions of this literature consist of songs, charms, and hymns. These were orally composed and transmitted to later generations by an amazingly meticulous retentive memory—a circumstance that accounts for their name *śruti*, "that which is heard". To us these come down in the form of enormous compilations (*saṃhitā*), a form traceable to considerable antiquity. Of these compilations, the earliest and regarded as fundamental is the *Ṛgveda*. There are in addition three others—the *Sāmaveda*, *Yajurveda* and *Atharvaveda*.

The *Ṛgveda* alone contains 1,028 songs in a total of 10,552 verses. Their total composition must have taken a long period of time. For modern scholars, its inner chronology is naturally a formidable problem, which they are still groping to solve. This much is certain that some of these songs are considerably earlier than others. Any hasty generalisation about the early Vedic people based on some stray Ṛgvedic evidence is liable to be fallacious.

The early songs of the *Ṛgveda*, which often surprise us by their primitive vigour and uninhibited imagination, are almost totally obsessed with the problems of physical survival. These express, so to say, without cessation the desire for food, cattle, progeny, victory, and so on. All this is mixed up with the mythological imaginings of a people, who see deities in many things that they do not understand and which fill them with awe easily passing into reverence. For instance, they see such deities in natural phenomena like the sun and wind, fire and forest, in the extraordinary might of their war chiefs or heroes, in the intoxicating power of their drink *soma*, and so on. The deities are important for them, because they are supposed to be aids to the fulfilment of elemental desires. As people with a rudimentary control over nature, the poets see deities even in their frankly pathetic wish-fulfilments like those of the prevention of abortion and the cure of phthisis.

People at such a stage of development are not expected to philosophise, and the fact is that the genuinely earlier songs of the *Ṛgveda* show no predilection for philosophy. Except for some admittedly later songs in this vast collection, speculations even in a proto-philosophical sense do not have a place in the *Ṛgveda* notwithstanding of course all the wild things often said about the great wisdom contained in it. As

H.P. Sastri[1] says, such statements are inspired more by an ignorant veneration for the *Veda* than an actual acquaintance with its contents.

The next phase of Vedic literary activity can be traced to the *Yajurveda.* This reaches its climax in colossal texts called the *Brāhmaṇas.* These texts are characterised by a shift of interest to discussion of the rituals or *yajña.* The rituals must have originally been something like the magical rites still to be observed among some present day primitive people surviving in certain pockets of the modern world. In their original primitive context, magical rites are not irrelevant. Their essence consists mainly in enacting "in fantasy the fulfilment of the desired reality. That is magic, an illusory technique, supplementary to real techniques. But though illusory, it is not futile." The ritual performance cannot have any direct effect on nature; but it can and does have an appreciable effect on the performers themselves. Inspired by the belief that it will bring into being the desired reality, they proceed to the task of actually bringing it into being with greater confidence and so with greater energy than before. And so it does have an effect on nature after all. "It changes their subjective attitude to reality, and so indirectly it changes reality."[2]

In this sense of being illusory techniques intended to aid real techniques, magical rites are originally connected with man's struggle with nature. As discussed in the *Brāhmaṇa* texts, however, the rituals are uprooted from their original context, and their function passes into its opposite. These become tools for a new technique—that of man's struggle against man. The point is too obvious to be missed and Eggeling[3] observes in the introduction of his English translation of the *Śatapatha Brāhmaṇa:*

"The *Brāhmaṇas,* it is well known, form our chief, if not our only, source of information regarding one of the most important periods in the social and mental development of India. They represent the intellectual activity of a sacerdotal caste which .... was ever intent on deepening and extending its hold on the minds of the people, by surrounding its own vocation with the halo of sanctity and divine inspiration. A complicated ceremonial, requiring for its proper observance and consequent efficacy the ministrations of the highly trained priestly class, has ever been one of the most effective means of promoting hierarchical aspirations. Even practical Rome did not entirely succeed in steering clear of the rock of priestly ascendancy attained by such-like means... The Roman statesmen submitted to these transparent tricks rather from considerations of political expediency than from religious scruples; and the Greek Polybius might well say that 'the strange and ponderous ceremonial of Roman religion was invented solely on account of the multitude which, as reason had no power over it, required to be ruled by signs and wonders'."

The change in the content of Vedic literature transforms also its form. In the *Brāhmaṇa* texts, instead of the inspired poetry of the *Ṛgveda,* we have only insipid prose—in fact the dullest and the most cumbrous style that we have in Indian literature. One reason for this insipidity is the tendency to evolve symbolic interpretations of ritual trivialities, in the course of which scraps of Ṛgvedic verses are often quoted without their context and with strange meanings read into them.

Such trivialities, though meaningless for us, are not irrelevant, for in terms of these the authors of the *Brāhmaṇas* also try to validate a new social norm, that emerges on the ruins of the ancient tribal one. The new norm is that of a split society in which the powers and privileges belong to the kings and nobles, though secondarily also to their ideological apologists—the priests. For the purpose of rationalising it, its essential features are sometimes projected on to ancient Vedic mythology. Thus the group of gods called Maruts are now made to stand for the common people while despotic power is represented by Indra and Varuṇa. Here are only a few examples from the *Śatapatha Brāhmaṇa:*

"Varuṇa, doubtless, is the nobility, and the Maruts are the people. He (the priest) thus makes the nobility superior to the people. And hence people here serve the Kṣatriya, placed above them" (ii. 5.2.6.).

"He muttered that verse addressed to Indra and referring to the Maruts. Indra, indeed is the nobility, and the Maruts are the people. 'They shall be controlled', he thought, and therefore that verse is addressed to Indra" (ii.5.2.27).

"Now some, on noticing any straw or piece of wood among the *soma*-plants, throw it away. But let him not do this; for—the *soma* being the nobility and the other plants the common people, and the people being the nobleman's food—it would be just as if one were to take hold of and pull out some food he has put in his mouth, and throw it away" (iii. 3.2.8.).

Some ritual details are sought to yield the symbolic interpretation of what "makes the *kṣatra* superior to the people. Hence the people here serve, from a lower position, the Kṣatriya, above them" (i.3.4.15). Similarly other ritual details are interpreted to show how "the Kṣatriya, whenever he likes, says, 'Hallo, Vaiśya, just bring to me what thou hast stored away'. Thus he both subdues him and obtains possession of anything he wishes by dint of his very energy" (i.3.2.15).

Many more examples like these may easily be quoted. But that is not necessary. What is necessary is only to note that in the *Brāhmaṇa* texts there clearly emerges a new political philosophy largely as a validation of the new social conditions. We shall mention it only in bare outlines, for without this we hardly understand the new philosophy of the *Upaniṣads*.

The political philosophy is traditionally expressed in terms of the four castes: Kṣatriyas (kings and nobles), Brahmins (priests and clerics), Vaiśyas (merchants and farmers) and Śūdras. What is meant by the last? The answer is suggested by a simple process of elimination. None of the first three classes is supposed to be responsible for the direct labour of production.[4] Besides, the three classes taken together can constitute no more than a negligible minority of the community visualised. It follows therefore that by the Śūdras the texts can only mean the vast majority of the direct producers. And the *Aitareya Brāhmaṇa*[5] declares that they are some sort of sub-human beings: they are only to serve the others, they can be thrown out at will and they can be slain at pleasure.

The contempt for manual workers—and therefore for manual labour—is quite clear. The counterpart of this is the exaltation of mental work—of thought, of consciousness, of pure reason. We have in this the clue to Upaniṣadic idealism.

The *Brāhmaṇa* texts are appended to the ancient compilations and these *Brāhmaṇas* appended another class of literature called the *Āraṇyakas* or *forest-texts.* "These texts comprised everything which was of a secret, uncanny character, and spelled danger to the uninitiated, and which, for that reason, might only be taught and learnt in the forest, and not in the villages" (Winternitz).

With all that is supposed to be so very mysterious about the *Āraṇyakas*—which, incidentally, is nothing but the lingering of the belief in the magical efficacy of their themes or words—the historical importance of these texts consists in their shift of interest to speculations on proto-philosophical questions, howsoever hesitant such a first step to philosophy may be. This tendency becomes all the more prominent in the still later class of literature, the *Upaniṣads,* which in their turn are appended to the *Āraṇyakas.*

With the *Upaniṣads* the Vedic literature comes to its end. Hence they are also called *Vedānta* or *Veda-end.* The new social conditions, sought to be validated in the *Brāhmaṇas* mainly in terms of ritual trivialities, are more stabilized in the Upaniṣadic age. In accordance with the theoretical temper of the age, the new norm of society is given a more philosophical form:

> Verily, in the beginning, this world was *brahma,* one only. Being one, he was not developed. He created still further a

> superior form, the *kṣatra*hood..... Therefore there is nothing higher than *kṣatra*. Therefore at the coronation ritual, the Brahman sits below the Kṣatriya. Upon *kṣatra*hood alone does he confer that honour. The same thing, namely *brahman*hood is the source of *kṣatra*hood. Therefore even if the king attains supremacy, he rests finally upon *brahman*hood....
>
> He was not yet developed. He created the commonality (*viś*)...
>
> He was not yet developed. He created the *śūdra*...
>
> He was not yet developed. He created still further a better form, Law. This is the power of the Kṣatriya class, namely Law. Therefore there is nothing higher than the Law. So a weak man controls a strong man by Law, just as if by a king. Verily, that which is Law is Truth.
>
> Therefore they say of a man who speaks the truth, 'He speaks the Law', or of a man who speaks the Law, 'He speaks the Truth'. Verily, both these are the same thing
>
> (Br. Up.i.4.11–4).

Is this a way of saying that philosophy is not unconnected with political power after all? What the philosophers strive after is truth. But truth is nothing but another way of looking at law. And it is from law that the kings and nobles derive their political power. The ruling ideas of the *Upaniṣads* are not unconnected with the ruling powers of the Upaniṣadic age.

It is important to see how the later Indian law-givers take up this Upaniṣadic suggestion and want to implement it on the Indian philosophical situation. That gives us some idea of the social function of Indian idealism.[6] For the present, we are concerned with the question of its origin.

We shall first describe the general process of the growth of the Upaniṣadic idealism and then pass on to see it in some detail.

2. EMANCIPATION OF CONSCIOUSNESS

In sheer bulk, Vedic literature is simply staggering. It must have taken more than a thousand years for the whole of it to be composed. What is nevertheless remarkable about it is the inner continuity of its development. It thus enables us to see how during a long period the material progress gained by successive generations of Vedic people enables them to reach a stage at which human labour is capable of producing much more than is necessary for its bare maintenance. A section of the community is thus no longer obliged to maintain itself by its own manual labour. Subsisting as it then does on the surplus produced by another section of the community, it finds leisure enough to specialise in speculative activity. Their thoughts and ideas, unlike those of their ancestors or the early Vedic poets, are no longer obsessed with the problem of physical survival only. They can more look forward to construct a speculative superstructure in its first real sense.

What is gained by this is undoubtedly of the most momentous significance. It is the realisation and recognition of the power of reason or of the creative role of consciousness. Without the emancipation of consciousness from the almost total preoccupation with the problem of survival, there is no beginning of theoretical activity in its full sense. In the *Ṛgveda* we come across poets and seers, who, however inspired they are, are inspired only by the vision of the fulfilment of elemental desires. Their consciousness is engrossed with the problem of the struggle with nature and they do not have the leisure to philosophise. In the vast *Brāhmaṇa* literature we have indeed the glimpse of the emerging leisured class. But it is engrossed with the problem of the stabilisation of the political power of the kings and their ideological apologists—with what is called "applied politics, or the practice of controlling men with fear".[7] The relative emancipation of consciousness of the leisured class is peculiarly consumed by this. The kind of intellectual atmosphere indicated by the texts is not the one in which the philosopher is encouraged to come to the fore. In the *Brāhmaṇas* we see priests rambling in the graveyard of primitive rituals; but we do not yet see the philosopher. The picture of the philosopher first emerges in the *Upaniṣads*, when the leisured class fully stabilises its own power and can afford to have the serenity and tranquillity of unruffled contemplation. The first philosophers of the *Upaniṣads* raise questions of immense theoretical significance and they earnestly seek answers to these.

At the same time, this progress—great though it is— also creates a very grave danger for thought, particularly in the view of those that visualise an ideal society in which the manual workers are shorn of all prestige and privilege. The tools and techniques by which nature is interrogated belong to these direct producers. But they recede to the background, and along with them the growing stock of their experience and understanding. Philosophical activity, in so far as it is cut off from all these, easily tends to lose the spirit of interrogating nature. The result is much worse than contempt for the physical sciences. It is the creation of an illusion, resulting from the coercion of consciousness to a peculiar process of introversion. Knowledge is no longer intended to be the knowledge of objects. It wants to be knowledge of the subject itself—of the bare ego or of the pure self. As the Upaniṣadic idealists put it, the ideal of the philosopher is *ātmaratirātmakrīḍa.*—'the libido fixed on the self, sporting with the self' (Ch. Up. vii. 25.2). Extreme introversion, we are told,[8] brings into operation a delusion of grandeur. It is the delusion of the ominipotence of the bare ego. This ego, this self, wants to dictate terms to reality and demands to be recognised as the only reality. 'I am that ultimate reality'—declares the Upaniṣadic idealist. The result is the lofty contempt for the material world, in which the philosopher himself has his being.

All this is putting the point in the terminologies of the psychologist. But that does not mean that we are trying to understand here the psychology of the Upaniṣadic idealists. If we are interested in their mental history, the reason is that it enables us to understand how the new world in which they live accounts for the fundamentals of their new world outlook. In their political philosophy, active intercourse with nature is no better than the forced labour of the Śūdras. The philosopher takes pride in disowning the spirit of interrogating nature and is hence under no obligation to admit its reality.

Thus cut off from active intercourse with nature, the philosopher's consciousness runs the risk of imagining that it can rise to ever higher and ever more remote conditions where only thought remains and the things thought of fade out. This is the cult of pure reason, i.e. of reason only as a faculty of illusion. Consciousness, estranged from concrete living, becomes a form of sick consciousness. It is no longer *consciousness of something* but *something like consciousness-in-itself*—just consciousness, sheer consciousness—not the consciousness of the real men and women engaged in the active intercourse with nature and getting progressively enriched by this intercourse. Consciousness is now viewed as a "deified absolute"—too mysterious to be grasped by mundane thought and too awesome to be described by ordinary language.

Not that the emancipation of consciousness has such a necessary fate. There are thinkers in Upaniṣadic India who do not share this line of thinking. There are even those who, instead of taking a deified view of consciousness, want to understand it in the sober scientific sense.[9] In all presumption, they are the pioneers of the scientific tradition in Indian philosophy. Their consciousness does not develop into the morbid consciousness of their idealist colleagues.

In Upaniṣadic India, however, their prestige is already on the decline and there is a growing contempt for whatever was evaluated as the positive science of the age.[10] In the new intellectual atmosphere, those whose glory is specially boosted are philosophers for whom consciousness, fully alienated from actual life, wants to oppose and undermine life.

Such a philosopher is the great Yājñavalkya. He declares that reality is just a mass of consciousness (*vijñānaghana*). It can neither be grasped by the normal organs of knowledge nor described in normal language. The only way of talking about it is to say, 'It is not this', 'It is not this'. While dreaming and further falling into the state of dreamless sleep, one gets progressively emancipated from the fetters of the material world and has a taste of this reality.

This is how the idealist outlook is first foreshadowed in Indian philosophy. But, as we shall presently see, it could hardly make any sense to the early Vedic poets, not merely because they are comparatively ignorant and do not know how to philosophise but because they are much too committed to the active intercourse with nature to afford such gambols of pure consciousness.

Thus for the understanding of the general history of ideological development, Vedic literature has great importance. It is a vast literature with an inner continuity of development, showing speculative consciousness not only in the making but also its eventual culmination in the cult of pure consciousness, the outcome of which is the idealist outlook.

An adequate survey of Vedic literature from this point of view forms the subject of an independent study. We have the scope here to note only a few salient points relevant for understanding the emergence of the idealist outlook.

3. CULT OF "SECRET KNOWLEDGE"

In the apparent chaos of the philosophical tendencies of the *Upaniṣads,* the more outstanding features with which the idealist outlook announces itself are on the whole clear. We have a clue to it in the name chosen for the texts.

The word *upaniṣad*—as suggested by its etymology and corroborated by its synonym *rahasyam*—means 'secret knowledge' or 'secret wisdom'. It is secret, because only a fortunate few of the age are supposed to be its custodians. At the same time, this knowledge is considered supremely important, because it is believed to have a marvellous potency of its own.

All this gives us some idea of the distinctive peculiarity of the *Upaniṣads.* Their main theme is knowledge, but not knowledge in the ordinary sense. It is knowledge restricted to a few of the community and is moreover believed to have a mysterious power of its own.

In the Vedic literature this is something new. The traditional way of admitting this is to describe the *Upaniṣad* as a new offshoot of the Vedic literature representing its 'knowledge branch' or *jñāna-kāṇḍa*. The concept of knowledge acquires in the *Upaniṣads* an altogether new and somewhat fabulous significance.

"Knowledge—not so much learning, but the understanding of metaphysical truths—was the impelling motive of the thinkers of the Upaniṣads... Knowledge was the one object of supreme value, the irresistible means of obtaining one's ends. The idea of the worth and efficacy of knowledge is expressed again and again throughout the Upaniṣads not only in connection with philosophical speculation, but also in practical affairs in life... So frequent are the statements describing the invulnerability and omnipotence of him who is possessed of this magic talisman, that *yaḥ evaṃ veda*—'he who knows this'—becomes the most frequently recurring phrase of the Upaniṣads."[11]

But this emphasis on the power of knowledge must not be misunderstood. It is not what Bacon means when he says that "the improvement of man's mind and the improvement of his lot are one and the same thing." Knowledge which is so much valued in the *Upaniṣads* is not at all intended to be a better insight into nature, serving as the basis of a better mastery of it. It is not supposed to be a guide to any course of action leading to some desired result. What is believed is that knowledge by itself fulfils all desires—i.e. fulfils these immediately, directly and automatically. How are we to understand such a belief?

There is only one answer to this. The belief is essentially magical. The typical Upaniṣadic way of expressing this magical belief is: "One who knows this reaches a full length of life, lives long, becomes great in offspring, great in cattle, great in fame." In so far as this is a belief in magic, there is nothing new about it in the Vedic tradition. The belief is overwhelmingly obvious in the *Atharvaveda* and *Yajurveda*; it assumes the most grotesque form in the *Brāhmaṇas*. As appended to the *Brāhmaṇas* the *Upaniṣads* do not outgrow the belief in magic. This is already discussed by Edgerton[12] in his remarkable paper "Upaniṣads: What do they seek and why?"

What Edgerton does not discuss, however, is another important point. In spite of the lingering of the magical belief in the *Upaniṣads*, there is also something strikingly new about the texts. In the earlier strata of the Vedic literature, the concept of metaphysical wisdom is itself absent. Hence there is no question of viewing it as possessing magical potency. In the early Vedic age, in other words, the belief in the potency of magic is there. But it is the belief in the magical potency of the ritual acts. In the *Upaniṣads*, the belief is clearly displaced. It is now the belief in the magical efficacy of secret wisdom, from which this literature receives its name.

If the persistence of magical belief indicates that the Upaniṣadic thinkers do not fully outgrow their ancestral convictions, the displacement of the belief to secret wisdom shows the new theoretical temper of the age. What is decisive about the *Upaniṣads* is this fetish of secret wisdom. In it is absorbed whatever still survives of the earlier ideas and attitudes. In the altered conditions in which they live, the Upaniṣadic thinkers find the mere stock of their ancestral convictions inadequate for their own purposes, however otherwise strong the hangover of these may be. Thus, though in a number of passages great veneration is expressed for the ancient compilations or *saṃhitās*, other passages of the *Upaniṣads* state in so many words that the mere knowledge of the *saṃhitās* is not enough for the new pursuit of metaphysical wisdom. An example of the latter is the story of Nārada and Sanatkumāra. Nārada approaches the latter and declares that in the stock of knowledge he already possesses are included the *Ṛgveda, Sāmaveda, Yajurveda* and *Atharvaveda.* Apparently dissatisfied with all this, he wants to be initiated into the secret wisdom of Sanatkumāra. And the first thing that the philosopher tells him is that all these branches of knowledge—inclusive of the knowledge of the four ancient compilations—are 'mere names' (*nāman*): these have no more value than a merely nominal one.

4. PHILOSOPHY AND NOBILITY

Who is this Vedic philosopher that has the audacity to declare that even the *Ṛgveda,* etc. are mere names? We do not know the exact answer. Keith[13] says that he is just a mythical sage of the *Upaniṣads.* But that is saying something too vague to have a meaning. The *Upaniṣad* that tells the story of Sanatkumāra declares, "People call him Skanda—yea, they call him Skanda." In Indian mythology Skanda is the name of the god of war. Does then Sanatkumāra belong to the class of the warrior nobles? Does the *Upaniṣad* want us to connect the new nobility with the new theoretical temper of the age?

The evidence of Sanatkumāra may itself be too thin to prove such a possibility. But the possibility is there and it cannot be easily dismissed. Many other legends of the *Upaniṣads* suggest it. Keith[14] sums these up as follows:

"In the *Chāndogya Upaniṣad* (v.11– 24) five learned Brahmins desire to learn from Uddālaka Āruṇi the nature of the Ātman Vaiśvānara; he doubts his ability to explain it, and as a result all six betake themselves to the king Aśvapati Kaikeya who gives them instruction, after first demonstrating the inaccuracy of their knowledge. In a narrative which is preserved in the *Bṛhadāraṇyaka Upaniṣad* (ii.1) and the *Kauṣītaki Upaniṣad* (iv) a scholar, Gārgya Bālāki, undertakes to set out the nature of *brahman* to the king Ajātaśatru of Kāśī: he propounds twelve views—or in the *Kauṣītaki* sixteen—which are all defective, and the king then explains the Ātman to him by the principle of deep sleep, prefacing the observation that it is a reverse of the rule for a Brahmin to betake himself to a Kṣatriya for instruction. Another legend in the *Chāndogya* (i.8.9) shows the Brahmin being instructed in the nature of ether as the ultimate basis of all things, by the king Pravāhaṇa Jaivali... Less important is the fact that the Brahmin Nārada is represented in the *Chāndogya* as being a recipient of information from Sanatkumāra, later the god of war, who tells the former that all this Vedic lore is mere name. The great text regarding the doctrine of transmigration is set out by Pravāhaṇa Jaivali to Āruṇi with the remark that the Brahmins have never before had this information, which so far had remained the monopoly of the Kṣatriyas. In a third version of this account, given in the *Kauṣītaki Upaniṣad*, the king is Citra Gāṅgyāyani."

What do all these legends imply? Keith[15] is inclined to view these as "delicate and effective pieces of flattery", i.e. of the kings by the priests who compile the *Upaniṣads*. This is taking a rather casual view of the Upaniṣadic material. The other way of misunderstanding the same is to take the Upaniṣadic legends at their face value. This is done by those who argue that the Upaniṣadic philosophy is the creation of the Kṣatriya caste. However, even assuming that the legends are to be taken seriously, the fact remains that, except perhaps the doctrine of the transmigration of the soul, the theoretical innovations attributed to the kings and nobles are on the whole secondary in importance. Compared to these, the speculative constructions attributed to a thinker like Yājñavalkya is much more imposing. But Yājñavalkya is a priest and not a noble. This easily disproves the theory of the Kṣatriya origin of the Upaniṣadic philosophy in the sense in which it is usually put. But it proves nothing against the fact connecting the nobility with the new philosophy, for without the patronage of the nobles even Yājñavalkya cannot philosophise. The point is not how much the kings and nobles directly contribute to the philosophical activity of the age. The point rather is that without their political and financial support, Upaniṣadic idealism is not adequately explained. This is best illustrated by the case of Yājñavalkya.

5. MATERIAL REQUIREMENTS OF AN IDEALIST

Secret wisdom of the age, as we have seen, is imagined to have the most wonderful power of its own. The power is so great that it promises not merely wordly things like cattle, offspring and fame; it can even assure something which nothing else can.

In an often-quoted legend of the *Upaniṣad*, Yājñavalkya —about to retire—wants to have his property settled between his two wives, called Kātyāyanī and Maitreyī.[16]

> Then said Maitreyī, 'If now, Sir, the whole earth filled with wealth were mine, would I be immortal thereby?'
>
> 'No', said Yājñavalkya, 'as the life of the rich, even so would your life be. Of immortality, however, there is no hope through wealth.'
>
> Then said Maitreyī, 'What should I do with that through which I may not be immortal? What you know, Sir, that indeed tell me.'

This delights the philosopher and he initiates the wife into the secret knowledge he possesses.

The importance of this story for illustrating the new attitude of the Upaniṣadic philosopher is often emphasised. That is rightly done. A considerable number of other passages of the *Upaniṣads* asserts that the secret wisdom of the age promises immortality.[17] This is one aspect. But Yājñavalkya's story has to be understood in more aspects than one.

The word for the immortal used in it is *amṛta*. The early poets of the *Ṛgveda* are aware of the word no doubt. They use it as a plain rhetoric, usually to describe euphoria induced by their intoxicating *soma*.[18] But the idea of 'secret wisdom' leading to immortality never occurs to them; nor the idea of 'property settlement' in the Upaniṣadic sense. The reasons for this are quite simple. They do not have property as Yājñavalkya does[19] and hence no opportunity to cultivate the cult of secret wisdom.

We shall presently see from where this property of the philosopher comes. But whatever its source, it obviously relieves him of the problem of maintaining himself by the manual labour of his own. How can he, without being thus relieved, devote himself to the cult of pure consciousness? The basic requirement for this is leisure enough for the purpose. The contempt for the verdict of practice on which depends the idealist outlook throughout its Indian career can be possible for the philosopher only in so far as he is relieved of the basic responsibility of practical life—in short, in so far as he is ensured of a leisured class existence.

By contrast the material conditions in which the early Vedic poets live do not permit them all this. With their comparatively rudimentary control over nature, they cannot but be obsessed with the problem of physical survival—a problem which is solved in ancient society by a greater degree of collective functioning of the community. The devotion of a selected few of the community to the cultivation of pure speculation is not yet objectively possible, for the community does not produce enough surplus to meet their material requirements. In the earlier strata of the *Ṛgveda,* songs ennobling the collective labour of the community are in fact innumerable. I have elsewhere quoted some of these.[20]

In the Upaniṣadic India—i.e. in the newly developed states of the Indo-Gangetic plain of about the eighth and seventh century B.C.—things are different. There is considerable progress in the control over nature, thanks mainly to the introduction of iron implements on some scale and the improved technique of agriculture and handicrafts, which are now added to cattle raising. Human labour acquires the ability to produce much more than is necessary for its bare maintenance. At the same time, the products of labour do not go to the labourers themselves, or, as the early Vedic poets put it, 'shared out' among the tribesmen. In fact, this activity of sharing out is so important to these early poets that in their mythological imagination it is raised to the status of veritable deities. They call these deities Bhaga and Aṃśa, literally 'the share'.[21] In the Upaniṣadic India, however, society is split into a ruling class and a toiling class. The former, consisting mainly of the king and nobles, usurp the surplus produced by the latter. An early Indian law-giver wants to rationalise this accomplished fact. Describing the ideal mode of living of the king or noble, he says:

"He shall live on the surplus."[22]

The accumulation of this surplus makes them enormously wealthy in terms of the age. Depending on this surplus to maintain themselves on a grand scale, they have all the leisure of life to pursue and patronise the cult of pure consciousness. The kings surrounded by their flatterers (*rājanya bandhu*) are often described by the *Upaniṣads* as taking a keen interest in philosophical discourses. But this does not mean that they have the monopoly of the 'secret wisdom'. Outside the circle of the nobility, there are persons with exceptional gifts claiming profounder wisdom endowed with more imposing power.

Such a person is the famous Yājñavalkya.

Attracted by the magical potency of his wisdom—and above all perhaps by the rumour that this wisdom ensures even immortality or an escape from death—one of the prosperous kings of the age, Janaka of Videha, is only too eager to part with a substantial portion of his own fortune to the philosopher as payment for being initiated into his secret wisdom. Without being a direct plunderer of the surplus, Yājñavalkya becomes entitled to a part thereof.

Nothing is more attractive for the kings than the prospect of overcoming death or attaining immortality. It is basically the same temptation that leads the Pharaohs of Egypt to waste the most colossal amount of wealth to build pyramids. Compared to them, the kings of the petty Upaniṣadic states have less to spend. But that is not the point. The point is that for these kings also the temptation of overcoming death is irresistible. They spend for it according to their means.

All this does not mean that for Yājñavalkya and his co-philosophers the promise of immortality ensured by their secret wisdom is necessarily a sales talk. It may as well be a part of their make believe. But whether make believe or not, it does pay. And because it pays, it can relieve the philosopher of the problem of maintaining himself by his own labour. It even enables Yājñavalkya to amass considerable property of his own—the property that he wants to settle before retirement. For him it is quite logical to tell the wife that this property does not ensure immortality; immortality is ensured only by his secret wisdom. Why else should his patron agree to pay him so well for being initiated into the secret wisdom? However, what he does not add is that though this property does not ensure immortality, it can and does ensure the leisure for cultivating the cult of pure wisdom. Without the solid support of this material wealth—the grand gift of his patron—the alternative for him is working for his living. His philosophy of pure contemplation does not harmonise with a life of manual labour. From this point of view, his worldly assets are not so unconnected with his world-denying philosophy as he wants his wife to believe.

Thus for understanding Yājñavalkya and his philosophy it is necessary to take note of his property and understand its sources. Where does it come from? The *Upaniṣads* are not at all vague about it. Here is a typical description of the general setting of his philosophical discourse[23]:

> Janaka, king of Videha, was seated.
>
> Yājñavalkya came up.
>
> To him the king said, 'Yājñavalkya, what brings you here? Is it because you want cattle or hair- splitting discussions?'
>
> 'Indeed both, your majesty', he said.

We shall presently see that in Upaniṣadic days material wealth is largely measured by cattle. Thus this great idealist philosopher, with his intense contempt for the material world, shows no hesitation to admit that he is not interested merely in philosophy; he is also interested in the payment for it. Metaphysically the cattle—like everything else in the world—are unreal no doubt. But these are not to be ignored, for without these the metaphysician is not ensured of his leisured class existence that enables him to spin the world-denying philosophy.

Yājñavalkya is thus confronted here with a question much more serious than that of mere theoretical consistency. It is too early for the Indian idealists to invent the philosophical trick of distinguishing between the purely provisional truth of practical life (*vyāvahārika* or *saṃvṛti satya*) and truth in its highest metaphysical sense (*pāramārthika satya*). Yājñavalkya does not say that the cattle, though ultimately unreal, are real for practical life only. Compared to the later idealists, he is naive enough to admit that he is interested in cattle, too, whatever may be their ultimate metaphysical status. How indeed can he be fully earnest about hair–splitting discussions without being provided with the material means for the purposes? Belonging as he does not to the class of the plunderers of the surplus produced by the direct producers, he has to depend on a part of the plundered surplus which he expects to receive from the king. And the king in his turn is only too eager to offer him the material wealth he needs, for his wisdom promises even immortality. At the end of each of his discourses on philosophy, the king offers him the gift of a thousand cows and a bull as big as an elephant—a very considerable amount of wealth for the Upaniṣadic age.

At the end of the final discourse Yājñavalkya declares, 'Verily, Janaka, you have reached fearlessness.' Janaka, king of Videha, says, 'My fearlessness comes unto you, noble Sir, you who make us know fearlessness. Adoration to you! Here are the Videhas; here am I at your service.'[24]

Fearlessness means here the fearlessness of death. Before passing on to see how Yājñavalkya's philosophy of the pure spirit creates such an assurance for the king, let us try to be clearer about Yājñavalkya's awareness—though in his own way—of the material basis of this idealist philosophy.

If Yājñavalkya is the greatest idealist philosopher of the *Upaniṣads*, he is also the most money-minded thinker of the age. Elsewhere he comes out with the rather startling admission that he has respect for metaphysicians interested in the ultimate reality, what he is interested over and above is the possession of cows. As he puts it, "Reverence be to him who is most learned in sacred writ! We are but hankering after cows."[25]

The legend in which this occurs brings us back to the same setting of philosophical discussion that we have just noted. Janaka, king of Videha, gets a sacrifice performed and lavishes gifts on the priests performing it. A large number of them are naturally attracted to his assembly. The king wants to find out who among these priests possesses the highest wisdom. So he has a thousand cows enclosed in a place, with ten pieces of gold tied to the horns of each. And he declares that the wisest of the priests is to take these away. While the other priests hesitate, Yājñavalkya asks his pupil to take them away on his behalf. This enrages the other priests. How is it that Yājñavalkya takes it for granted that he is the wisest among them all? To this the philosopher comes out with the statement just quoted. He has respect for metaphysics; but he is also aware of the need of material wealth.

But the other priests want him to prove his philosophical superiority. So they start questioning him. Significantly their first question is whether he knows the secret to immortality: "Since everything here is coextensive with death—everything is overpowered by death—how can the sacrificer (i.e. the royal donor) move beyond death?"

The *Upaniṣad* wants us to believe that Yājñavalkya alone knows the answer to this. But what is the answer? The metaphysical discourse attributed to him is a long one. Its main point is the gradual unfolding of the idealist outlook. But how is this outlook supposed to overcome death and ensure immortality? There is only one way of doing this and that is to remove from the realm of reality the physical world as a whole, and along with this the physical facts of birth and death. As Yājñavalkya argues, the soul which is pure consciousness and bliss, is the only reality. Being completely uncontaminated by anything material, it is by nature aloof from what appears to the mortal eyes as birth and death. Thus death, like birth, is completely unreal. How can one who knows this be any longer haunted by the fear of death?

This is not ensuring oneself against the fact of death, before which the philosopher is as helpless as any other mortal. But it is a way of inducing a subjective change into oneself which helps one to overcome—though only in ideas and imagination—the sense of death and the terrors thereof.

Significantly, being conscious in his own way of the material basis of his idealism, Yājñavalkya never forgets his patron while talking of immortality. He declares that the immortality he is talking of is to be attained not only by the metaphysician who knows the ultimate reality to be pure spirit but also by his patron on whose gifts the metaphysician subsists[26]:

> When born, indeed, he (the spirit) is not born,
> Who would again beget him?
>
> Reality is pure consciousness and pure bliss.
>
> It is the goal reached by the donors of wealth,
>
> As well as by those who are firmly established on the knowledge of this.

At least one point of this declaration is striking and it is in need of some discussion. The donor and the philosopher reach the same goal. What needs to be added to it, however, is that they reach it in different ways. The philosopher creates for the donor the illusion of immortality. The donor creates for the philosopher the material conditions for this illusion-making.

These conditions are in short the conditions of social parasitism. It kills the philosopher's spirit of interrogating nature, coerces his consciousness to total introversion and makes him a philosopher of pure spirit, for which death is as meaningless as birth.

For our understanding of the sources of idealism, this parasitism of the philosopher is of crucial importance. One way of judging it is to have some concrete idea of the philosopher's material assets. We begin with some clues to these as preserved in the *Upaniṣads.*

In the account of the *Bṛhadāraṇyaka Upaniṣad* just quoted, Yājñavalkya's pupil drives away for him one thousand cows, with ten *pādas* of gold tied to the horns of each. In the next account of the same *Upaniṣad,* king Janaka—awed by Yājñavalkya's breath-taking flights of pure reason—four times offers him 'a thousand cows and a bull as large as an elephant'.[27] This is immediately followed by another account of the same text in which the same philosopher receives from the same donor for the same reason five thousand cows, in instalments of one thousand each.[28] This is immediately followed in the *Upaniṣad* by the account already referred to—the account in which the philosopher wants to have his property settled between his two wives, Kātyāyanī and Maitreyī.

The logical sequence followed by the text is not to be overlooked. It tells us of the need felt by the philosopher for property settlement only after describing the process of its accumulation.

Let us try to be clearer about the property accumulated. Not to speak of other accounts, the three that we have just mentioned tell us of a total of ten thousand cows, besides the ten thousand *pādas* of gold. But this is only elementary arithmetic, and lest we be misled by it the *Upaniṣad* tells us also of the bulls as big as elephants. The cows accumulated by the priest-philosopher also multiply. We have in another *Upaniṣad* a rough calculation of the rate of this multiplication. Satyakāma Jābāla goes to Haridrumata Gautama, desiring to be a student of sacred knowledge.

> After having received him as a pupil, he (the priest-philosopher) separated out four hundred lean, weak cows and said, 'Follow these, my dear.'
>
> As he was driving them on, he said, 'I may not return without a thousand.'
>
> So he lived away a number of years. When they came to a thousand, the bull spoke to him, saying: 'Satyakāma!'

'Sir', he replied.

'We have reached a thousand, my dear. Bring us to the teacher's home.'[29]

If this rate of increase satisfies the Upaniṣadic calculation in one case, there is no reason why it should not be applicable to another. The ten thousand cows received by Yājñavalkya only according to three accounts of the *Bṛhadāraṇyaka Upaniṣad* are soon supposed to multiply into twenty-five thousand. It does not take much time again for the twenty-five thousand to multiply into 62,500. And so on.

All this is talking too much of cows no doubt. Why do the *Upaniṣads* do it? Keith answers: "It is clear that cattle, not land, was the real foundation of wealth, just as in Ireland, Italy (cf. *pecunia*), Greece, etc. Cattle could be, and were, used individually, but land was not open to a man's free disposal; no doubt, at any rate, the consent of the family or of the community might be required."[30]

Thus assuming that the *Upaniṣad* does not want us to look at the priest-philosopher as a member of the landed aristocracy, there is no doubt that it wants us to look at him as an extremely wealthy person—a real aristocrat of the age. Besides, the question of land is not to be totally dismissed, for there is the physical problem of accommodating the cattle. How does the priest-philosopher solve this problem?

Whatever may be the system of land tenure in Upaniṣadic India, there are in these texts unmistakable accounts of the gift of villages by the kings and nobles to the custodians of secret wisdom.[31] We read of this more explicitly in the Pāli canonical literature of the Buddhists, which give us an idea of the social conditions not much later than that of the *Upaniṣads:*

"The Brahmin villages of settlements were mainly in the Magadhan and Kosalan regions ... The reason for the presence of the Brahmin *gāmas* in these two regions is likely to be found in the early development of *brahmadeyya* land ownership in these areas. *Brahmadeyya* was the royal gift of land or an estate to well known Brahmins and others, for the services, probably ritual in nature, which they rendered to the king. Some of the *brahmadeyya* lands are specially described as Brahmin *gāmas*. Khanumata and Opasads, which are given respectively by kings Pasenadi and Bimbisāra to the Brahmin Kūṭadanta and Canki are thus described. On the other hand, Campā, Ukkattha and Salavatika, although these places belong to the Brahmins Sonadanta, Pokkharasādi and Lohicca respectively, are known only as *brahmadeyya* lands... In Ekanala, the Brahmin farmer *Bharadvāja* has so much land that he needs 500 ploughshares to plough it."[32]

We do not read in the *Bṛhadāraṇyaka Upaniṣad* of any royal gift of a village to Yājñavalkya. But the presumption is that he has some villages or at least pens vast enough to accommodate his ever-multiplying thousands of cows. If so, the further presumption is that there is also need for him to have proper security arrangement for such an enormous amount of wealth.

This leads us to the description of the prosperous Brahmin given by the Buddha—the Brahmins who "have themselves guarded in fortified towns, with moats dug out round them and cross-bars let down before the gates, by men girt with long swords."[33]

The picture of the parasitism of the priest-philosopher is not difficult to reconstruct. It is in this parasitism that we have the clue to his world-denying idealism.

The Buddha is himself inclined to look at these new parasites—the prosperous Brahmins of his age—as a fall from the simple moral grandeur of the ancient Vedic poets. He asks one of them[34]:

"But just so, Ambaṭṭha, those ancient poets (or seers)... the authors of the verses... whose ancient form of words so chanted, uttered or composed, the Brahmins of today chant over again and rehearse, ...that you should on that account be a seer or have attained the state of a seer...? Now, what think you Ambaṭṭha? What have you heard when Brahmins old and well stricken in years, teachers of yours or their teachers, were talking together—did these ancient poets, whose verses you chant over and repeat, parade about, well groomed, perfumed, trimmed as to their hair and beard, adorned with garlands and gems, clad in white garments, in the full possession and enjoyment of the five pleasures of sense, as you and your teacher too do now?"

The Buddha is evidently transforming the reality of the rudimentary control over nature of the ancient Vedic poets into a romantic picture of their great asceticism. The primitive poets are really not so ascetic as he wants us to think. At the same time, where the Buddha is unquestionably correct is that these ancient poets live a life quite different from the parasitical one of their later champions. As a result, the philosophy of the pure spirit of the Upaniṣadic idealists can hardly make any sense to them.

We shall have a brief note on the general theoretical temper of these ancient poets and then pass on to see why this is so different from that of the Upaniṣadic idealists.

6. PRIMITIVE PROTO-MATERIALISM OF THE ANCIENT VEDIC PERIOD

Among the later Indian philosophers those who want to take their stand exclusively on Upaniṣadic idealism are the Advaita Vedāntins. According to them, an appropriate descriptive epithet of their philosophy is *Śārīraka-mīmāṃsā* or Śārīraka philosophy. *Śārīraka* means the body that is filthy. Upaniṣadic idealism is given such a name because it is the philosophy of the pure spirit or soul which, much to the annoyance of the idealists, remains imprisoned as it were in the defiled body.

The underlying idea is strongly reminiscent of the ancient Greek idealist, Plato, who—disgusted with the body as a prison for the soul—goes to the extent of describing the desire for death as the right mood of the philosopher. A few centuries before Plato, Yājñavalkya also gives an enviable description of a dying man who, while dying, gets released from the fetters of the defiled body and the deceptions of the sense-organs. It is tempting to quote here a few lines from these two eminent ancient idealists and see how intense a contempt for the body is characteristic of the ancient idealist outlook. Argues Plato:

"As long as we are encumbered with body, and our soul is contaminated with such an evil, we can never fully attain what we desire; and this, we say, is truth. For the body subjects us to innumerable hindrances on account of its necessary support... and it fills us with longings, desires, fears, all kind of fancies, and a multitude of absurdities, so that, as it is said in real truth, by reason of the body it is never possible for us to make any advance in wisdom... It has then in reality been demonstrated that if we are ever to know anything purely, we must be separated from the body, and contemplate the things themselves by mere soul. And then, as it seems, we shall obtain that which we desire, and which we profess ourselves to be lovers of—namely wisdom—when we are dead, as reason shows, but not while we are alive. For if it is not possible to know anything purely in conjunction with the body, one of these two things must follow: either that we can never acquire knowledge, or only after we are dead, for then the soul will subsist apart by itself, separate from the body, but not before."[35]

Such is the *śārīraka* philosophy of ancient Greece. The way in which Yājñavalkya puts it is to give an enviable description of a dying man—enviable, because while dying, he is getting progressively relieved from the fetters of the body:

> He is becoming one, they say, he does not see.
> He is becoming one, they say, he does not smell.
> He is becoming one, they say, he does not taste.
> He is becoming one, they say, he does not speak.
> He is becoming one, they say, he does not hear.
> He is becoming one, they say, he does not think.
> He is becoming one, they say, he does not touch.
> He is becoming one, they say, he does not know.

The point of his heart becomes lighted up. By that light the self departs, either by the eye, or by the head, or by other bodily parts. After him, as he goes out, the life goes out. After the life, as it goes out, all the breaths go out. He becomes one with intelligence...[36]

This, in short, is an important feature of the philosophy of the pure spirit. It is a philosophy of the most intense contempt for the body, so much so that it goes to the extent of glorifying death as by far the greatest bliss conceivable. Paradoxically, the cult of death is also made to pass as the philosophy ensuring immortality. This combination of the opposites is possible, because in the philosophy of pure spirit birth is as fictitious as death.

For understanding the development of Vedic thought, however, it is necessary to note that a philosophical view like this would have gone completely over the heads of the early Vedic poets, who feel that nothing is more important than nourishing the body with food and drink. The feeling is so intense that they are led even to conceive food—called *pitu*—as one of their deities. The way in which they praise this deity, though primitive, is also quite refreshing, particularly when we return to it after the morbid speculations on the desirability of death. We quote in rough rendering a part of the song in praise of food from the *Ṛgveda*[37]:

"Savoury food, honeyed food, we welcome thee; be our protector. Come to us, beneficial food, we welcome thee; be our protector. Come to us, beneficial food—a source of delight, a friend of the well-respected, and having no enemy. Your flavours, oh food, are diffused through regions, as the winds are spreading through the sky. These men, oh food, who are your distributors—oh most sweet food— they who are the eaters of thee and thy juices, increase like you with elongated necks. The minds of the mighty deities, oh food, are fixed upon thee... Oh food, the wealth which is associated with the mountains went to thee. Oh sweet one, listen to us and be accessible to our eating. And since we enjoy the abundance of the waters and plants, therefore, oh body, may you grow fat. And since we enjoy the drink *soma*, the mixture with boiled milk and boiled barley, therefore, oh body, may you grow fat..."

Specially striking is the last refrain: *vātāpe pīva it bhava*, 'Oh body, may you grow fat.'

This is not a philosophical view, of course, and it is not meant to be one. But its evidence is not to be overlooked. It does represent a theoretical temper and that is fully opposed to the *śārīraka* philosophy of the *Upaniṣads.* And the point is that the general theoretical temper underlying the song just quoted, rather than being exceptional, is really typical of the ancient songs of the *Ṛgveda.*

It is tempting to raise here another question.

In later Indian philosophy, the most outspoken materialists are called the Lokāyatas or Cārvākas, according to whom there is nothing over and above the body. They are despised in various ways. One of these is to say that the very name *Cārvāka* is indicative of the vulgarity of the philosophy. It is supposed to be derived from the root *carv*, meaning 'to eat' or 'to chew'. These philosophers are called the Cārvākas because—unaware of any lofty ideal—they allegedly care only for eating and drinking.

Such an etymology of the name is probably fanciful. But even admitting it, we cannot escape a simple question. Which of the later philosophical views—the Cārvāka and the Śārīraka—suits the theoretical temper of the early Vedic poets? There is only one answer to it : the poets go into ecstasy over food for the solid reason that it makes the body fat. It is possible to imagine the ancient poets understanding the Cārvāka philosophy, but not the Śārīraka. This is one of the reasons why I have elsewhere[38] tried to describe the ancient Vedic thought as indicative of primitive proto-materialism. It is on the ruins of this that later emerges the idealistic outlook.

7. PRIMORDIAL UNITY OF WISDOM AND ACTION

It remains for us to discuss only another point in this connection. What is it that accounts for the difference in the theoretical temper of the early Vedic poets from that of the Upaniṣadic idealists?

Compared to the Upaniṣadic philosophers, the Ṛgvedic poets are undoubtedly ignorant people. Their stock of ideas is very poor; their capacity for conceptual construction is so limited that they can only imagine deities in things they do not understand. The significance of evidence and reasoning for answering questions concerning truth and reality is something beyond their mental horizon. Indeed they are not even properly aware of such questions, not to mention answering these. The Upaniṣadic philosophers are far ahead of them. For them these questions acquire great importance and they try to answer these on the strength of evidences and arguments.

All these are quite on the surface. But these do not answer the question we are asking ourselves. It is not the question concerning the richness of thought but rather of its general direction. The want of richness of early Vedic thought compared to the Upaniṣadic one is easily understood in terms of the progress of thought. But the point is that in the Upaniṣadic idealism, we see not only a progress of thought but also a dangerous turn taken by it. In spite of developing superior equipment for knowing, the idealists proceed with its aid only to condemn the objects of knowledge. Their way of knowing becomes hostile to what is known, i.e. what is known by experience and the application of reason. This hostility of knowledge to the things known is not to be found in the poets of the *Ṛgveda*, however limited may be the range of their experience and however imperfectly developed may be their power of the application of reason.

In short, the general direction of their thought is different. It is in need of an explanation. How are we to explain it?

We have tried to understand the general direction of

thought of the Upaniṣadic idealists in terms of their cult of secret wisdom—wisdom estranged from action. It will negatively confirm this understanding if we can now see that the absence of such a general direction of thought of the early Vedic poets is correlated to the absence in their consciousness of any separation of wisdom from action.

Is there this negative confirmation?

It is there and the unique advantage of the Vedic literature is that it enables us to see it clearly. Composed over a period of a thousand years or more, it retains a close continuity of inner development. From the *Upaniṣad* or *Veda*-end we can move backwards to the earlier strata of the Vedic literature. When we do this, we have the glimpse—distant and dim though it may be—of at least the relics of the primitive past qualitatively different from that of the Upaniṣadic age. What is so important about it is that it enables us to see—depending all the time on definite literary records—that just as the Upaniṣadic society emerges on the ruins of an ancient undifferentiated community, so also the theoretical temper of the Upaniṣadic idealists emerges on the ruins of an ancient theoretical temper, which is perhaps best described as representing a primordial complex of wisdom and action. Wisdom, far from becoming the secret possession of a fortunate few, is not yet dissociated from action. Hence it does not develop any contempt for nature with which, through action, men have intercourse. We have in this the clue to the primitive proto-materialism of the early Vedic period.

I have elsewhere discussed the relics of the primitive undivided community in the *Ṛgveda*. I shall try to discuss here some of the relics of the primordial unity of wisdom and action as found in the *Ṛgveda*.

Mental labour in its most exalted form, as known to these pre-literate poets, is the oral composition of songs, or, in their own words, 'making verses by the mouth'.[39] However, to themselves it is only a craft and its glory is best understood on the model of the other craft they know so well, viz. that of the carpenter fashioning the chariot.

For understanding the general theoretical temper of the early Vedic poets, this point is of crucial importance. We shall discuss a few evidences in some detail.

An entire hymn of the *Ṛgveda*[40] has for its theme the drunken monologue of Indra, the war–chief. It describes all sorts of great feats that he boasts of performing under the influence of *soma.* One of these is that of composing the Vedic song as beautifully as the carpenter makes the chariot. As Indra puts it, *ahaṃ taṣṭeva vandhuraṃ paryacāmi hṛdā matim* (x.119.5). Sāyaṇa, the most orthodox Vedic commentator, interprets it as meaning the act of 'marking by the mind' the hymn in the way in which the carpenter makes the chariot-seat. This cannot be said by one for whom mental labour is superior to manual labour. The ancient poet knows nothing about the mysterious power of pure reason.

This evidence cannot be dismissed as drunken raving only, for the way in which Indra here views the art of poetry is a frequently recurring theme of the *Ṛgveda*.

In a song in praise of Indra, the poet Purucchepa says: this song is fashioned for you by one desirous of wealth, just as the carpenter endowed with wisdom (*dhīraḥ*) fashions the chariot (i.130..6). The adjective *dhīraḥ*, 'endowed with wisdom', for the carpenter may appear to us as unconventional, for we are not accustomed to associate wisdom with manual operation. We think of the wise man mainly as a contemplator, not a craftsman. But the ancient poets do not think so. For them manual skill is itself a mark of wisdom. Wisdom is yet to be dissociated from action in the consciousness of the Vedic poets.

As if to leave nothing vague about their own attitude, these poets freely use the words *atakṣāma* and *atakṣam* for poetry-making. These words, derived from the root *takṣ*, 'to make or to fashion', refer primarily to the carpenter's craft. It is this root that gives to the Vedic people the words for the carpenter—*takṣan* and *taṣṭṛ*.[41]

In a song in praise of Agni, the poet says, 'I have fashioned this song for thee just as the wise carpenter fashions the chariot' (v.2.11). The expression used is: *ratham na dhīraḥ svapā atakṣam*. As describing the art of poetry, such an expression appears extraordinary particularly for people to whom this art represents intellectual work par excellence. But exactly the same expression is used in another song—this time in the context of offering to Indra freshly composed songs along with clothes and chariot (v.29.15). Elsewhere, a poet says, 'Let these songs please the deities Aśvins—songs that are fashioned by us (*takṣāma*) as beautifully as the carpenter fashions the chariot.' (v.73.10). Describing his own composition another poet says, 'This extensive hymn of mine, shining with brightness, is moving towards the sun and brings welfare to men. I have composed it in the way in which the carpenter makes a strongly built chariot fit for being drawn by the horse' (x. 93.12).

Even today, we talk of 'brushing up a poem'. The ancient poets also speak of it. But they speak of it in their own way—in the analogy of scraping the wood as is done by the carpenter. Thus the poet says, *abhi taṣṭeva didhayā manīṣām*, 'brighten up the song like the carpenter' (iii.38.1). Sāyaṇa interprets it to mean brightening up the song in the way in which the carpenter makes a piece of wood shining by scraping it.

In accordance with the general attitude underlying all this, the *Ṛgveda* conceives the poets as a *kāru* (ii.39.8; viii. 62.4; etc.). Derived from the root *kṛ*, 'to make', it means the maker. As the maker of song the poet has neither more nor less of social prestige than any other—the carpenter working on wood, the physician healing diseases, the girl grinding corn on the stone, the arrow-maker making arrows with sticks, stones and feathers. This is the impression we have from the often-quoted labour song of the *Ṛgveda* (ix.112), which in spite of describing the division of labour in society, harps on the theme of the harmonious working of all.

Certain philological evidences indicate that in the ancient

period any sharp distinction between wisdom and action is practically unknown. What the ancient poets are aware of is some kind of a primordial unity of the two—a point not easy to understand in accordance with later preoccupations. Here are a few examples.

In the *Ṛgveda,* we come across an apparently peculiar word, *vidmanāpasaḥ.* We can perhaps best translate it as those that possess 'the wisdom of action' or 'knowledge which is also the know how'. Understandably, it is used in the context of both manual and mental work: chariots with excellent wheels are fashioned with its aid (i.111.1) and it also forms the basis of the poets' craft (i.31.1).

This is a rather rare word in the *Ṛgveda* no doubt. It occurs only twice in the vast collection. But not so are certain other words of more decisive significance. The Vedic poets freely use certain words to mean sometimes wisdom and sometimes action. Such words are *dhī, śaci, kratu.* These mean wisdom; but these also mean action. All this creates an obvious problem for the compiler of the *Nighaṇṭu,* the earliest glossary of Vedic words. Are these to be put in the list of 'words meaning wisdom' (*prajñā nāmāni*) or in the list of 'words meaning action' (*karma nāmāni*)? The problem is solved by him by putting the words in both the lists.

These words, therefore, tell their own story. To the ancient poets, wisdom may as well be viewed as action, and action as wisdom. They are not yet aware of a sharp difference between the two. The only wisdom they care for is that of practical activity. Though primitive, it represents the attitude of uniting theory with practice. Incidentally, even the word *māyā,* which in the Advaita Vedānta philosophy means the inscrutable principle of cosmic illusion, retains in the *Ṛgveda* the sense of the primordial unity of wisdom and action.

Philological evidences like these are reminiscent of ancient Greece before the birth there of the idealist outlook[42]:

"Prior to the fifth century, not the contrast but the unity of thought and deed is uppermost. In the epic and lyric, knowledge is practical; to know is to know how; wisdom is still in action and therefore power to act. Heraclitus, the first of the philosophers to turn to this theme, assumes as a matter of course that *logos* and *sophia* carry the double reference to true words (and thought) and right deed."

With the growth of slavery and the consequent degradation of manual labour as something by nature slavish, wisdom wants to free itself from its old bond with action, and therefore also from the material world with which, through action, man has intercourse. This tendency culminates in Plato:

"For Plato wisdom meant not the knowledge of nature, but of super–nature constituted by ideas... As for art—that power to control nature, the slow acquisition of which by man Democritus regarded as identical with the self-differentiation with animals—it was relegated by Plato to a kind of limbo. It belonged to the sphere of opinion, the bastered knowledge of the slave, not the truth of the philosopher."[43]

A similar development takes place in India and culminates in Upaniṣadic idealism. For the present, we are trying to explore the sub-soil of this idealism. The art of poetry as understood by the ancient poets gives us a clue to it. Let us take up this clue again.

We hear of a few female poets whose compositions find place in the *Ṛgveda* (Bṛhaddevtā ii.82–4). One of them is called Ghoṣā. She sums up her song, saying, 'Oh Aśvins, I have composed this song for thee in the way in which the Bhṛgus fashion the chariot' (x.39.14). Though expressed in different words, the idea reoccurs in the *Ṛgveda*: We shall make songs for Indra in the way in which the Bhṛgus fashion the chariot (iv.16.20).

Who are the Bhṛgus, whose manual skill the poets want so admiringly to imitate? Commenting on Ghoṣā's poem, Sāyaṇa answers: 'Because of their connection with action (*karmayogāt*), the Ṛbhus are here referred to as the Bhṛgus.' The answer is apparently peculiar. The Ṛbhus stand for a community of Vedic deities while the name Bhṛgus 'appears in the historical character of the designation of a tribe.'[44] Why should the 'connection with action' create in the commentator's imagination such a substitution of the deities by the tribesmen?

Sāyaṇa mentions no ground for this and thus leaves us only to conjecture. One of the conjectures is that the commentators's imagination is saturated with Vedic mythology, in which the Ṛbhus occupy a peculiar position. They are originally only human beings, but they are eventually raised to the status of the deities because of 'their connection with action'—their craftsmanship or labour skill —a very important form of which is making excellent chariots. Could it be that all this leads the commentator so easily to associate the Ṛbhus with the Bhṛgus because of the mention of the activity of chariot-making?

In any case, one point is beyond doubt. Discussing the manual skill of chariot making, Sāyaṇa is easily reminded of the Ṛbhus. This is important, because it leads us to see a fascinating feature of early Vedic mythology: manual work, far from carrying any social stigma about it, is considered so important that it raises ordinary human beings to the status of the Vedic deities. We quote Macdonell's summary[45] of the relevant evidences of the *Ṛgveda*:

"Besides the higher gods of the Veda there are a number of mythical beings not regarded as having the divine nature fully and originally. The most important of these are Ṛbhus. They are celebrated in eleven hymns of the *Ṛgveda* and are mentioned by name over a hundred times... The Ṛbhus are about a dozen times called by the patronymic name of Saudhanvana, son of Sudhanvan, 'the good archer'... With Indra they help mortals to victory (iv.37.6) and are invoked with him to crush foes (vii.48.3). They are said to have obtained the friendship of Indra by their skilful work (iii. 60.3; iv.35.7 & 9), for it is they who fashioned his steeds... The Ṛbhus are characteristically deft-handed (*suhastāḥ*) and skilful (iv.33.1. & 8; etc.), their skilful deeds being incomparable (iii.60.4). They are frequently said to have acquired the rank of gods in consequence of their marvellous skill. Through their wondrous deeds they obtained divinity (iii.60.1). By their skilful deeds they became gods and immortal, alighting like eagles in heaven (iv.35.8). They are men of the air who by their energy mounted to heaven (i.110.6). For their skilful services they went on the path of immortality to the host of the gods (iv. 35.3), obtaining immortality among the gods and their friendship (iv. 33.3 & 4; iv. 35.3; iv. 36.4). But they were originally mortals, children of Manu, who by their industry acquired immortality (iii. 60.3; i.110.4)... They went to the gods and obtained the sacrifice, or a share of the sacrifice, among the gods through their skilful work (i.20.1 & 8; i.21.6 & 7)... They are thus sometimes expressedly invoked as gods (iv.36.5; iv.37.1). Like the higher gods they are besought to give prosperity and wealth (iv. 33.8; iv.37.5) in cattle, horses, heroes (iv.34.10) and to grant vigour, nourishment, offspring, dexterity (i.111.2). They grant treasure to the *soma* presser (i.20.7; iv.35.6). He whom they help is invincible in fight (iv.36.6)."

Such then is the peculiarity of the mythological imagination of the ancient Vedic people. Excellence in manual skill is so marvellous that it raises ordinary human beings to the status of the gods. Since mythology does not grow out of nothing, all this wants us to infer a society— with its characteristic mode of consciousness—in which the craftsmen along with their craft retain great prestige.

Let us try to follow up the suggestion of Vedic mythology a little further.

How do the Ṛbhus acquire so much excellence in arts and crafts? From whom do they receive the training for it? The *Bṛhaddevatā* answers[46]:

"They became pupils of Tvaṣṭṛ. Tvaṣṭṛ instructed them in every art in which he was a master (*tvaṣṭra*). The All-gods, who are thoroughly versed in the arts, challenged them. They then made for all the gods vehicles and weapons. They made the nectar-yielding cow... of Bṛhaspati, then for the Aśvins a divine car with three seats, and for Indra his two bay steeds;

also what they did through Agni who had been dispatched to them by the gods... And Tvaṣṭṛ and Savitṛ, and the god of gods Prajāpati, summoning all the gods, bestowed immortality on the Ṛbhus."

This leads us to see the greatest craftsman of Vedic imagination. The poets call him Tvaṣṭṛ and describe in various ways his skill in arts and crafts[47]:

"He is a skilful workman (i.85.9; iii.54.12) producing various objects showing the skill of an artificer. He is in fact the most skilful of workmen, versed in crafty contrivances (x.53.9). He is several times said (v.31.4; etc.) to have fashioned (*takṣ*) the bolt of Indra. He also sharpens the iron axe of Brahmaṇaspati (x.53.9). He formed a new cup (i.20.6) which contained the food of the *asura* (i.110.3) or the beverage of the gods (i.161.5; iii.35.5). He thus possesses vessels out of which the gods drink (x.53.9)."

Interestingly, these ancient poets—because they are yet to know the mystery of biological reproduction—are inclined to see the hands of the great craftsman even behind the creation of men and animals[48]:

"The *Ṛgveda* further states that Tvaṣṭṛ adorned all beings with form (x.110.9.). He develops the germ in the womb and is the shaper of all forms, human and animal (i.88.9; viii.91.8; x.184.1). Similar statements are frequently made in later Vedic texts, where he is characteristically a creator of forms. He himself is called omniform (*viśvarūpa*) more often than any other deity in the *Ṛgveda*. As fashioner of living forms, he is frequently described as presiding over generation and bestowing offspring (iii.4.9; etc.). Thus he is said to have fashioned husband and wife for each other from the womb (x.10.50). He has produced, and nourishes, a great variety of creatures (iii.55.19)... He is indeed a universal father, for he produced the whole world."

Even some of the great Vedic gods—Bṛhaspati, Agni, Indra—are sometimes conceived of as being created by this master craftsman.[49]

But who is this great god that gives shape practically to

everything known to the Vedic poets? The best clue to him is to be found is his name[50]:

"The word (*tvaṣṭṛ*) is derived from a rare root *tvakṣ*, of which only one verbal form, besides some nominal derivatives, occurs in the *Ṛgveda*, and the cognate of which, *thwaks*, is found in the *Avesta*. It appears to be identical in meaning with the common root *takṣ*, which is used with the name of Tvaṣṭṛ in referring to the fashioning of Indra's bolt. The meaning therefore appears to be the 'Fashioner' or 'Artificer'."

There are thus grounds to think that this god is only a personification of craftsmanship. In any case, his name is precariously near the Vedic word for the carpenter—*takṣan* or *taṣṭṛ*—both derived from the root *takṣ*, meaning manual skill. In the songs ennobling the activities of his apprentices—the Ṛbhus—the most frequently recurring verb is the same. "The same verb *takṣ*, 'to fashion', is generally used with reference to the manual skill of the Ṛbhus as that of Tvaṣṭṛ."[51]

From what we can infer about the general theoretical temper of the early Vedic poets, therefore, it is only to be expected that in their view the "working hands" still retain a great deal of glory and there is no question of these being pushed to the background by the glory of the products of the head—pure wisdom or pure reason as conceived by the Upaniṣadic idealists. Vedic mythology satisfies this expectation.

Macdonell notes[52] that Vedic poets take no special care to describe the physical features of Tvaṣṭṛ and the Ṛbhus. But there is a significant exception to this. The poets do take special care in describing the glory of their working hands. Thus we are repeatedly told that Tvaṣṭṛ has wonderful hands: he is *supāṇi* (3.54.12; 7.34.20; 6.49.9), he is *suhasta* (7.35.12), he is *su-gabhasti* (6.49.9)—all referring to the dexterity of his hands. Sometimes these adjectives are repeated in the same verse, evidently for placing special emphasis on this feature of the god. The same is true of the Ṛbhus. The praise of their working hands is about the only important aspect of their physical feature that we read in the *Ṛgveda*.[53]

As if to make their own attitude to manual labour fully clear, the poets tell us that some of the great Vedic gods share this glory of Tvaṣṭṛ and the Ṛbhus. Excellent working hands are also possessed by Mitra and Varuṇa[54], Indra[55], Agni[56], Savitṛ[57], and others. One of the lesser poets of the later period, described as the son of the female poet Ghoṣā already quoted, has the name Suhastya, 'one with dextrous hands'. In the poem attributed to him (x.41), he praises his own working hands (x.41.3) evidently in imitation of the gods.

Such then are the ancient conditions as remembered by the Vedic literature. In the later Vedic period, however, things are strikingly different. In the words of Engels[58],

"... the more modest productions of the working hands retreated into the background, the more so since the mind that planned the labour was able, at a very early stage of the development of society, to have the labour that had been planned carried out by other hands than its own. All merit for the swift advance of civilisation was ascribed to the mind, to the development and activity of the brain. Men became accustomed to explain their actions as arising out of thoughts instead of their needs; and so in the course of time there emerged that idealistic outlook on the world which, specially since the fall of the world of antiquity, has dominated men's minds. It still rules them."

This brings us to the Upaniṣadic period—the period in which, along with the new norm of living on the surplus produced by the labour of others, there emerges the cult of secret wisdom, supposed to be the possession of a fortunate few of the times. This wisdom, completely cut off from action, develops a sense of delusional omnipotence of its own: it wants to dictate terms to reality and to be recognised as the only reality.

REFERENCES

1. Haraprasada Racanāvalī (in Bengali) Vol. ii, Calcutta 1960, 389ff. This remarkable paper remains yet to be translated from Bengali.
2. G. Thomson, *Studies in Ancient Greek Society*, Vol. i, London 1949, 440.
3. J. Eggeling, in : *Sacred Books of the East*, Vol. xii, Introduction IX–X.
4. To the evidences mentioned by me in my *Indian Philosophy*, New Delhi 1964, 87ff., the following may be added:
   Gautama x.5: Agriculture and trade are also lawful for a Brahmin provided he does not do the work himself.
   Gautama xvii.7: A Brahmin may eat the food given by a trader who is not at the same time an artisan.
   Manu x. 99–100: But a Śūdra being unable to find service with the twice-born and threatened with the loss of his sons and wife, may maintain himself by handicrafts. Let him follow those mechanical occupations and those various practical arts by following which he can best serve the twice-born.
5. Aitareya Brāhmaṇa vii.29. This may be read along with the typical *dharmaśāstra* passages defining the cultural and economic status of the Śūdras:
   Gautama xii. 4–7: Now if he listens intentionally to a recitation of the *Veda*, his ears shall be filled with molten tin or lac. If he recites Vedic texts, his tongue shall be cut out. If he remembers them, his body shall be split in two. If he assumes a position equal to that of the twice-born in sitting, lying down, in conversation or on the road, he shall undergo corporal punishment.
   Gautama x.50: The Śūdra belongs to the fourth caste, which has one birth only. For him also are prescribed truthfulness, meekness, and purity. He shall use the cast-off shoes, umbrellas, garments; and mats of the higher castes and eat the remnants of their food, and live by practising mechanical arts.
   Manu x. 129: No collection of wealth must be made by a Śūdra, even though he be able to do it; for a Śūdra, who has acquired wealth gives pain to a Brahmin.
6. I have tried to go into some details of this in *Essays in Honour of Professor Susobhan Sarkar* (New Delhi 1976).
7. B. Farrington, *Greek Science* (Penguin 1963 ed.) 27.
8. K. Abraham (the Psycho-Sexual Differences Between Hysteria

and Dementia Praecox, 1908) starts this line of analysis in recent psychology.

9. The most outstanding Upaniṣadic philosopher representing this line of thought is Uddālaka Āruṇi (Chāndogya Upaniṣad vi). See particularly W. Ruben, *Studies in Ancient Indian Thought*, Calcutta 1966, 77ff.
10. Ch. Up. vii. 1.1–4; Māṇḍ. Up. i. 1.5. The most dreadful feature of this is the contempt for medical science. See Manu iii.152; iii.180; iv.212; iv.220; etc. Interestingly, the Aśvins—the greatest of the physician-gods of the Ṛgveda (i.57.6; viii.18.8; viii.86.1; x.39; viii.9.6 & 15; etc. etc.)—require in the *Brāhmaṇa* period ritual purification for their medical past: see Śat. Br. iv. 1.5.1ff. This changed attitude to medical science is traceable to the Yajurveda: Tait. Sam. vi. 4.9; Mait. Sam. iv. 6.2.
11. R. Hume, *Thirteen Principal Upaniṣads*, Oxford University Press, 1951 ed., 58-59.
12. JAOS 1929, 97ff.
13. A. B. Keith, *Vedic Index*, London 1958, 422; *Religion and Philosophy of the Vedas and Upanishads*, Harvard 1925, 497.
14. Keith, *Religion and Philosophy*, 493.
15. Keith, *Vedic Index* i, 206.
16. Bṛ. Up. ii.4; iv.5.
17. This is a persistent theme of practically all the principal Upaniṣads—Ait. Up. iv. 6; v.4; Kauṣ. Up. ii.14; Kena Up. xii; Ch. Up. i.4.5; Bṛ. Up. ii.4.3; etc.; Iśā Up. xi; Maitrī Up. vi.9; Śvet. Up. iii.7; Muṇḍ. Up. ii.2.11; Kaṭha Up. vi.8; vi.18; Praś. Up. iii. 11–12; etc. etc.
18. Ṛv. i.43.9; i.84.4; viii. 48.12; ix.3.1; etc.etc.
19. The songs in praise of gifts (*dāna-stutis*) are very late and do not prove a vastly propertied class in the early Vedic period.
20. D. Chattopadhyaya, *Lokāyata*, New Delhi 1959, Ch. viii.
21. Ib. 565 ff.
22. Gautama x.29–30.
23. Bṛ. Up. iv.1.1.
24. Ib. iv. 2.4.
25. Śat. Br. xi.6.3.2; Bṛ. Up. iii.1.2.
26. Bṛ. Up. iii. 9.28.
27. Ib. iv. 1.3; iv.1.5; iv.1.6; iv.1.7.
28. Ib.iv.3.14; iv.3.15; iv.3.16; iv.3.33; iv.4.7.
29. Ch. Up. iv. 4.5–iv.5.1.
30. Keith, *Vedic Index* i, 100.
31. Ch. Up. iv. 2.3; cf. Kauṣ. ii. 1 & ii. 2.

32. N. Wagle, *Society at the Time of the Buddha*, Bombay 1946, 18–19.
33. *Ambaṭṭha Sutta*, Translated by Rhys Davids, *Dialogues of the Buddha*, vol. ii, Oxford 1923, 130.
34. Rhys Davids ib. 129.
35. Plato, Phaedo 66. Tr. H. Cary (Everyman's Library).
36. Bṛ. Up. iv. 4.2.
37. Ṛv. i.187.
38. Chattopadhyaya, *Lokāyata* Ch. viii.
39. Ṛv. i.38.14.
40. Ṛv. x.119.
41. Keith, *Vedic Index* i, 297, 302.
42. G. Vlastos, quoted by B. Farrington in *Philosophy for the Future*, New York 1949, 4.
43. Farrington ib. p. 5.
44. Ṛv. vii.13.6; viii. 3.9; viii.6.18; etc.
45. Macdonell, *Vedic Mythology*, Strasbourg 1897, 131-132.
46. Bṛhaddevatā iii.83–8. Tr. Macdonell.
47. Macdonell, *Vedic Mythology* 116. Ṛv. x.8. describes Indra decapitating the three-headed son of Tvaṣṭṛ while an Indus seal depicts somebody with three heads. These are about the only solid evidences for D.D. Kosambi's strange conjecture that Tvaṣṭṛ is originally an Indus priest (or deity?). In defence of this conjecture, it is necessary not only to depend on a large number of further assumptions but moreover to overlook many positive evidences of the Vedic literature.
48. Macdonell, *Vedic Mythology* 116.
49. Ib.
50. Ib. 117.
51. Ib. 132.
52. Ib. 116, 131.
53. Ṛv. iv. 33.8; iv. 35.3; iv. 35.9; v. 42.12; x. 66.10.
54. Ṛv. i. 71.9; iii. 56.7; iii. 57.2.
55. Ṛv. iii. 33.6.
56. Ṛv. i. 109.4.
57. Ṛv. iii. 55.4.
58. F. Engels, *Dialectics of Nature*, Moscow 1964 ed., 180.

7

Material Basis of Idealism

We do not expect the idealists to raise the question concerning the material basis of idealism. The question, by implying that there is such a possible basis, amounts to a surrender of the primacy of spirit to nature, the very foundation of idealism. In defence of their own position, therefore, the idealists have to reject the question as illegitimate.

With the materialists—particularly the Marxists—it must be different. The general structure of the idealistic outlook, whatever might have been the variations and however much it might have reacted back on the material conditions, is of the nature of superstructure: it cannot be without a material basis. The circumstance that the materialists have not so far raised the question sufficiently seriously does not imply that the question itself is unimportant from their point of view. Rather the importance of the question is not confined to the understanding of idealism alone. It may help us to understand, though negatively, something basic about the materialistic outlook itself, which is, on the Marxist understanding, the only consistent alternative to idealism.

We shall try to understand here the position of Marxism with regard to this question. It will be a discussion of the *origin* of the idealistic outlook and not of its significance or historical role. Secondly, any *evaluation* of the Marxist view itself would be outside our present discussion. We shall, therefore, try to stick as closely as possible to the actual writings of Marx and Engels.

Character of Class Society

Already in the *Communist Manifesto,* Marx and Engels observed: 'The history of all past society has consisted in the development of class antagonisms, antagonisms that assumed different forms at different epochs. But whatever form they may have taken, one fact is common to all past ages, namely the exploitation of one part of society by the other. No wonder, then, that the social consciousness of past ages, despite all the multiplicity and variety it displays, moves within certain common forms, or general ideas, which cannot completely vanish except with the total disappearance of class antagonisms.'[1]

It is well-known that when Marx and Engels drafted the *Manifesto,* 'the social organisation existing previous to recorded history was all but unknown.' Thanks mainly to the epoch-making work of Morgan, to our knowledge of social development was added the facts of primitive pre-historic society which had yet to witness class-differentiation and class-antagonism. This was the primitive communist society. We may thus identify three main stages in the development of human society: the primitive pre-class society, class society and the classless society of the future.

This point is important. It implies that the general ideas or the common forms within which, according to Marx and Engels, the social consciousness of the past ages had moved—because it was intimately related to class-antagonism and class-exploitation—are not to be sought either in the pre-class society of the past or in the classless society of the future.

But what did they mean by these general ideas or common forms of social consciousness characteristic of the class-society as a whole? Elsewhere, Marx called these the *mystical veil* of the life-process of class-society: 'The life-process of society, which is based on the process of material production, does not strip off its mystical veil till it is treated as production by freely associated men, and is consciously regulated by them in accordance with a settled plan.'[2] And

Engels, borrowing the Hegelian terminology, characterised the same as *false consciousness:* 'Ideology is a process accomplished by the so-called thinker consciously, it is true, but with a false consciousness. The real motive forces impelling him remain unknown to him; otherwise it simply would not be an ideological process. Hence he imagines false or seeming motive forces. Because it is a process of thought, he derives its form as well as its content from pure thought, either his own or that of his predecessors. He works with mere thought material, which he accepts without examination as the product of thought, and does not investigate further for a more remote source independent of thought; indeed this is a matter of course to him, because, as all action is *mediated* by thought, it appears to him to be ultimately *based* upon thought.'[3]

One point is clear. The common form of the social consciousness of the entire period of class society is a false consciousness because it is imagined to be under the autonomy of pure thought, as made of mere thought-elements both in form and in content. We shall presently see the significance of this. For the moment there is another question. In spite of there being some general characteristic of class-society as a whole, its successive stages are marked by real differences as well. From the Marxist point of view, therefore, the general false consciousness of the class-society as a whole is expected to reveal different specific forms in the successive epochs of the class-society. How are we to understand these specific forms? George Thomson has suggested that the answer is to be found in what Marx and Engels, in the *German Ideology,* called the *illusion of each given epoch.*[4] 'The illusion of a given epoch is the false consciousness of that epoch. Thus, one of the achievements of socialist society is that it frees itself from false consciousness, which is a general characteristic of class society, its particular form varying from one epoch to another ("the illusion of that epoch").'[5]

Idealist Outlook

What concerns us, first of all, is a clue to this false consciousness. We have to seek for it in that which, according to the Marxist understanding, emerged at the superstructural level as a result of society splitting up into antagonistic classes and which, further, dominated human consciousness throughout class-society. Here is how Engels explained what it was: 'From generation to generation, labour itself became different, more perfect, more diversified. Agriculture was added to hunting and cattle-breeding, then spinning, weaving, metal-working, pottery and navigation. Along with trade and industry, there appeared finally art and science. From tribes there developed nations and states. Law and politics arose, and with them the fantastic reflection of human things in the human mind: religion. In the face of all these creations, which appeared in the first place to be products of the mind, and which seemed to dominate human societies, the more modest productions of the working hand retreated into the background, the more so since the mind that planned the labour process already at a very early stage of development of society, was able to have this planned labour carried out by other hands than its own. All merit for the swift advance of civilisation was ascribed to the mind, to the development and activity of the brain. Men became accustomed to explain their actions from their thoughts, instead of from their needs (which in any case are reflected, come to consciousness in the mind)—and so there arose in the course of time that idealistic outlook on the world which, especially since the downfall of the ancient world, has dominated men's minds. It still rules them...'[6]

If this is how Engels wanted us to look at the origin of the false consciousness characteristic of the class-society as a whole, we must infer that the idealistic outlook *is* the false consciousness that took different forms in the different epochs of class-society.

Engels also pointed out why the emergence of the idealistic outlook along with the emergence of the class-society cannot be looked at as an accidental coincidence. There was something inherent in the latter which accounted for the former. With society splitting up into classes, there was a divorce of thought from action—of mental labour from manual labour—and also a sense of degradation attached to the latter: 'the growth of slavery,' as Engels said elsewhere, 'already began to brand working for a living as slavish and more ignominious than engaging in plunder.'[7] By contrast, all merit for the swift advance of civilisation was ascribed to the mind because it was the mind that planned the labour process. That is, mental labour became the concern of the ruling class and thus, in the consciousness of the ruling class the verdict of the mind or thought or ideas acquired a stupendous significance. The result has been that the primacy of the spirit of thought became the dominant characteristic of the world-outlook throughout class-society, for the main characteristic of the world outlook of an age is determined by the dominant mode of the consciousness of the ruling class of the age. 'The ideas of the ruling class are in every epoch the ruling ideas, i.e. the class, which is the ruling material force of society, is at the same time its ruling intellectual force. The class which has the means of material production at its disposal, has control at the same time over the means of mental production, so that thereby, generally speaking, the ideas of those who lack the means of mental production are subject to it.'[8]

If this explains why, throughout the history of class-society, the consciousness of the toiling class failed to become the dominant mode of consciousness, the explanation of the domination by the idealistic outlook of the consciousness of the ruling class throughout class-society is to be sought in the circumstance that in all the epochs of the class-society the ruling class remained the leisured class, that is the class that could withdraw itself from the direct responsibility of material labour, there being always the toiling class to shoulder it. Already in their first full statement of Marxism, Marx and Engels made this point quite clear: 'Division of labour only becomes truly such from the moment when a division of material and mental labour appears. From this moment onwards consciousness can really flatter itself that it is something other than consciousness of existing practice, that it is *really* conceiving something without conceiving something *real;* from now on consciousness is in a position to emancipate itself from the world and to proceed to the formation of "pure" theory, theology, philosophy, ethics, etc.'[9]

Labour Process

Thus, in order to proceed to the formation of the idealist outlook, consciousness has to emancipate itself from the world and the precondition of this is the emancipation of the thinking class from the obligation of manual labour. The reason for this is clear. The labour process, being essentially a transaction between nature and the material human body as a natural phenomenon, carries within itself a sense of objective coercion. That is, the reality of the material world, of nature, forces its stamp on the human consciousness so long as man remains engaged in the process of the mutual operation. This is borne out by Marx's well-known analysis of the labour process. 'Labour is, in the first place, a process in which both man and nature participate, and in which man of his own accord starts, regulates, and controls the material reactions between himself and nature. He opposes himself to nature as one of her own forces, setting in motion arms and legs, head and hands, the natural forces of his body, in order to appropriate nature's productions in a form adapted to his own wants.'[10]

Marx went into much greater details in his analysis of the labour process and we can see from this how much this process owes to the acceptance of the material reality of the objective world or nature. All the factors involved in the labour process—the personal activity of the man, the subject of the work (which, when filtered through previous labour, is called the raw material), and the instruments of labour—

all these are the product of the material world or nature. 'The soil in the virgin state in which it supplies man with necessaries or the means of subsistence ready to hand, exists independently of him, and is the universal subject of human labour. All those things which labour merely separates from immediate connection with their environment, are subjects of labour spontaneously provided by nature... An instrument of labour is a thing, or a complex of things, which the labourer interposes between himself and the subject of his labour, and which serves as the conductor of his activity. He makes use of the mechanical, physical, and chemical properties of some substances in order to make other substances subservient to his aims... Thus nature becomes one of the organs of his activity, one that he annexes to his own bodily organs, adding stature to himself in spite of the Bible. As the earth is his original larder, so too it is his original tool house.'[11]

If the labour process is so much under obligation to nature or the objective world, how can human consciousness, without emancipating itself from its verdict, move towards an idealistic outlook, the primary prerequisite of which is the denial of the self-sufficient or independent existence of nature? But there are more points involved in the Marxist understanding of the idealistic outlook. For, idealism is not merely the negative doctrine of the denial of nature; it is the *positive theory of spirit or consciousness being the ultimate reality,* of thoughts and ideas dictating terms to reality. Secondly, on the Marxist understanding, the idealist outlook was the result of a process of *social evolution,* the characteristic of which is not the cessation of the role of manual labour but rather the receding of it to the background of social reality—to such a position of degradation and contempt as hardly to have any longer a claim to contribute to the predominant world outlook.

For an understanding of these two points we have to analyse further characteristics of the labour-process to which Marx drew our attention: 'We presuppose labour in a form that stamps it as exclusively human. A spider conducts operations that resemble those of a weaver, and a bee puts to shame many an architect in the construction of her cells. But what distinguishes the worst architect from the best of bees is this, that the architect raises his structure in imagination before he erects it in reality. At the end of every labour-process, we get a result that already existed in the imagination of the labourer at its commencement. He not only effects a change of form in the material on which he works, but he also realises a purpose of his own that gives the law to his *modus operandi*, and to which he must subordinate his will.'[12]

In the beginning, thus, there is an idea. Of course, this idea is not pure subjectivity in any abstract sense because it is itself the product of the material conditions: it arises from the concrete material needs felt by the living human individuals in their relation to the rest of the world. Nevertheless, the idea as idea is not the same as the material condition originating it. The two are qualitatively distinct. That is, as an idea it acquires a kind of real subjectivity which it would be vulgar materialism to overlook. And the decisive characteristic of human labour is that such an idea exists at the beginning of the labour-process and initiates it. At the end, again, there is only the realisation of this idea in the objective world—the objective world satisfying the idea that initiates the labour-process. And everything in human labour that carries the sense of the objective coercion, i.e. the process of the manual operation strictly speaking, occurs between these two extremes. However, when the ultimate result is reached, the stamp of the intermediate steps involved is no longer apparent. As Marx said, 'The process disappears in the product, the latter is a use-value, nature's material adapted by a change of form to the wants of man. Labour has incorporated itself with its subject: the former is materialised, the latter transformed.'[13]

It is not difficult to see what happens when the importance of the entire intermediate process involving the material transaction between man and nature snaps off from human consciousness, i.e. the ruling-class consciousness. There remains only the idea at the beginning and at the end only the realisation or the satisfaction of the idea in the objective world—an appearance of the subordination of nature to the demands of the spirit or consciousness. Human ideas do appear to dictate terms to the world and consciousness does assume the semblance of the ultimate reality. And here we have the essence of the idealistic outlook.

Standpoint of the Leisured Class

So long as it is the question of the individual labourer, there is obviously little possibility of the development of such an outlook. Engaged as he is in the labour-process itself, the stamp of the immediate reality of the objective world—the objective world as the subject of his labour, the toolhouse of his instruments and the basis of his sheer physical existence—cannot be washed away from his personal consciousness. So long, again, as it was the collective life of the pre-class society, there could be no question of anybody having such an outlook, for there could be no existence in it without a share in the labour of the community as a whole. However, while explaining the sources of the idealistic outlook Marx and Engels were not speaking of either of these two standpoints. They were discussing specifically the breakdown of society into antagonistic classes and the effect of this on the world outlook of the leisured class.

The crucial point is that with the emergence of class-differences, 'the plan, the purpose, the piece of imagination' sought to be realised in the material world through the labour-process gets detached from the aspect of the manual operation proper, because the former becomes the concern only of the ruling class while the latter that of the toiling class. The idea given shape to by the labourers is no longer their own; those whose idea is realised through the labour-process, again, have no share in the labour-process itself. The beginnings of this is to be traced when the division between the actual producers and the organisers of production took place and it assumed a well-defined form when these organisers of production—originally only the custodians of the means of production—converted themselves into the owners thereof. At this stage society finally split up into the ruling class and the toiling class.

It is only from the standpoint of the former that we may understand the real force of the idealistic argument. The Pharaohs thought, let there be the pyramids and the pyramids were there. Thought did indeed dictate terms to reality. And since it was the thought of that class in whose consciousness the manual operation of the million slaves had no longer any validity, the intermediate steps involved between the demand of thought and the satisfaction of it in reality lost all claim to contribute to the general world outlook. The result was a delusion of the omnipotence of thought and it is here that we find the real source of the idealistic argument—the false consciousness of class-society as a whole.

French and British Materialism

It naturally remained for materialism to be the philosophy of revolution—the materialism of the British revolution and the materialism of the French Revolution. For these were the products of situations in which the toiling class did move to the forefront of the social reality. Engels observed: 'And although, on the whole, the bourgeoisie in its struggle with the nobility could claim to represent at the same time the interests of the different labouring classes of that period, yet in every great bourgeois movement there were independent outbursts of the class which was the more or less developed forerunner of the modern proletariat... Alongside these revolutionary armed uprisings of a class which was as yet immature, corresponding theoretical manifestations made their appearance.'[14]

We have here the clue to the materialistic philosophies of those periods. At the same time, corresponding to the limitations of those revolutions, the materialist philosophies, too, had their limitations. Rather than establishing the social superiority of the toiling class, these revolutions simply replaced one exploiting class by another. And these materialist philosophies, too, already pregnant with their opposites, had eventually to culminate in disguised or over idealism.

Illusion of the Modern Epoch

It is interesting to observe how the false consciousness of class-society has, in the modern period, taken the form of the specific illusion of the epoch.

The social root of the idealistic outlook—the separation of thinking from the manual operation—started quite early in the history of social development. Further advance in the productive technique went on nourishing it until in the modern period the whole thing took the form of what Marx called 'industrial pathology.' Referring to the division of labour in modern manufacture, Marx observed: 'It converts the labourer into a crippled monstrosity, by forcing his detail dexterity at the expense of a world of productive capabilities and instincts... Not only is the detail work distributed to the different individuals, but the individual himself is made the automatic motor of a fractional operation.'[15] And again, 'The knowledge, the judgement, and the will, which, though in ever so small a degree, are practised by the independent peasant or handicrafts man... these faculties are now required only for the workshop as a whole. Intelligence in production expands in one direction, because it vanishes in many others. What is lost by the detail labourers, is concentrated in the capital that employs them. It is a result of the division of labour in manufacturers, that the labourer is brought face to face with the intellectual potencies of the material process of production, as the property of another, and as a ruling power.'[16]

Marx quoted Adam Smith: 'The man whose whole life is spent in performing a few simple operations has no occasion to exert his understanding... The uniformity of his stationary life naturally corrupts the courage of his mind... But in every improved and civilised society, this is the state into which the labouring poor, that is, the great body of the people, must necessarily fall.'[17]

Commented Marx: 'For preventing the complete deterioration of the great mass of the people by division of labour, A. Smith recommends education of the people by the state, but prudently, and in homoeopathic doses. G. Garnier, his French translator and commentator, who, under the first French empire, quite naturally developed into a senator, quite as naturally opposes him on this point. Education of the masses, he urges, violates the first law of the division of labour, and with it "our whole social system would be proscribed." "Like all other divisions of labour," he says, "that between hand labour and head labour is more pronounced and decided in proportion as society (he rightly uses this word for capital, landed property and their state) becomes richer. This division of labour, like every other, is an effect of past, and a cause of future progress... Ought the government then to work in opposition to this division of labour, and to hinder its natural course? Ought it to expend a part of the public money in the attempt to confound and blend together two classes of labour, which are striving after division and separation?"'[18]

Ferguson, added Marx in his footnote, had already said, 'And thinking itself, in this age of separations, may become a peculiar craft.'[19] It is no wonder, then, that the philosopher of the age should come out with the most outspoken manifesto of pure thought—the sharp declaration that of all his activities he could feel most indubitably certain only of pure thinking. As is well-known, Descartes made the bare *cogito*—the bare 'I think'—the starting point of his philosophy: 'Can I affirm that I possess any one of all those attributes of which I have lately spoken as belonging to the nature of body? After attentively considering them in my own mind, I find none of them that can properly be said to belong to myself. To recount them were idle and tedious.

Let us pass, then, to the attributes of the soul... Thinking is another attribute of the soul; and here I discover what properly belongs to myself. This alone is inseparable from me. I am—I exist: this is certain; but how often? As often as I think; for perhaps it would even happen, if I should wholly cease to think, that I should at the same time altogether cease to be.'[20]

Descartes, they say, was the father of modern philosophy. This is true. For he was the first to give the most momentous expression to the illusion of the modern epoch. Subsequent development of modern European philosophy has largely been the development of this Cartesian principle of the bare *cogito* as the most indubitable starting point of philosophy. It remained for Hegel and his followers to carry this principle to its furthest logical limits: 'Thus Hegel restores to thought its own right. Thought is not one existential form of the absolute beside others; it is the absolute itself in its concrete unity of self; it is the idea come back to itself—the idea that knows itself to be the truth of nature and the power in it.'[21]

Refutation of Idealism

However, if this modern manufacturing period created conditions for the sharpest expression of the idealistic outlook, it also enhanced the process leading to the final refutation of it. For the same division of labour in the modern manufacturing period has developed the productive power to such an enormous extent and given it such a highly socialised form that it ultimately rebels against the production relations and threatens the very structure of class-divided society. The Marxist analysis of this is well-known. What particularly interests us here is the consequence of this for the philosophical issue.

The earlier materialists tried to refute and reject the idealistic outlook. Where they failed, however, was to see its social roots. Diderot, for example, felt frankly exasperated: "Those philosophers are called *idealists* who, being conscious only of their existence and of the sensations which succeed each other within themselves, do not admit anything else. An extravagant system which, to my thinking, only the blind could have originated: a system which, to the shame of human intelligence and philosophy, is the most difficult to combat, although the most absurd of all.'[22] And Lenin commented that Diderot came very close to the standpoint of contemporary materialism (Marxism) namely 'that arguments and syllogisms alone do not suffice to refute idealism.'[23]

The point is, it is impossible to refute idealism on the strength of mere philosophical arguments however acute. The very effort at a purely theoretical refutation of idealism is doomed to an ultimate surrender to it, as has historically happened in the case of many philosophers. Such an effort is after all an appeal to the verdict of pure thought—the acceptance of the detached consciousness as having the highest verdict on the nature of reality—and this is the basic claim of idealism itself. As is argued by the idealists, it is impossible to prove the primacy of matter because the very organ of such a proof would be thought itself and as such would imply the primacy of the spirit. However, the premise of the detached thought, upon which such arguments rest, is itself the product of the social conditions under which thought is actually detached from action and exalted over it.

However, if the idealistic outlook is the result of the separation of thought from action, it can be refuted not by appealing to one fragment of these separated elements but only by restoring the lost union of these two, which, in its turn, cannot be restored without changing the very structure of the class-society. In other words, the false consciousness of class-society can be finally overthrown only by overthrowing the class-structure of society itself. While explaining their own materialistic conception of history, Marx and Engels observed, 'It has not, like the idealistic view of history, in every period to look for a category, but remains constantly on the real ground of history; it does not explain practice from the idea but explains the formation of ideas from material practice; and accordingly it comes to the conclusion that *all forms and products of consiousness cannot be dissolved by mental criticism,* by resolution into "self-consciousness" or transformation into "apparitions", "spectres", "fancies", etc., *but only by the practical overthrow of the actual social relations which gave rise to this idealistic humbug;* that not criticism but revolution is the driving force of history, also of religion, of philosophy and all other types of theory.'[24] It is from this point of view alone that we can understand the philosophical significance of revolutionary practice emphasised by Marx in his oft-quoted eleventh thesis on Feuerbach: 'The philosophers have only *interpreted* the word in various ways; the point however is to *change* it.'[25]

Pre-class Consciousness

If the idealistic outlook represents the false consciousness of class-society, a special problem arises with regard to the general nature of the world outlook of primitive pre-class society. Being based upon the collective labour of the entire community, such a society is obviously yet to create the material conditions for the emergence of the idealistic outlook in human consciousness. But what could be the positive characteristic of this primitive pre-idealistic world outlook?

Since, because of uneven development, some human groups are actually living even today at a stage through which our ancestors passed several thousand years ago, a solution of the problem could possibly be obtained on the basis of a study of their actual world outlook. This suggestion is important. But there are certain special difficulties involved in the procedure. First, the primitive peoples are known to us only in so far as they are already penetrated by civilised men—the traders, missionaries, recruiting agents, colonial administrators, and, following them, the academic-anthropologists. It is not unlikely, therefore, that these primitive groups, as known to us, are already contaminated by the ideas and institutions distinctive of civilised man. As George Thomson, referring to the Australian aborigines, has observed, 'Backward though they are, these tribes have been in continuous contact for a century or more with European gold-diggers, sheep-farmers, missionaries, policemen and other champions of our own culture. They have imbibed respect for private property along with belief in God.'[26]

Secondly, it is not improbable that the civilised student of these primitive peoples is unconsciously inclined to read in them the beliefs and ideas ingrained in himself, i.e. accepted by him as but natural or human and, therefore, eternal. The magical rites of the primitive peoples are often misinterpreted as their religion and, as we shall see, when Tylor and others have discussed animism, what they have in fact done is largely to project their own idealistic preoccupations on to the pre-idealistic ideas of the primitive peoples.

Thanks to the greater objectivity of Frazer and others, we are now beginning to understand the qualitative difference between the ideas of the primitive peoples and ours. However, before proceeding to analyse the results of these studies, it may be useful for the Marxist to discuss a question of more general theoretical interest. Assuming beliefs and ideas to be vitally related to the social structure, it may be possible to arrive at some idea of the general relationship between the world outlooks of pre-class society, class-society and the classless society of the future on the basis of a clear idea of the general relationship between these three stages of social development.

Engels concluded his *Origin of the Family* with a quotation from Morgan: 'A mere property career is not the final destiny of mankind, if progress is to be the law of the future as it has been of the past. The time which has passed away since civilisation began is but a fragment of the past duration of man's existence; and but a fragment of the ages yet to come. The dissolution of society bids fair to become the termination of a career of which property is the end and aim, because such a career contains the elements of self-destruction.

Democracy in government, brotherhood in society, equality in rights and privileges, and universal education foreshadow the next higher plane of society to which experience, intelligence and knowledge are steadily tending. *It will be a revival, in higher form, of the liberty, equality and fraternity of the ancient gentes.*'[27]

This should be read side by side with the following from Marx: 'The first reaction against the French Revolution and the Enlightenment bound up with it was naturally to see everything as mediaeval, romantic; even people like Grimm are not free from this. The second reaction is to look beyond the Middle Ages into the primitive age of every nation, and that corresponds to the socialist tendency, although those learned men have no idea that they have any connection with it. Then they are surprised to find what is newest in what is oldest—even equalitarians, to a degree which would have made Proudhon shudder.'[28]

That the *socialist tendency* corresponds to *finding what is newest in what is oldest*, is indeed a very clear formulation. Only the question is: are we to restrict its implication to the consideration of the material basis only? Or, is there any definite ground preventing us to extend its implication to the consideration of the superstructural elements as well? From the Marxist point of view, there can be only one answer to these questions. For there cannot be one consideration for the material basis and another—altogether different—for the superstructure. Now, the classless society of the future, by destroying the social roots of spiritualism and idealism, is going to see the final victory of science and the materialistic outlook. And, if we are to see what is newest in what is oldest, the general character of the world-outlook of the primitive pre-class society is only expected to be of the nature of proto-science and proto-materialism. Further, this primitive proto-materialism would have the same relation with scientific materialism as primitive communism to the civilised communism of the future.

Magic and Religion

We may now turn to the characteristic primitive belief, as actually observed. Said Frazer: 'Among the aborigines of Australia, the rudest savages as to whom we possess accurate information, magic is universally practised, whereas religion in the sense of a propitiation or conciliation of the higher powers seems to be nearly unknown... But if in the most backward state of human society now known to us we find magic thus conspicuously present and religion conspicuously absent, may we not reasonably conjecture that the civilised races of the world have also at some period of their history passed through a similar intellectual phase ... in short that, just as on the material side of human culture there has everywhere been an age of Stone, so on the intellectual side there has everywhere been an Age of Magic?'[39]

What, then, is magic? 'Magic rests on the principle that by creating the illusion that you control reality you can actually control it. In its initial stages it is simply mimetic. You want rain, so you perform a dance in which you mimic the gathering clouds, the thunderclap, and the falling shower. You enact in fantasy the fulfilment of the desired reality.'[30]

What particularly interests us is the question, how far the attitude implicit in it can be assessed in our terms of idealism and materialism. We quote Frazer again: 'Wherever sympathetic magic occurs in its pure unadulterated form, it assumes that in nature one event follows another necessarily and invariably without the intervention of any spiritual or personal agent. Thus its fundamental conception is identical with that of modern science; underlying the whole system is a faith, implicit but real and firm, in the order and uniformity of nature.'[31] It is from this point of view that Frazer characterised magic as next of kin to science and as such basically opposed to religion. Religion, he pointed out, 'stands in fundamental antagonism to magic as well as to science, both of which take for granted that the course of nature is determined, not by the passions or caprice of personal beings, but by the operation of immutable laws acting mechanically. In magic, indeed, the assumption is only implicit, but in science it is explicit.'[32]

Thus with all its limitations of objective knowledge, the primitive world outlook remains yet to be emancipated from the acknowledgement of the reality of nature as governed by natural laws and as such it would not be correct to attribute to the primitive people any spiritualist or idealist view. However, this does not mean that we may attribute to them any materialist world outlook in our sense. For the primitive consciousness is yet far from acquiring any clear sense of the independent existence of the objective world, i.e. a sense of objectivity as exclusive of their own existence. The primitive view of nature is yet largely an extension of the experiences of the primitive peoples, of the relations which they have established among themselves in the development of production. 'So long as labour remained collective, the process was necessarily incomprehensible to the individual participants. As an organic sequence of collective and concerted bodily movements, it presented itself to the individual consciousness as a combined act of will, which achieved in the end of the process its natural and necessary result; and, if it failed, as it often did, its failure seemed to arise from resistance on the part of the subject of labour, which had a will of its own, too strong to be overcome. In these conditions the process assumed the form of a conflict, in which the labourers endeavoured by a mimetic act to impose their will on the subject of their labour.'[33]

However, what needs specially to be noted is that neither the will of the labourers themselves nor the will imagined by them to be possessed by the subject of their labour could, at this stage, be conceived as disembodied or purely psychical. The reason is simple: the very concept of the purely psychical—the disembodied, the purely spiritual—could not as yet dawn on them. As their own will is conceived by them largely in terms of their physical abilities, so also the will opposing them—imagined by them as belonging to the subject of their labour—contained, as we have seen, the rudiments of the ideas of the laws of nature, however unconsciously conceived. It is true that the primitives do not distinguish between the two clearly and separately, that they are incompletely aware of the distinction between themselves and the environment around them, which they were changing and to which they were therefore opposed. In this sense, they have not yet learned the distinction between themselves and nature. This is primitive ignorance, a mental poverty that corresponds to the material poverty of technological development.

It was only by interpreting this primitive ignorance in terms of his own idealistic preoccupations that Tylor was led to formulate his well-known theory of animism. The primitive peoples, he imagined, saw spirits everywhere and in everything—a view that would probably be acclaimed by some civilised philosopher but would remain totally ununderstood by the primitives themselves. The word "spirit" in Tylor's sense is yet to make any sense to them. Even their gods and ghosts, so often spoken of, are far from being "spirits" of our imagination. For these are as concrete and material as any material entity; they leave footprints on the mud and cast shadows while walking in the sun. Tylor himself wondered at this peculiarity of the primitive belief. However, granting this to be true, granting, in other words, that the primitive idea of the so-called "spirit" is as much material as our idea of any material body, it will not be logical to project on the primitive consciousness any "spiritualist" or idealist outlook in our sense of these. If Tylor actually did it, the reason was his own idealistic preoccupations.

It is for the same reason, again—namely the idealistic preoccupations of the modern scholars—that Frazer's view of magic as distinct from and prior to religion and as, in fact, an instinctive or unconscious groping at natural laws is often criticised these days and even discarded as old-fashioned. What particularly interests us is to see how these criticisms of Frazer have missed the real weakness of Frazer's own views in so far as these were themselves inspired by the idealistic outlook. He wanted to look at both magic and religion as mere matters of knowledge and ignorance—as made of mere thought materials rather than as linked up with the material intercourse and the material activity of real human beings.

This is most conspicuous in his conjecture concerning the transition from magic to religion. He imagined the whole process as due to the sudden discovery by some gifted individuals of the futility of magic and the consequent substitution of it by them of a more logical alternative which formed the original core of religion. 'The shrewder intelligences must in time have come to perceive that magical ceremonies and incantations did not really effect the results which they were designed to produce... This great discovery of the inefficacy of magic must have wrought a radical though probably slow revolution in the minds of those who had the sagacity to make it... If the great world went on its way without the help of him or his fellows, it must surely be because there were other beings, like himself but far stronger, who, unseen themselves, directed its course and brought about all the varied series of events which he had hitherto believed to be dependent on his own magic.'[34] These mighty beings eventually became the gods of religion and the disillusioned magicians, in worshipping them, gained back quietude of heart.

However, it is impossible to understand the whole problem of magic and religion only in terms of knowledge and ignorance. If it be true that throughout the whole world and throughout the vast period of primitive existence, human beings have in fact attached the most stupendous significance to the magical beliefs and practices, and further, if it be also true that before the breakdown of the primitive life magic did not yield to religion, the presumption would rather be that with all the ignorance involved in it magic did have a functional role in the life of the primitive people, i.e. it was somehow or other linked up with their struggle against nature. Others, working on some such presumption, have arrived at the view that though an illusory technique magic was nevertheless supplementary to the real technique: 'The Maoris have a potato dance. The young crop is liable to be blasted by east winds, so the girls go into the fields and dance, simulating with their bodies the rush of wind and rain and the sprouting and blossoming of the crop; and as they dance they sing, calling on the crop to follow their example. That is magic, an illusory technique supplementary to the real technique. But though illusory it is not futile. The dance cannot have any direct effect on the potatoes, but it can and does have an appreciable effect on the girls themselves. Inspired by the dance in the belief that it will save the crop, they proceed to the task of tending it with greater confidence and so with greater energy than before. And so it does have an effect on the crop after all. It changes their subjective attitude to reality, and so indirectly it changes reality.'[35]

In short, by representing the desired reality as if it were actually present, magic does lead the primitive peoples to overcome the felt-helplessness in the face of hostile nature. And it needs to be remembered that the lower the development of the productive technique, the greater the necessity for patience, foresight and faith.

Thus, the efficacy of magic is psychological. However, it cannot be understood in terms of individual psychology. The wish of an individual, represented as fulfilled, results only in a dream. The desire of the group, represented as fulfilled—though equally illusory—becomes a guide to action. For the emotional tension created by such a representation surcharges the group as a whole and makes it ready to burst forth into action: 'Collectivity and emotional tension, two elements that tend to turn the simple reaction into a rite, are—specially among primitive peoples—closely associated, indeed scarcely separable. The individual among savages has but a thin and meagre personality; high emotional tension is to him only caused and maintained by a thing felt socially; it is what the tribe feels that is sacred, that is matter for ritual.'[36]

However, this collectivity is undermined by the advance of the productive technique. It creates surplus and as such the possibility of a few to live on the labour of many. But the memory of the primitive efficacy of magic dies hard. It is eventually rationalised as a mysterious power, the secret possession only of the few. That is superstition and, as superstition, it becomes a hindrance to the actual productive technique. Magic passes into its opposite. It becomes religion.

Early Materialists

If magic rests upon the instinctive recognition of nature as governed by the natural laws, and in this sense, the next of kin to science, and if further, it represents the beliefs and practices characteristic of the primitive pre-class society, then it would be wrong to expect in the pre-class society any world-outlook other than the instinctive proto-materialist one. Naturally enough, the more advanced works on the ancient cultures are leading us to a progressive recognition of the role of magic in the development of the early scientific ideas. 'Science and magic are, in their earliest stages, indistinguishable.'[37] This is a point, according to Needham, the importance of which 'one cannot emphasise too much.'[38] Again, 'magic and science were originally united in a single undifferentiated complex of manual labour.'[39] All these are to be understood along with the consideration that science is impossible without the recognition of the extra-mental reality of nature, i.e. the materialist outlook.

We may be yet far from a full knowledge of the instinctive materialism of the primitive pre-class society and of its influence on the materialist outlook of the early philosophers. However, we may again point out that the more advanced researches are leading us to a progressive recognition of both. Here are, for example, the bold formulations arrived at by George Thomson with regard to the early Greek philosophers: 'The greatness of the Milesians lies precisely in this, that they expressed in a new form, abstract and objective, the fundamental truths which had forced themselves on the consciousness of primitive man, but had previously found expression only in the concrete, subjective form of myth.'[40] Again 'Classical scholars have often debated with their scientific colleagues the extent to which the Greek philosophers deserve credit for having anticipated the discoveries of modern science. The debate is always inconclusive, because the question is misconceived. The truth of the matter is not that these ancient Greeks anticipated the results of modern science, but that modern scientists have succeeded in reaffirming certain fundamental but forgotten truths and establishing them securely on the basis of experimental proof. The early Greek philosophers stood near the beginning of class society; the modern bourgeois scientists stand near its end. In the work of Anaximander, the mythical cosmogony of primitive communism is in process of being transformed by the "pure reason" of the new ruling class, but with its dialectical content still unimpaired; in the work of Kant, and still more of Hegel, the new dialectical content, immeasurably richer than the old, is on the point of bursting the bonds imposed on it by the "pure reason" of bourgeois society. The primitive dialectics of these early Greek materialists stands to the dialectical materialism of the present day in the same relation as primitive communism stands to modern communism.'[41]

We have here an example of 'finding what is newest in what is oldest,' and this, as Marx showed, 'corresponds to the socialist tendency.'

REFERENCES

1. Marx and Engels, *Selected Works* (Moscow 1946) Vol. I. 129.
2. Marx, *Capital* (Moscow 1954) Vol. I. 80.
3. Marx and Engels, *Selected Correspondences* (Moscow) 541.
4. Marx and Engels, *German Ideology* (Calcutta) 29.
5. *Communist Review*, August 1952, 240-1.
6. Engels, *Dialectics of Nature* (Moscow 1954) 238-9.
7. Engels, *The Origin of the Family, Private Property and the State* (Moscow 1952) 269.

8. *German Ideology* 37-8.
9. Ib. 19-20.
10. *Capital* I. 177.
11. Ib. 178-9.
12. Ib. 178.
13. Ib. 180.
14. *Selected Works* I. 152.
15. *Capital* I. 360.
16. Ib. 361.
17. Ib. 362.
18. Ib. 362-3.
19. Ib. 362 n.
20. Descartes, *Meditations* (Everyman) 87-8.
21. Schwegler, *History of Philosophy,* 316.
22. Quoted by Lenin, *Materialism and Empirio-Criticism* (Moscow 1947) 27.
23. Ib.
24. *German Ideology* 27. (Italics added).
25. *Selected Works* I. 354.
26. G. Thomson, *Studies in Ancient Greek Society,* Vol. I. (London 1949) 74.
27. *Origin of Family* 291-2.
28. *Selected Correspondence* 242.
29. J. Frazer, *The Golden Bough* (Abridged ed. London 1949) 55.
30. G. Thomson, *Religion* (London 1950) 9.
31. *The Golden Bough* 48-9.
32. Ib. 51.
33. *Studies in Ancient Greek Society* Vol. II (London 1955) 46-7.
34. *The Golden Bough* 57-8.
35. *Studies in Ancient Greek Society* Vol. I. 440.
36. Jane Harrison, *Ancient Art* and *Ritual* (London 1935) 36.
37. J. Needham, *Science and Civilisation in China* Vol. II (Cambridge 1956) 34.
38. Ib. 33.
39. Ib. 426.
40. *Studies in Ancient Greek Society* Vol. II. 160.
41. Ib. 162.

8

Tagore and Indian Philosophical Heritage

Of the most tediously verbalised ideas, some are 'the love of truth' and 'the love of liberty'. But the courage required to profess these in the real sense is not always met. There are difficulties about it, and the difficulties are both external and internal. The external difficulties are rather well-known. These are created by organised political and economic power. The internal difficulties, however, are often unsuspected. The love of truth and the love of liberty, in so far as these are intended to be more than mere words, require the strength to overcome mental inertia and the courage to introduce corrections into time-honoured ideologies.

The point sought to be emphasised in the present lecture is that Rabindranath Tagore showed this strength and this courage. What was exceedingly remarkable about him is that the more he approached the end of his life the sharper became the expressions of this strength and this courage. It became so sharp indeed that he went to the extent of questioning some of his earlier basic commitments. To bring this point into focus, only one type of his observations are quoted here—observations which, when pieced together, give us a rather uncommon profile of the poet.

I have myself felt that this aspect of Tagore's stand is exceedingly important for uplifting our own morale, specially in those grim days when the forces of disintegration are posing real threats to our national life. I am deeply grateful to the University of Mysore for giving me the opportunity to present a brief sketch of this profile of the poet.

I am personally very thankful to Professor H.M. Nayak, who, often with profound differences with my own understanding, had, since 1971, given me many chances of expressing my ideas as representing a possible point of view. Whether—or how much—he actually shares the ideas is besides the point. The point rather is that he does not believe in suppressing the ideas that are opposed to his own, or, positively speaking, he believes in discussing and debating—in moving forward through the clash of ideas. The general intellectual climate of the country would have been healthier with more people like him at the helm of academic affairs.

I

There once swarmed with a piercing clarity before the vision of Rabindranath Tagore the fact of philosophy being sometimes directly related to politics. I shall begin with an account of this.

It happened in 1932. Air travel then was not what it is today. The poet had an invitation from Persia, now Iran. Arrangements were made for his travel by air. This was his second experience of air travel, the earlier one having been a brief hop from London to Paris.

En route to Persia, the poet with his party had a stopover at Baghdad. There he was told of the British air force carrying on regular bombing missions to the villages of some dissenting Sheikhs.

Rabindranath wondered! For him it was sheer murder and massacre. Yet, how simple it was! How incredibly simple indeed it was for human beings to kill the fellow beings without even bothering to discriminate between the guilty and the innocent—between men, women and children. It was just a question of releasing some weapon from the high altitude, which, when reached, the material world faded out, and with it everything that gave sense to such discriminations.

Apparently, there was something about the technique of attaining altitude that made such an inhuman act so simple for human beings. Tagore pondered over the whole thing and wanted to understand it in terms of his own experience of air travel. This led him to review the technique of attaining altitude in another recognised form, namely that of the free flight of metaphysical speculation. Dramatically enough, the political function of certain time-honoured philosophical views—specially those that undermined the reality of the world—leaped before his eyes.

We shall try to follow his train of thought, though inevitably missing the tremendous power of persuasion of his original writing in our rough English rendering of it. Observed Tagore:

"As the aircraft takes off and goes on gaining altitude, the connection of the earth with our five sense-organs becomes thin and thinner. It is eventually reduced to a connection with the visual sense alone, and that too without any immediacy about it. The reality of the earth with its infinite variety carried hitherto a sense of certainty about it. Henceforth, however, it became increasingly indistinct. That which had been a three-dimensional reality got reduced to a flat two-dimensional sketch. It is only within the well-defined context of space and time that the varieties of creation retain their distinct individuality. With the loss of this context, creation tends towards dissolution. The earth looked involved in this process of dissolution. It was fading out and its claim to reality was no longer pressing on our consciousness. In such a state of mind when one showers the weapons of annihilation, the terror one masters knows no bounds. One's hands no longer suffer the hesitation caused by an assessment of the actual crime committed by those that one is about to kill. The assessment is not there, because the facts and figures on which it can be based just disappear. Man is by nature attached to the earth. With the fading out of its reality, that which sustains this attachment just snaps.

"The philosophy preached by the *Gītā* was also some kind

of an aircraft like this. It carried the compassionate mind of Arjuna to such a dizzy height from where, when he looked below, there remained hardly any distinction between the killer and the killed, between the kin and the foe. There are in human arsenal many a weapon like this made of philosophical stuff. These serve the purpose of concealing the real. These are to be found among the theories of the imperialists, in sociology and in religion. Those on whom death is showered therefrom are left only with one consolation: *na hanyate hanyamāne śarīre*—It [the soul] is not slain when the body is slain."[1]

I am aware, of course, that this passage can surely be better translated. But that will only make its logic far more devastating. In any case, there is no getting away from a simple fact. Tagore sees in certain trends of philosophy the most sinister social and political function. He sees in these malevolence and murder. For him, these are but treasons to human conscience.

When Rabindranath wrote this, he was over seventy. He had not even a decade more to live. One wonders how he would have looked at the ideological waste land of contemporary imperialism, the essence of which is mindlessness combined with brutality. One wonders how he would have reacted to the news of the actual use of the atom bomb on Hiroshima, specially when the political and military collapse of Japan was imminent, and there was no need whatsoever of this wanton murder of men, women and children—inclusive of the most innocent ones. However, from Tagore's observations just quoted, we can perhaps understand a few points. For the pilots that released the bomb it was possibly as simple a matter as pressing certain buttons. But could they actually do it with the full awareness of the number of innocent human beings that were going to be snuffed out by this simple act? The question was apparently not so relevant for them, for they were at too high an altitude to visualise these men, women and children with flesh and blood. There were undoubtedly bitter protests against the whole affair. The biologist Theodor Hauschka wrote an open letter to Oppenheimer, the main architect of the atom bomb, saying that the prestige of the new scientists came chiefly from the fact that "they had become brilliant collaborators with death." For Oppenheimer—who incidentally, had a smattering knowledge of Indian philosophy—there was perhaps nothing new about this. While witnessing the sinister and gigantic cloud released by the first experimental atomic explosion, he is said to have recited what Krishna, the lord god, said to Arjuna in the *Gītā*: "I am become Death, the shatterer of the worlds." We are, thus, back again to Death and the philosophy preached by the *Gītā* that Tagore spoke of.

But let us not digress to Oppenheimer and the atom bomb. Our purpose here is to try to understand Tagore.

What he said about the *Gītā* was surely highly heretical not only from the viewpoint of Hindu orthodoxy but also from those of many accredited leaders in the country—Bankimchandra, Vivekananda, Tilak, Aurobindo and Gandhi. But that is not all. What made Tagore's train of thought all the more appalling for many of his contemporaries—inclusive of some of his closest associates—needs at once to be noted. The Sanskrit sentence with the most biting satire on which he concluded the observation just quoted—*na hanyate hanyamāne śarīre*—is generally known as occurring in the *Bhagavat-gītā*. That is true; but not the whole truth. In the *Bhagavat-gītā* itself, it is actually quoted from the *Kaṭha Upaniṣad*, where, read in full, the passage is:

> This wise one [i.e. the soul] is not born, nor dies.
> This one has not come from anywhere, nor has
> it become anyone.
> Unborn, constant, eternal, primeval, this one
> Is not slain when the body is slain.
> If the slayer think to slay,
> If the slain think himself slain,
> Both these understand not.
> This one slays not, nor is slain.

The *Bhagavat-gītā* [ii. 19-20] quotes practically verbatim this passage from the *Kaṭha Upaniṣad* [ii.18-19].

For any student of the Upaniṣads, this passage is a very famous one. But Rabindranath Tagore was much more than just a student of the Upaniṣads. It is well-known that from his early adolescence, he was literally saturated with Upaniṣadic studies. It will, therefore, be totally gratuitous to imagine that he could by any chance be unaware of what in fact he was indicting. He was indicting an Upaniṣadic idea as re-occurring in the *Gītā*.

To this, there remains to be added another simple point. One cannot evade in this context the question of philosophical coherence. In other words, the central idea conveyed by the statement that the soul is not killed when the body is killed does not represent a stray or isolated thought in the Upaniṣad itself. It is impossible to scrap it without seriously mutilating—or even totally negating—the general philosophical view of which it is but an exemplification.

What, then, is this philosophy?

It is the philosophy of the Pure Spirit or Pure Soul, exalted to the status of the ultimate reality. Hence its association with the mundane body, though temporary, is viewed as some kind of aberration. That is why, one of the names chosen for the philosophy is *śārīraka*. The name tells its own story. It is derived from the word *śarīra* or 'the body' by adding to it the suffix *kan* for conveying the sense of degradation. *Śārīraka*, in short, means the Pure Soul somehow debased because of dwelling for the time being in the defiled body.

According to Advaita Vedānta—a comparatively later school of Indian philosophy which continues to be extremely powerful even today—it is *the philosophy* of the Upaniṣads. That is why Śaṁkara, the most renowned champion of the Advaita Vedānta, chose for his *magnum opus* the title *Śārīraka-bhāṣya*. It is actually a commentary on the *Brahma-sūtra* or *Vedānta-sūtra*, a work intended to systematise the philosophy of the Upaniṣads.

Whether Advaita Vedānta or the Śārīraka philosophy

represents the only trend in the Upaniṣadic literature is not our main point of discussion here. The point, on the contrary, is that it has at least a very prominent place in Upaniṣadic thought. In other words, the idea that the soul is not slain when the body is slain must be viewed as having a profound importance in the Upaniṣads.

In the *Bhagavat-gītā* the Lord God himself is made to preach this philosophy with a metaphor exquisite in its beauty and simplicity. The soul moves from one body to another in the way in which you cast off your tattered clothes in favour of the fresh ones. As a poet, Tagore was perhaps expected to admire above all the beauty of such a literary technique. However, when confronted with a situation in which basic humanism was directly debauched, the poet was apparently left with little patience for this kind of literary beauty. He was appalled instead by the ugliness of the socio-political function that the philosophy itself was liable to serve. And he saw this ugliness being shared in common by many a weapon in the ideological armoury of the imperialists and by many a theory in sociology and religion.

But that is not all. The poet further felt that all these theories were based on a simple trick. It is the trick of concealing the real—of luring your thought to a certain metaphysical altitude which, when reached, the felt reality of the material world vanishes as it were.

Basically speaking, all this is saying something which a modern materialist or a modern revolutionary usually says, though he says this in his own way, using his own terminologies. Not that terminologies do not matter. When it comes to the question of scientific precision, it is desirable to avoid loose expressions, often with more or less confusing overtones. But that does not mean that terminologies are more important than the basic thought-content, of which the terminologies are but vehicles. Therefore, whatever may be the poet's way of expressing the thoughts, what concerns us here above all is this train of thought itself. And, to say the least, the train of thought in the passage quoted surprises us, because of its contiguity to what the materialists and revolutionaries today are found to profess.

I need not be told, of course, that Rabindranath Tagore was neither a materialist nor revolutionary in the contemporary sense. He was indeed often furthest from both. I have before me his collected works of over ten thousand closely printed pages, with which I am reasonably acquainted. I am aware of his family background and of the general intellectual climate in which he grew up. Nor am I unaware of the impact of the national awakening on him and of his own contribution to it, notwithstanding his committed internationalism. He had, besides, great expectations from modern European civilisation—specially from the liberalism of the nineteenth century England—about which, particularly at the last stage of his life, he was thoroughly disillusioned. All this made the development of his personality and personal convictions a highly complex phenomenon, any generalised view of which is liable to be fallacious.

So I have myself wondered at the courage of those who have written on *the philosophy* of Rabindranath Tagore, professing to read a monolithic view as it were throughout his poems and songs, his short stories, novels and plays, his essays, discourses and public declarations. I am myself too timid to construe a systematic philosophy in the generally accepted sense out of what I have read and known about Tagore. I am not even sure how far the poet himself would have genuinely endorsed such a tendency. In his last birthday message of 1941, published under the title *Crisis in Civilisation,* he opened with a note on the profound change in his personal convictions:

"Today I complete eighty years of my life. As I look back on the vast stretch of tears that lies behind me and see in clear perspective the history of my early development, I am struck by the change that has taken place both in my own attitude and in the psychology of my countrymen—a change that carries within it a cause of profound tragedy."[2]

It is no use trying to understand the poet without understanding the changes in his own understanding. But this does not at all mean that there is any scope to doubt or deny certain fundamental facts about him. By far the most important of these is that he was a profoundly religious person, and specially during the earlier part of his life, was passionately committed to the spiritual heritage of India, with the most decisive dedication to the teachings of the Upaniṣads. It is precisely because of this reason that his observation we have quoted appear to be so extraordinary. Whether one likes it or not, one only expects the revolutionaries and materialists to talk like that. What one does not at all expect is Tagore saying as these.

Yet there is no getting away from the fact that this profoundly religious person—remembered not without reason as an apostle of Upaniṣadic wisdom—came out at his grand old age with a train of thought that had almost the appearance of a total indictment of his own early convictions in the Upaniṣads. We shall see that this was not fully true, that even while taking a strikingly radical attitude in roughly the last ten years of his life he did not allow his convictions in the Upaniṣads to be totally snapped. But we shall also see how difficult and even tortuous was the way in which he hoped to effect some kind of working adjustment of his new realisations with his earlier convictions.

I do not know how those who specialise in Tagore studies would like to reconcile the observations we have quoted with the rest of his life-pattern and his teachings. This much I know, however, that those who profess to write on the philosophy of Rabindranath Tagore—generally speaking, prefer to overlook the passage we have quoted. A blanket of silence is usually drawn over it, as if it represented some kind of poetic aberration or something like a vagary of the god-intoxicated *gurudeva* of the Santiniketan *āśrama*. However, it is not necessary to take such a superficial view, which incidentally, is rather disparaging for Tagore's intellectual integrity. We have, in other words, to try to understand Tagore, inclusive of his observations of 1932, which we have quoted for the main reason that it appears to be a pointer to the directions to which his ideas were moving in the last phase of his life.

How, then, are we to understand these observations?

Tagore's religious convictions, deep though these were, were rooted after all in profound humanism. It is true that specially during the earliest part of his life—and also in his sermons collected under the title *Śāntiniketan* as well as in his lectures on the *Religion of Man*—the prevailing mood was that of expounding this humanism mainly in terms of the idealist metaphysics. He was talking of MAN in all capitals as it were—as if it were some kind of transcendental category or something more or less wrapped up by a mystical or quasi-mystical veil. But something extra-ordinary happened during the last phase of his life—or, to be more precise, during the last ten years of his life—as a consequence of which this quasi-mystical veil on MAN was torn to shreds, and, to the foreground of his vision moved forward the struggling millions of men, women and children who for ages were kept suppressed by the most brutal force—both political and ideological. In short, humanism acquired for him a strikingly new dimension. This humanism—or humanism with this new dimension—was totally outraged when, in 1932, he was told of the massacre of men, women and children, without discrimination between the innocent and the guilty. The poet came out with the denunciation of the brutal force responsible for the outrage. It was inclusive of the denunciation of the philosophy that could, and, as a matter of fact did, sanctify the act of killing.

What I am trying to drive at is that Tagore's observation of 1932 can be explained. But it cannot be explained if taken as an isolated phenomenon or as a statement taken out of its real context. It can be explained only in the broader context of the turn his thoughts were taking in the last phase of his life.

II

Professor Niharranjan Ray, whose eminence as a historian of Bengal and also as a commentator of Tagore is well-known, draws our attention to the special importance of understanding the last phase of Tagore's life for a proper appreciation of the full formation of the poet's historical consciousness. It is true, observes Niharranjan, that Tagore was "never far removed from the inner realities of the people" even in his earlier poems and in his short stories and symbolical dramas and novels of urban life. "But", adds Niharranjan with emphasis, "it was left to his mature years, indeed after he was 70, to impart into this sense of reality the background of a historical consciousness... But he had to wait till the declining years of life for the complete liberation of his intellect, for attaining a true detachment that gives a clear vision into the intricate process through which the world and humanity moves from progress to progress. In fact, the last ten years of life open a new phase of creative activity, new but not inherently unconnected from his earlier phases; indeed the last phase crowns the earlier phases with a final efflorescence which can be historically interpreted as the fulfilment of a logical process."[3]

This development of the poet during the last ten years of his life was indeed a very complex process. Things happening in India and abroad had a good deal of impact on him, rudely shaking up much of his earlier dreams, his sense of serenity and tranquility, his meditations and mystical raptures. In 1931, there was the disintegration of the second Civil Disobedience movement followed by imperialist repression and undermining of civil liberties all over India. Perhaps more appalling for the poet's committed internationalism were things happening in the world abroad. As Niharranjan sums up: "Abroad, in 1932 greedy Japan preyed upon historic but struggling China, in 1935 came Fascist Italy's murderous attack upon the dark and weak Abyssinia, and in 1936 the German and Italian Fascism started their attack upon the

Republican Spain. All over Europe and the Western world standards of political and economic morality speedily dropped down to an incredibly low ebb and released forces that sought to strangle humanity's voice. Man, the one love of the poet, was everywhere in chains, humanity which had been his only altar of worship was everywhere in desecration, till finally, in 1939, the destiny of man and the future of humanity were cast into the whirl of death and destruction.[4]

But Rabindranath did not write anything like *The Waste Land*. Nor did he seek refuge in the intensification of his earlier religious convictions and metaphysical commitments. His thoughts and ideas took a turn, which, superficially viewed, may appear to be quite strange. On the basis of a survey of Tagore's writings of the last ten years of his life, Niharranjan Ray sums it up as follows: "During the last ten years of life, Tagore was growing more and more secular in the innermost depths of his existence... The more he approaches death the more worldly he becomes, the more he loves man, the more he drinks into the fountain of life. It is not without reason he questions his Master if He has loved those who are the instruments of tyranny and oppression of the lowliest of the low, questions the justice of the continued existence of the present social organisation that desecrates humanity. This total attitude of the mind then is at the background of the last phase of Tagore's creative genius."[5]

As we have just said, this turn in the poet's attitude cannot but appear to be quite strange. Ordinarily speaking, with age one grows more conservative, more religious, sometimes also more superstitious, for one listens to the footsteps of death and becomes afraid. In the poems of the last phase of his life—specially those in the *Rogaśajyāya* [In the Sick Bed: 1940], *Árogya* [Recovery: 1941] and *Janmadine* [On the Birthday: 1941]— it is easy to judge how the poet himself was very clearly visualising his approaching end. What was most remarkable about him, however, was that this did not at all have a crippling effect on his consciousness. The approaching death did not frighten him, for in the meanwhile he had developed a death-defying philosophy, which was his humanism with a totally new dimension added to it. As Niharranjan Ray has very aptly described it, "The demand of man, of humanity free from outworn traditions and prejudices is the only claim that he came to recognise, humanity freed from social and economic serfdom, men free from all kinds of tutelage is the ideal he came to stand for. To that claim and to that ideal Tagore brought the offerings of the last ten years of his life crowned finally by the thundering voice that frowned grimly on those who are the enemies of the Eternal Man. The sentinel is gone but his grim warning yet abides in *Crisis in Civilisation*."[6]

This is about the finest way of describing the attitude of the poet that took shape during the last phase of his life. However, what needs perhaps to be added to it are a few points of explanation.

The Eternal Man just mentioned is no longer the quasi-metaphysical category of his earlier understanding. This category is, in the meanwhile, pushed to the background in the poet's consciousness to make room for the struggling millions of men and women of flesh and blood. Not that they did not exist in his earlier writings. We see them teeming his exquisite short stories and his no less exquisite songs and poems. He felt the agony of their suffering more intensely than perhaps anybody else. But, then, he also felt somewhat helpless. What he could suggest was some kind of palliative remedy for their misfortune, but nothing of the nature of a total and radical transformation of their lot.

And then, in 1930, he experienced something that appeared to him as some kind of miracle of miracles. With the metaphor drawn from traditional India, he described it as "the light of the mightiest sacrificial fire that has been lit in the world's history."[7] He visited the Soviet Union and said: "Had I not come, my life's pilgrimage would have remained incomplete."[8] And yet what he was talking of was not what the pilgrims rush after. What he was talking of was something else altogether. As he himself put it: "The dumb have found their voice, the ignorant have cast the veil from their minds, the helpless have become conscious of their own power and those who were in the depths of degradation have come out of society's 'black hole' to claim equality with everybody else. This is Soviet Russia's achievement in less than eight years' time." (p. 40)

We have so long been trying to understand the new dimension added to Tagore's humanism during the last phase of his life, or, to be more specific, during the last ten years of his life. It begins from 1930, with the experience of his visit to the Soviet Union. How this experience initiated a qualitative change in his fundamental convictions was best described by the poet himself:

"Throughout the ages, civilised communities have contained groups of nameless people. They are the majority—the beasts of burden, who have no time to become men. They grow up in the leavings of society's wealth, with the least food, least clothes and least education, and they serve the rest. They toil most, yet theirs is the largest measure of indignity. At the least excuse they starve and are humiliated by their superiors. They are deprived of everything that makes life worth living. They are like a lampstand bearing the lamp of civilisation on their heads: people above receive light while they are smeared with the trickling oil.

"I had often thought about them, but came to the conclusion that there was no help for them. If thre were no one below, how could there be anyone above, and it is necessary to be there above. If there is nobody at the top, it is impossible to see anything beyond one's immediate ken; mere animal existence can never be man's destiny. His civilisation consists in going beyond bare subsistence. The most cherished fruits of civilisation have flourished on the field of leisure. There is need to preserve a corner for leisure in human civilisation. So I used to think that the utmost should be done to improve the education, health and comfort of those who are compelled to labour at the bottom of society not merely through circumstances, but by reason of their body and mind...

"In any case I have not been able to think it all out satisfactorily, but to think that it is inevitable that the progress of civilisation could be maintained only by keeping down the bulk of humanity and denying it its human rights is a reproach to the human mind.

"A radical solution of this problem is being sought in Russia. It is not time yet to consider the final fruit of this attempt, but for the present whatever catches my eye strikes me with amazement. The royal road to the solution of all our problems is education... It is astonishing to watch the extraordinary vigour with which education spreads throughout Russian society... What abundant preparation, what tremendous effort, so that no one should remain helpless or idle. Not in European Russia alone, but also among the semi-civilised races of Central Asia, they have opened the flood-gates of eduction. Unending efforts are being made to bring the latest fruits of science to them. The theatres here are crowded, but those who come to them are peasants and workers. Nowhere are they humiliated. In the few institutions I have visited so far, I have seen the awakening of their spirit and the joy of their self-respect... A few years ago the condition of the masses here was fully comparable with that of the Indian masses: things have rapidly changed in this short period, whereas we are up to the neck in the mud of stagnation."[9]

On his own admission, therefore, what he saw happening in the Soviet Union resolved at one stroke as it were a fundamental problem with which Tagore had earlier been confronted in his commitment to humanism. This meant the turning point for the ideas and attitude of the last phase of his life. Not that he became a Marxist or a communist. He expressed many reservations for Marxism in various writings of the last phase of his life. Nevertheless, the impact of his experience of the Soviet Union on his ideas and attitude was stupendous. He could never forget for the rest of his life that certain basic problems concerning the destiny of the vast masses of the toiling people, posed by many theoreticians as insoluble, were in fact not so. These could as a matter of fact be solved—and solved in an admirable way—as proved by the great experiment in human history which he saw taking place in the Soviet Union. This became some kind of an unshakable conviction for him for the rest of his life. Thus, in his last birthday message which he called *Crisis in Civilisation* and which is for us his last testament, we read:

"I have also been privileged to witness, while in Moscow, the unsparing energy with which Russia has tried to fight disease and illiteracy, and has succeeded in steadily liquidating ignorance and poverty, wiping off the humiliation from the face of a vast continent. Her civilisation is free from all invidious distinction between one class and another, between one sect and another. The rapid and astounding progress achieved by her made me happy and jealous at the same time. One aspect of the Soviet administration which particularly pleased me was that it provided no scope for unseemly conflict of religious differences nor set one community against another by unbalanced distribution of political favours. That I consider a truly civilised administration which impartially serves the common interests of the people.

"While other imperialist powers sacrifice the welfare of the subject races to their own national greed, in the USSR I found a genuine attempt being made to harmonise the interests of the various nationalities that are scattered over its vast area. I saw people and tribes who only the other day were nomadic savages being encouraged and indeed trained, to avail themselves freely of the benefits of civilisation. Enormous sums are being spent on their education to expedite the process. When I see elsewhere some two hundred nationalities which only a few years ago were at vastly different stages of development—marching ahead in peaceful progress and amity, and when I look about my own country and see a very highly evolved and intellectual people drifting into the disorder of barbarism, I cannot help contrasting the two systems of government, one based on cooperation, the other on exploitation, which have made such contrary conditions possible."[10]

It is, thus, impossible to imagine that the enthusiasm the poet felt for the Russian revolution was only a temporary phase for his convictions. From 1930, when he visited the Soviet Union, to 1941, the year he died, it remained as some kind of unshakable conviction for the poet that the humanism he always dreamed of could be scientifically implemented by following the path of the Russian revolution, I am aware, of course, that it is possible to quote isolated passages from his writings of these last ten years, showing some kind of a return to romantic rapture and fascination for Upaniṣadic idealism characteristic of his early life. Nevertheless, Niharranjan Ray is fully justified in drawing our attention to the fact that during this last phase of the poet's life there was some kind of fundamental shift in his total attitude. Tagore of his maturest days is hardly understood without understanding this fundamental shift in his own understanding. But the most fundamental shift in Tagore's convictions itself remains ununderstood without taking note of the fact that this began in 1930, when he had the first direct experience of the most momentous historical transformation going on in human history.

It remains for us to add only a few more points. In 1930, when Tagore visited the Soviet Union, there was much emphasis on an organised campaign against religion. How did the poet with his own profound religious convictions—the god-intoxicated *gurudeva* of the Śāntiniketan *āśrama*—react to it? His reaction, to say the least, was most unexpected. As he himself wrote:

"The Soviet revolutionaries have uprooted the old religious organisation and the political system, both of which for centuries had subdued their minds and sapped their vitality. Because even a king, however much he may limit the freedom of his subjects from without, cannot be a greater enemy than the religion which kills man's freedom of mind by taking advantage of his ignorance. It has been observed so far that the king who wants to keep his subjects in bondage finds his chief support in the religion which keeps them blind. That religion is like the poison-princess who fascinates by embracing and kills by fascinating. The arrow of piety enters the heart deeper than the arrow of death, because it kills without hurting.

"The Soviets have saved the country from the insults of the Tsars and self-imposed humiliation; however much the devout people of other countries may reproach them, I personally cannot. Far better is atheism than religious infatuation that darkens the mind and keeps the soul in a dungeon."[11]

In the poet's own assessment, there could have been certain excesses no doubt in the organised propaganda in favour of the Marxist economics in the Soviet Union. Even then, the poet had the patience to try to understand it. As he put it:

"They are wont to say 'Let us attain our objectives first: we shall attend to other things later.' The situation in Russia resembles wartime conditions. She is beset with enemies at home and abroad. There is ceaseless manoeuvring all round to wreck the entire experiment. The foundations of their structure therefore must be strengthened as quickly as possible; hence they have no qualms about using force."[12]

Not that Tagore really approved of the method; he would have been happier indeed had the Russians been able to do without the use of force. As the poet added, "Nevertheless, however insistent the necessity may be, force is one-sided. It destroys, it does not create."[13]

At the same time, the poet wanted us to take note of another exceedingly important fact. Throughout the history of exploitative society, another technique of destroying basic humanism is known to be in operation. It is not brute force but the clever use of ideology—specially religious ideology.

And the poet was happy to see that the Russian revolution did away with tyranny in this form. As he observed:

"Those who really want to tyrannise kill man's mind first, while here on the contrary they are strengthening the vitality of his mind."[14]

As is perhaps only to be expected of Rabindranath, all this immediately reminded him of his own people and of the tyranny of regimented religion on them for centuries—a tyranny from which he saw actual emancipation in Soviet Russia achieved only in a few years. As he observed, "I thought of the peasants and workers in my own country. It all seemed like the work of the Genii in the Arabian Nights. Only a decade ago they were as illiterate, helpless and hungry as our own masses: equally blindly superstitious, equally stupidly religious. In their misery and trouble they knocked their heads against the door of their God; in fear of the other world their mind was held in bondage by the priests, and in fear of this world by the king, merchants and landlords: their task was to clean the boots of those who kicked them with these very boots. Their customs had not changed for a thousand years: their carts, spinning wheels and oil presses belonged to their grandfathers' times: any suggestion of change would provoke them to revolt. The ghost of Time sits on the back of our three hundred million and blindfolds them from behind: with them too it was the same. Who could be more astonished than an unfortunate Indian like myself to see how they had removed the mountain of ignorance and helplessness in these few years?"[15]

In 1930, only the most radical of the radicals in India could dare say such things, though there was hardly any to put it as powerfully and passionately as the poet did.

But let us return to another point. When the poet had this new realisation, what happened to his earlier religious convictions and specially to his commitment to the Upaniṣads characteristic of his early life? Could he and did he go to the extent of renouncing these altogether? The answer is that he did not. What nevertheless he tried to do was something else.

He wanted to effect some kind of working adjustment of his new realisation with his old convictions. The way he actually did it was, to say the least, really extraordinary: he went to the extent of reading the essential point of the Bolsheviks in the ancient Upaniṣads. As he put it:

> Since my visit to Russia I have realised a saying of the Upanishads: *mā gṛdhaḥ*—do not covet. Why not? Because everything is pervaded by the one truth: personal greed alone impedes its realisation. *Tena tyaktena bhuñjīthāḥ*—enjoy only that which issues from this unity. The Bolsheviks are saying the same thing about the material side of life. They recognise only one absolute human truth in all humanity: enjoy only that, they say, which is produced by this unity: *mā gṛdhaḥ kasyasviddhanam*—do not covet others' possessions. But greed is bound to arise wherever there is personal division of wealth. By sweeping this away they want to say: *tena tyaktena bhuñjīthāḥ*.[16]

The quotations are well-known. These are from the *Īśa Upaniṣad*—a text commented upon by many, from Śaṁkara to Sri Aurobindo. I do not know how far they and their followers would agree with Tagore and read in this Upaniṣad the essential programme of the Bolsheviks about the material side of life. But that is another point into which let us not at present digress. We are trying now to understand Tagore. Would it be permissible from this point of view to ask ourselves a simple question? Could it be that the poet was putting a condition to his old conviction? Could it be that he was accepting the Upaniṣad on condition that it accepted the Bolshevist programme? The question is important, because without answering it we hardly understand the last phase of the poet's life.

I want to be permitted to add only one more point. The tremendous impact of the Bolshevik revolution on Rabindranath is an undeniable fact. But it is also an uncomfortable fact specially to those that want to make a pure aesthete or a pure mystic of him. What they can try, therefore, is to look at it as but a temporary emotional outburst of the poet. But would Tagore himself permit us to do it? Before answering this question, we have to read and re-read his last testament—*Crisis in Civilisation*. When we do it, we cannot escape a simple fact. He saw, in 1941, European Civilisation in the grip of a very grim crisis. But there was one exception to it. He saw no crisis in the socialist civilisation. Instead of crisis, he saw there the hope for the future. We shall not understand Rabindranath Tagore—not at least the last phase of his life—so long as we fail to see what he saw in the socialist civilisation.

REFERENCES

1. *Pārasye* (In Persia). *Rabīndra Racanāvali*, Government of West Bengal, Vol. X, p. 754.
2. *Crisis in Civilisation*, 1941. p. 1.
3. N. Ray, *Tagore : The Last Phase.* The Calcutta Municipal Gazette, Tagore Memorial Supplement, September 1941. p. 25.
4. Ibid. 26.
5. Ib.
6. Ib. 28.
7. *Letters from Russia*, Eng. tr. Visvabharati 1960. p. 14.
8. Ib. 10.
9. Ib. 1-4.
10. *Crisis in Civilisation*, pp. 7-9.
11. *Letters from Russia*, p. 11.
12. Ib. 114.
13. Ib. 114-5.
14. Ib. 93.
15. Ib. 27.
16. Ib. 53–4.

Index